THE CLASSICS OF WESTERN SPIRITUALITY

Safed Spirituality

Rules of Mystical Piety, The Beginning of Wisdom

TRANSLATION AND INTRODUCTION BY
LAWRENCE FINE

PREFACE BY
LOUIS JACOBS

PAULIST PRESS
NEW YORK • RAMSEY • TORONTO

Cover Art:
The 13 *middot* ("attributes") of God's mercy represented as the beard of one of the *parzufim* ("divine configurations") according to the Zohar and the interpretation of Isaac Luria. Used by permission of the Jewish Theological Seminary, New York.

Library of Congress
Catalog Card Number: 84-60735

ISBN: 0-8091-2612-5 (paper)
        0-8091-0349-4 (cloth)

Published by Paulist Press
545 Island Road, Ramsey, N.J. 07446

Printed and bound in the United States of America

Contents

Editor of this Volume

LAWRENCE FINE is Associate Professor of Religious Studies at Indiana University. His research is in the field of Jewish mysticism, especially sixteenth-century Safed. His published work has been particularly concerned with the study of theories and techniques of mystical meditation among the Safed Kabbalists. His articles and essays have appeared in various scholarly journals and books.

Author of the Preface

LOUIS JACOBS is the rabbi of the New London Synagogue in England and Professor of Talmudic Studies at Leo Baeck College for the training of rabbis. He is the author of *Principles of the Jewish Faith; A Jewish Theology; Studies in Talmudic Logic*, and a number of books on Jewish mysticism including *Jewish Mystical Testimonies* and *Tract on Ecstasy*, a translation of one of the very few direct reports of their experience by the Jewish mystics.

Preface

"Religion is a way of walking, not a way of talking." This saying, attributed to Dean Inge, a pioneer in the study of mysticism for its relevance to the world of the twentieth century, provides an adequate summary of the particular thrust of the sixteenth-century mystics who come so vividly alive in Lawrence Fine's lucid presentation of their thought and practice. Activists as well as contemplatives, their profound meditations on God in the heavens resulted in a heroic attempt to walk humbly with Him on earth.

Thanks to the massive researches of Gershom Scholem and his school, the literary, philological, and historical investigation into kabbalistic texts is a significant branch of Jewish studies. It has acquired the full status of an academic discipline in which the most rigorous canons of scholarship are followed. It is no longer necessary to be a Kabbalist in order to study the Kabbalah. All that is required is a mastery of the source material—a pretty big "all," let it be said, in view of the extremely difficult style and language of these texts. No compromising of scholarly objectivity is apparent if the question is put: how can this kind of material assist in the spiritual quest of those who cannot share the basic presuppositions of the Kabbalists—who do not believe that, for example, there really are ten *Sefirot* and both a male and female element in the Godhead whose "sacred marriage" is dependent on human virtue, but who do find meaning in the idea of a soul hungry for God, in Otto's "the numinous," and in the maxim of Rabbi A. I. Kook that man is by nature a mystic? There is no simple answer. With admirable, scholarly restraint, Fine does not advance one, leaving it to the readers of his book for whom the texts he has chosen ring a bell to work out their own method of demythologization. For, on any showing, the Safed Kabbalists were mighty God-seekers; at times, perhaps, overcredulous and superstitious from the contemporary point of view, but daring stormers of the heavens who taught that God needs man for his grace to flow throughout all creation and that no human deed is trivial since, for good or for ill, it has a tremendous cosmic effect. A Neo-Kabbalism may be in the process of emerging, one in which the rich insights of the masters can be assimilated into modern thought without any attempt at bypassing the findings of the historians.

It should be noted that the authors of the *Hanhagot*, contained in the first part of the book, and De Vidas and his popularizer, Poyetto, in the second part, were learned men. Intellectual capacity, the use of the mind in the service of God, was a *sine qua non* for aspirants to the religious life at the mystical level, even though, as Fine remarks, some of the *Hanhagot* were also directed for the use of the ordinary folk. Far from piety and learning being seen as in conflict (a phenomenon certainly not infrequent in the history of religion), holy living was, for these masters, inconceivable without a grounding in holy thinking. The nature of this thinking was not, to be sure, rational inquiry into the nature of the universe; still less was it a matter of philosophical argument for the existence of God and the truth of Judaism. It consisted rather of a determined effort by the mind to grasp the kabbalistic gnosis, the "wisdom" referred to in the title of De Vidas's work. The contemplative exercises involved deep reflection on the intricacies of the whole kabbalistic scheme; on the relationships among the *Sefirot*; the parallels between the worlds on high and the human body below; the various combinations of divine names and concentration on these during prayer. While the mystics used the term *gerushin* (divorces) for their absences from home in order to visit the graves of departed saints, they strove effectively to prevent any severance of mind from heart. Nor did they allow a divorce to take effect between their religious and their ethical stance or between the individual and the group, as the very existence of the brotherhoods demonstrates. Almsgiving; tendering assistance, both spiritual and material, to those in need; the avoidance of spite, envy, bad temper, pride, and malice; the cultivation of humility, compassion, and love for all creatures; these were all essential ingredients in the mystical life. The mystics would not have accepted George Orwell's contention that you cannot love both God and man. Yet for all their recognition that the two are in no way incompatible (quite the contrary), their emphasis was on the love of God, which, for them, as De Vidas states, was to be far more powerful than any human love. A man must love his God more than he loves his wife and children. In a sense, ethical conduct, strictly enjoined, was more a means to an end than an end in itself, the end being the close attachment to God that they called *devequt*. The Hasidic movement, in the eighteenth century, drawing on the writings of the Safed mystics, similarly made the attainment of *devequt* its chief aim and could teach that a man should mix socially and engage in conversation with his fellows with his mind all the time on God—an idea, incidentally, that can be traced back through the Safed mystics to Bahya's "Duties of the Heart," Bahya being influenced, in turn, by the Sufis. Kierkegaard's distinction between "ethical man" and "the knight of faith" receives some support in the Safed documents.

Fine rightly observes that *devequt*, attachment to God, does not mean for the Safed mystics the *unio mystica* in which the soul of the mystic becomes absorbed in God. They believed in all probability that it was impossible for the finite soul of man to merge with the Infinite. It may be worth noting, however, that for all the influence of the Safed mystics on Hasidism, the Hasidic masters repeatedly speak of *bittul ha-yesh*, "self-annihilation," as the ideal and come very close to identifying *devequt* with this ideal, one that does imply the complete *unio mystica*.

It is frequently asserted that normative Judaism is opposed to asceticism. Leaving aside the question of whether there is any such entity as normative Judaism and, if there is, how we go about detecting it, there is an inherent absurdity in treating Cordovero, Karo, Luria, De Vidas, and the others, all of them severe ascetics, as Jewishly abnormal, in view of their preeminence in Jewish thought and their wide influence on Jewish life. All the masters of Safed seemed to have pursued the ascetic way, believing that it is necessary to lose the world if the soul is to be gained. The saint who crawled into a sack—his tale is told in this book—to be dragged along the floor of the synagogue and pelted with stones until he was bruised all over, and who, in addition, urged this penance on his fellow-worshipers; the mystics who rolled in the snow and stung themselves with thorns; the husbands who restricted congress with their wives to certain prescribed periods and even then performed the act without pleasure or passion with their minds on the *Shekhinah;* those who denied themselves sleep to rise for the midnight vigil and who fasted for days on end; these can hardly be set up as advocates of worldly enjoyment as a religious imperative. It is precarious to speak of their activities as morbid; one man's morbidity is another man's healthy religious outlook. And there was little gloom in the lives of the Safed mystics, even in their mourning over the destruction of the Temple. Joy, they taught, can alone have redemptive power. Man must take delight in serving his Maker. The fruits of *devequt* are such rapture and ecstasy that no sacrifice for them to be attained can be too great and once realized, they make all pain and suffering on the road pale into insignificance. For all that, the practices described will strike the average reader as extravagant, not to say bizarre. The mystics themselves no doubt succeeded in counterbalancing their sense of guilt with their appreciation of the elevated role they played in upholding the heavens. For lesser mortals to emulate them would probably result in overwhelming guilt feelings. It is reliably reported that the famous nineteenth-century rabbinic authority R. Moses Sofer of Hungary, noticing that a pupil of his was prone to fits of melancholia, urged the young man to give up his daily reading of De Vidas!

William James's analysis of saintliness in his *The Varieties of Religious Experience* is pertinent. After describing saintly practices similar to those followed by the Safed mystics, James goes on to discuss the one-sidedness of such conduct. Is it necessary to be quite so fantastically good as that? James implies that in every area of human endeavor, whether in art, music, science, or politics, one-sidedness is the price to be paid for worthwhile achievement and that it is possible both to admire the saints and be repelled by them:

> We are proud of a human nature that could be so passionately extreme, but we shrink from advising others to follow their example. The conduct we blame ourselves for not following lies nearer to the middle line of human effort. It is less dependent on particular beliefs and doctrines. It is such as wears well in different ages, such as under different skies all judges are able to commend.

James may be right. Who can tell how many sensitive Jewish souls tortured themselves, like the pupil of R. Moses Sofer, through the desire to make the ideas and ideals found in De Vidas and Poyetto their own while knowing only too well how remote they were from the quality of life envisaged in these tomes. And yet how does one account for the many editions both works went into and what is the secret of their constant appeal unless they sound an echo in the Jewish soul? Readers of this book, Jewish or non-Jewish, will now be able to examine this topic for themselves. Whatever their conclusions, they will remain indebted to the author for enabling them to embark on a fascinating journey through the sea of Jewish spirituality, to compare notes on their return with voyagers on the same ocean but on other waters and in different climes.

Foreword

A Renaissance

The renaissance of Jewish mystical life that took place in the Galilean city of Safed in the sixteenth century is one of the most significant and remarkable chapters in the history of Judaism. The ideas that developed there, the rich literature that was produced, the stunning array of teachers it nurtured, established Safed as one of the great centers of Jewish creativity. It is here that Jewish mystical spirituality, in the form of the kabbalistic tradition, merged with intense messianic enthusiasm. The combination of these two religious tendencies—more often seen independently of one another—proved to have powerful consequences.

The members of the Safed community regarded themselves as possessing extraordinary responsibility, not only for the well-being of the Jewish people and its redemptive aspirations, but for the well-being of the divine realm itself. The Safed mystics appropriated a basic kabbalistic notion, that the deeds of individuals have repercussions in the world of God, the world of the *Sefirot*. In the wake of historical crisis—the expulsion of the Jews from the Iberian peninsula in the late fifteenth century—the conviction that individual actions have profound consequences was transformed into a *social* ideal. It was now the collective action of a single-minded community that had the power to achieve that which no previous generation had achieved.

It is this more than anything else that is so striking about the community whose ideas and way of life are presented in this volume. There were other periods of Jewish history in which impressive works of ethics were written, in which the spiritual ideals of love for God and one's fellow human beings were espoused, in which devotional piety was intense and vigorous. But one is hard pressed to find another community that exceeded this one in its dedication to the notion that collaborative religious activity could reestablish order in the cosmos, an order that was believed to have been tragically rent asunder. In comparison with our own time, often characterized by the fear that social action, no less private action, holds little possibility of "repairing" the world, the Safed mystics call to mind a very different point of view.

Something else that will strike the reader of Safed literature is the unusual willingness of these individuals to invigorate and reshape older Jewish symbols, motifs, and rituals. Sabbath and festival worship, prayer, ethical behavior—every dimension of religious life—was transformed and revitalized by the strength of the spiritual impulses at work. Yet, unlike the Sabbatian movement of the seventeenth century, the Safed mystics remained wholly situated within the boundaries of "orthodox" Judaism.

The present selections are introduced by a broad overview of the historical circumstances that gave rise to the Safed community and the central features of Safed piety. The texts themselves are of two types. First, I have provided important examples of *Hanhagot*, brief descriptions of and prescriptions for religious behavior. These include the practices of Moses Cordovero, Abraham Galante, Abraham ben Eliezer ha-Levi Berukhim, an anonymous Safed scholar, Joseph Karo, and Isaac Luria. The devotional rites and rules of each of these men are preceded by short introductions. The second part of the volume contains selections from the mystical-ethical treatise known as *Reshit Ḥokhmah* (The Beginning of Wisdom) by Elijah de Vidas. These are drawn from the most important condensation of de Vidas's work, which was prepared by an Italian scholar and Kabbalist, Jacob Poyetto. This part too is preceded by an independent set of introductory remarks. It is hoped that, taken together, these texts will open a window on the world of sixteenth-century Safed.

I was first introduced to the literature of Safed in a class at the Hebrew University taught by Professor Joseph Dan. The excitement of that encounter—with both texts and teacher—was to help determine the direction of my scholarly interests. It was my great fortune to be able to pursue those interests under the guidance of Professor Alexander Altmann at Brandeis University. Through their critically important studies on the literature and life of sixteenth-century Safed, Gershom Scholem, Isaiah Tishby, and Zvi Werblowsky have also been my teachers. All who follow in their path are in their debt.

It is also my pleasure to acknowledge those who have had a more direct role in the preparation of this work. I am grateful to my friend and colleague Arthur Green for suggesting that I edit a volume for the series of which this book is a part, and for his valuable comments on portions of this work. Other colleagues and friends who read all or parts of the manuscript are Louis Jacobs, Daniel Matt, and George Savran. To each of them, I am

FOREWORD

most thankful. I wish also to acknowledge the kind patience and assistance of Richard Payne, originator, and John Farina, editor, of this series. David Smith, former chairman of the department of Religious Studies at Indiana University, extended to me his support and generosity of spirit beyond the call of duty. To my wife Deborah (whose great-grandfather traveled from Eastern Europe to settle in the holy city of Safed), and to my sons Jacob and Aaron, I express my love. They are ever my deepest source of joy and inspiration.

Abbreviations

Biblical

Gen.	Genesis
Ex.	Exodus
Lev.	Leviticus
Num.	Numbers
Deut.	Deuteronomy
Is.	Isaiah
Jer.	Jeremiah
Ezek.	Ezekial
Mal.	Malachi
Ps.	Pslams
Prov.	Proverbs
Lam.	Lamentations
Ecc.	Ecclesiastes
Dan.	Daniel
I Sam.	I Samuel
I Ch.	I Chronicles
II Ch.	II Chronicles

Talmudic Tractates

Ber.	Berakhot
Pes.	Pesaḥim
Meg.	Megillah
Hag.	Ḥagigah
Ned.	Nedarim
San.	Sanhedrin

Midrashic

Lev. Rabbah	Leviticus Rabbah
Ecc. Rabbah	Ecclesiastes Rabbah

Introduction

Historical Background

Following centuries of flourishing social, cultural, and religious life in Spain, the Jews of that country were expelled in the year 1492. The Expulsion represented the culmination of a century of deteriorating relations between Jews and Christians. From the Iberian Peninsula tens of thousands of Jews seeking refuge migrated to the Muslim countries of North Africa, to Italy and to various parts of the Ottoman Empire. It was the Ottomans who actively welcomed the Jews of Spain.[1] The Sultan Bayazid II is reported to have been pleased to receive the Sefardim (Spanish and Portugese Jews and their descendants) into his midst, and is alleged to have said of the Spanish king Ferdinand: "Can you call such a king wise and intelligent? He is impoverishing his country and enriching my kingdom."[2] The exiles settled in the large cities of Constantinople, Salonika, Adrianople, and Nicopolis, as well as in numerous smaller towns across the empire. Whereas those in each of the large centers founded various synagogue communities named after the town or region from which they had come, Jews in the smaller localities tended to organize around one general congregation.

On the whole, the exiles thrived and enjoyed economic prosperity. The sentiment allegedly expressed by Bayazid concerning the enrichment of his empire by the Sefardim was not without foundation. The exiles brought with them valuable talents and expertise. Some served as courtiers of the sultan, while others became physicians, bankers, and diplomats.

---

1. For an overview of the history of the Jews in the Ottoman Empire, see I. Ben-Zvi, "Eretz Yisrael Under Ottoman Rule," in *The Jews, Their History, Culture and Religion*, ed. L. Finkelstein (New York, 1960), vol. I, pp. 602–89.

2. This report is attributed to Bayazid's courtiers by Eliyahu Caspali, *Seder Eliyahu Zuta*, ed. A. Shmuelevitz (Jerusalem, 1975). Immanuel Aboab ascribed it to Bayazid himself in his *Nomologia o Discursos legales compuestos* (Amsterdam, 1629), p. 195.

INTRODUCTION

The majority turned to commerce and crafts, including the manufacture of weapons and gunpowder, a skill of which the Ottomans were eager to take advantage.

An event of decisive importance for Jewry occurred in the years 1516–1517 under the rule of Selim I when the Turks succeeded in extending their territory in the East by overpowering the Mamluks, thus gaining control over Egypt, Syria, Palestine, and the Arabian Peninsula. As a result of these events, Jews were able to settle in Palestine under highly favorable conditions. The ensuing immigration, which reached into the end of the sixteenth century, brought to Palestine former exiles and their descendants who were already living under Ottoman rule, as well as Jews from North Africa, Italy, and the Germanic states. Many of these were individuals who had been forcibly converted to Christianity and were interested in openly returning to Judaism, and in doing penance for their sins. These immigrants joined Arabic-speaking Jews (*Musta'rabim*) who had lived in the land even before the Arab conquest in the seventh century. It is estimated that by the middle of the sixteenth century there were approximately ten thousand Jews in Palestine.[3]

For a variety of reasons Safed, a small town located high in the Galilean hills, approximately twenty miles north of the Sea of Galilee, experienced the largest increase in population. Safed was the choice of many, in part, on account of the far greater economic opportunities available there as compared with Jerusalem. Safed became especially known as a textile center, in which industry the Jews played an important part.[4] In addition to the weaving of cloth, Jews who settled there engaged in the practice of various crafts, agriculture, shopkeeping, peddling, and international trade. Moreover, Safed was the Jewish center closest to Syria, itself the home of a strong Jewish community and the route by which Jews arrived from other provinces in the northwestern part of the Ottoman Empire. Finally, the region around Safed was the burial place of numerous sages from the talmudic period, lending it an aura of importance. Of particular significance in this regard was the presence, just a few miles from Safed in Meron, of the grave of Rabbi Shimon bar Yohai, to whom tradition ascribes authorship of the Zohar.

The relatively stable political situation in Safed, along with a healthy

---

3. B. Lewis, *Notes and Documents from the Turkish Archives: A Contribution to the History of the Jews in the Ottoman Empire* (Jerusalem, 1952), p. 10.

4. S. Avitsur, "Safed—Center of the Manufacture of Woven Woolens in the Fifteenth Century," *Sefunot* 6 (1962): 41–69 (Hebrew).

economic base, provided the conditions under which a rather extraordinary community began to develop from about 1530 on. Safed attracted an unusual array of scholars and rabbis. Religious life took on a vitality the Jewish community in Palestine had not experienced for centuries as Safed began to emerge as a great spiritual center, not only for the Jews of that country, but for Near Eastern Jewry as a whole.

In the study houses, synagogues, and academies, religious life and intellectuality flourished. In several different fields of Jewish literature, Safed scholars made contributions that were to exert enormous influence on Judaism. It was in Safed, for example, that Joseph Karo (1488–1575) composed the *Shulḥan 'Arukh*, which is to this day regarded as the authoritative code of rabbinic law for traditional Jewish practice. Religious poetry of high quality, much of which made its way into the prayer book, was written by men such as Israel Najara, Eleazar Azikri, Solomon Alkabez, and Isaac Luria. Influential and innovative homiletical writings were composed by Moses Alsheikh, Elisha Gallico, and others.[5]

It was in the realm of Kabbalah, however, that Safed made its most distinctive contribution, influencing the course of Jewish history in fundamental ways. Building on the kabbalistic tradition, the roots of which go back to twelfth-century Provence and thirteenth-century Spain, Safed became the scene of a mystical renaissance of considerable proportions. As we shall see, the Safed mystics promoted a radically innovative doctrine according to which the practice of mystical devotion was no longer to be restricted to small conventicles or groups of initiates as had been the case at an earlier time; instead, it was held to be the legitimate domain of each and every individual. This attempt to democratize and popularize the mystical life, advanced by the leading Kabbalists of this community, proved to have historical consequences, the impact of which was felt long after Safed itself began to decline toward the end of the sixteenth century. The widespread and disastrous messianic movement of the seventeenth century known as Sabbatianism, which galvanized around the personality of Sabbatai Sevi, had its roots in Safed Kabbalism. Further, it is difficult to imagine the rise of Hasidism, the popular mystical movement that flourished among the masses of Eastern European Jewry beginning in the eighteenth century, and that exists to this day, without the contribution made by sixteenth-century Kabbalah.

---

5. Concerning the poetry of Israel Najara, see A. Mirsky, "New Poems of R. Israel Najara," *Sefunot* 6 (1962): 259–302 (Hebrew). Moses Alsheikh's work is analyzed by S. Shalem, *Sefunot* 6 (1962): 197–258; idem, *Sefunot* 7 (1963): 179–197 (Hebrew).

INTRODUCTION

The Religious World of Safed

Between approximately 1530 and 1590, the Kabbalists of Safed evolved a theological world view and a religious way of life that exhibited a highly distinctive character. This new religious outlook may be analyzed by examining five essential features of Safed piety: (a) messianic fervor, (b) organized brotherhoods, (c) ascetic behavior, (d) ritual innovation, and (e) contemplative exercises.

Messianic Fervor

It was not long after the Expulsion that efforts were made to impose some meaningful religious perspective on the terrible events that had recently taken place. In this period before the ascendancy of Safed, one of the most outstanding and influential advocates of an emerging messianic response was Isaac Abrabanel (1437–1508). Abrabanel was the author of a number of exegetical works that expressed hopes for redemption and interpreted contemporary events as messianic tribulations. He sought to convince the exiled Jews that the tragedy they were experiencing was *purposeful*, that it was a prelude to the arrival of the messianic age, which he calculated would begin in 1503. At that time, according to Abrabanel, the Jews would avenge themselves on their enemies, the dispersed would return to the Land of Israel, the resurrection and judgment would take place, and all Jews would live under the leadership of the Messiah.[6] Numerous other authors followed Abrabanel's path, producing various kinds of exegetical, homiletical, and apocalyptic treatises aimed at representing the Spanish Expulsion as the "birthpangs" of the messianic age.

In this early post-Expulsion period, a Jerusalem Kabbalist named Abraham ben Eliezer ha-Levi (ca. 1460–ca. 1530) became well known as a zealous messianic propagandist and preacher of repentance.[7] Drawing on a wide array of sources, including the Zohar, ha-Levi composed several apocalyptic treatises in which he attempted to prove that the year 1524 would witness the beginning of the messianic deliverance, and that the Messiah would appear in 1530–1531. Through his writings and preaching he sought to inspire Jews to engage in penitence in order to ready them-

---

6. The very titles of Abrabanel's works suggest his messianic preoccupation: *Ma'yenei Yeshu'ah* (Fountains of Deliverance), *Yeshu'ot Meshiḥo* (The Deliverance of His Anointed), and *Mashmi'a Yeshu'ah* (Announcing Deliverance).

7. Concerning the activities of this sage, see G. Scholem, *Qiryat Sefer* 2 (1925) and 7 (1931).

selves for the inevitable messianic coming. Messianic excitement was aroused further during this period by the extraordinary activities of David Reuveni and the Marrano Solomon Molkho, whose frequently wild political exploits were based on apocalyptic expectations and personal messianic pretensions. From this same period comes the anonymously authored *Kaf ha-Qetoret* (The Spoonful of Incense) which was written as a commentary on the book of Psalms. The Psalms were interpreted as alluding to the imminence of redemption and were said to constitute battle hymns for the final apocalyptic war![8]

This acute eschatalogical fervor, which hinged all its hopes on the conviction that the Messiah was about to appear soon, eventually dissipated after 1530 when these hopes went unfulfilled. It gave way to a rather different mood, which can be felt in the writings of the Safed community. This new mood differed from the older one in at least two basic respects.

In the first place, the view of the apocalypticists and messianic calculators toward the Expulsion was, paradoxically, a positive one. Inasmuch as it fit into God's overall plan to usher in the messianic era, the tragic suffering brought on by the exile was ultimately a good thing, an unfortunate but indispensable element within the broader eschatalogical scheme of things. The view that emerged among the Safed Kabbalists differed in that for them the exile ceased to have such positive meaning. Instead, they came to regard it more as the catastrophe it actually was, as another powerful illustration of the reality of Israel's exile and the severe bitterness of unredeemed existence. Israel's condition was as serious and problematic as ever. The earlier apocalyptic tension, oriented primarily toward the external dynamics of history, now gave way to the search for a resolution to the problem of exile on a deeper level of spirituality.[9]

The second and closely related departure from the earlier outlook was the appropriation of Kabbalism on the part of the Safed community. While Abraham ben Eliezer ha-Levi may have drawn on kabbalistic sources for the purpose of building a case for the imminence of redemption, he did not synthesize Kabbalah with messianism in any fundamental way. In Safed, however, messianic views were from the start bound up with the deepest

---

8. *Kaf ha-Qetoret* is extant in a Paris MS, Bibliotheque Nationale, no. 845.

9. Despite the fact that they were residing in the Land of Israel, the new immigrants still regarded themselves as living in an exiled condition. Redemption involved far more than mere physical residence in Palestine; it included the ingathering of the Jewish people from the diaspora, as well as the appearance of the Messiah. Nevertheless, the migration of Jews to their homeland, even on a small scale, was viewed with messianic significance. For a discussion of the transition from apocalyptic messianism to Safed's new outlook, see G. Scholem, *Major Trends in Jewish Mysticism* (New York, 1943), pp. 244–251.

INTRODUCTION

kabbalistic themes. Here we must say a few words about some of the relevant motifs of the older Kabbalah.[10]

According to kabbalistic theology, the life of the divine is comprised of two parts, the first of which is known as *'Ein-Sof* (literally, "Infinite" or "Without End"). *'Ein-Sof* is that aspect of God which is utterly unknowable and concealed beyond all human apprehension. The hidden and perfect root of all reality, it can be neither positively named nor imagined. At most it can be described as "that which thought cannot attain," "the concealed light," or "indistinguishable unity." *'Ein-Sof*, then, constitutes that dimension of the divine life which is absolutely transcendent, God as He is known only to Himself. According to some Kabbalists in fact, even the Scriptures make no reference to God as *'Ein-Sof*, so great is His ineffability.

The doctrine of *'Ein-Sof*, with its insistence on the inability of human beings to know God's essence, strongly resembles the *via negativa* or "negative theology" of the medieval philosophers. The Kabbalists, however, go far beyond the philosophers by means of the notion of *Sefirot*, ten aspects of the divine that emanate from the inner wellsprings of *'Ein-Sof*. Described as the hidden *'Ein Sof's* "garments," "crowns," "lights," or "colors," the *Sefirot* flow out of *'Ein-Sof*, revealing and making manifest the life of the Godhead. According to this doctrine of divine emanation, the *Sefirot* are not mere external attributes of God but aspects of His very Self, intrinsic dimensions of His being through which He continuously manifests Himself. They are symbols that point to spiritual realities comprising the life of deity. While virtually nothing can be said of God as *'Ein-Sof*, the realm of the *Sefirot* is accessible to human contemplation and description. Together, *'Ein-Sof* and the ten *Sefirot* comprise what the Kabbalists refer to as the upper world. (A description of the ten *Sefirot* and their symbolic associations is found in the Appendix.)

Below the sefirotic realm is the lower world or the world of separation. What is the relationship between these two levels of reality? In the first place, the early Kabbalists described the divine unfolding that occurs in the upper world, and the creation of our world, as two aspects of the very same process. Creation takes place on two levels simultaneously, the material world being a visible manifestation of a process that takes place in a concealed way in the sefirotic realm. The essential difference between

---

10. For introductions in English to the ideas of the Kabbalah of the twelfth and thirteenth centuries, see L. Fine, "Kabbalistic Texts," *Back to the Sources: Reading the Classic Jewish Texts*, ed. B. Holtz (New York, 1984); L. Jacobs, *Seeker of Unity* (New York, 1966), pp. 27–48; D. Matt, *Zohar: The Book of Enlightenment* (New York, 1983); Scholem, *Major Trends*, pp. 205–243.

the two realms is that whereas the world of unity is one in which there is, ideally, perfect harmony and integration, the world of separation is characterized by flaw and materialization. Nevertheless, inasmuch as the lower world was created as a result of the emanation of divine life from above, it corresponds to and parallels that world in its very structure. Everything in our world has a counterpart, a correspondence in the world above. The earth, moon, sun, stars, rivers, oceans, and all of the processes of nature of which they are a part, reveal to us the processes of dynamic life that take place on the level of the *Sefirot*.

Not only does everything in the material world *mirror* a spiritual reality above, but everything in creation is *invested* with divine vitality or abundance from the *Sefirot*. There is a continuous flow of divine nourishment and blessing from one realm of existence to the other, endowing all things in the lower world with life. In order to express this relationship the Kabbalah uses the image of a cosmic chain in which everything is linked to everything else. All the elements of existence—from the most hidden to the most visible—are intimately and inextricably bound to one another. All things trace their roots back to the inner recesses of the Source of all being, *'Ein-Sof*.

Where do human beings fit into this mythological scheme? To the Kabbalists, the human personality represents the totality of the sefirotic structure and, even more, is imbued with divine life. This is especially true of the soul, the *neshamah*, which is regarded as deriving from God. The soul, then, establishes a direct link between the *Sefirot* and every person. On the basis of this doctrine, the Kabbalists teach a remarkable idea, namely, that human deeds have an effect on the upper world. Every action reverberates on the level of the *Sefirot!*

The early Kabbalists taught that prior to Adam's sin there was no material world at all. Adam himself was of a purely spiritual nature. Moreover, the *Sefirot* stood in a relationship of perfect harmony with one another. This situation ended with Adam's sin. Adam assumed corporeal form and was no longer located in the upper world; the intrasefirotic relationship was no longer one of unceasing unity. Instead, a degree of disharmony was introduced. This disharmony or flaw is most frequently conceived of as separation between two of the *Sefirot*, *Tif'eret* and *Malkhut*, male and female aspects of God. The task of all human beings is to *restore* the original harmony that existed prior to Adam's fall. Every proper deed contributes to the well-being of divine life. In turn, the momentary reunification of God brought about by such an action enables divine light to flow downward into the material realm. That is, virtuous earthly action reunites God's various aspects, primarily by restoring the love between *Tif'eret* and *Malkhut*, and reestablishes the relationship between a person and the *Sefirot*.

This doctrine of the cosmic repercussions of religious deeds consti-tutes one of the most far-reaching conceptions of Kabbalah. The effect of such theology—though the Kabbalists themselves do not explicitly draw such a conclusion—is to thoroughly revise the notion of God's autonomy. God is no longer conceived to be in control of all history in the conven-tional theological sense. Rather, God's *own* well-being is determined by what human beings do or fail to do. The mystic's religious observance takes on altogether new meaning by investing his every deed with enor-mous significance.

It is this set of mystical ideas that the Safed Kabbalists brought to the situation in which they found themselves. The intense sense of exile to which we have already referred expressed itself in the preoccupation of these individuals with the fate of the *Shekhinah*, another name for the *Sefirah Malkhut*. As a feminine principle within God, the last of the ten *Sefirot* who has no divine light of Her own but who only reflects the light of the upper *Sefirot*, the *Shekhinah* was regarded as having been cut off from the source of Her nourishment. The external realities of history, most recently the tragedy of the Expulsion, were considered to have their parallel in the life of God. Just as the people Israel had been dealt a terrible blow, sent yet again into exile, so too God himself had suffered a great rending, the sep-aration of the *Shekhinah* from the rest of God. Even more, the sins of the Jewish people themselves—reiterations of Adam's sin—were considered to have brought on the exile in the first place. The pietists of Safed, many of whom were exiles or the descendants of exiles from Spain, held themselves responsible for the tragic breach that they believed had taken place within the realm of the *Sefirot*.

Even though the earlier Spanish Kabbalah had already spoken of the *Shekhinah*'s exile, it was the Kabbalists of Safed, now consumed by the hor-rors of historical exile, who took up this theme and pushed it to its ex-treme. In the process, they achieved a personal identification with the *Shekhinah*, the intensity of which was unknown among the earlier Kabbal-ists. An excellent illustration of this may be seen in a practice of Moses Cordovero and Solomon Alkabez. In a small book called *Tomer Devorah* (The Palm Tree of Deborah), Cordovero described how they used to wan-der among the gravesites of rabbinic sages believed to be buried in the en-virons of Safed. They did so in imitation of the wandering of the exiled *Shekhinah*!

INTRODUCTION

> One should wander, as if exiled from place to place, purely for the sake of Heaven, and thereby make oneself a vessel for the *Shekhinah* in exile. . . . Thus one should humble one's heart and bind it to the Torah, even as Rabbi Shimon bar Yohai and his associates used to wander about and discuss Torah. And if one trudges on foot from place to place, without horse or cart, so much the better.[11]

Cordovero indicates in another source that this practice resulted in experiences of automatic speech, in which interpretations of scriptural verses would gush forth from their mouths without prior reflection:

> . . . what I and others have experienced in connection with *gerushin* ["exiles" or peregrinations], when we wandered in the fields with the Kabbalist Rabbi Solomon Alkabez, discussing verses from the Bible suddenly, without previous reflection. On these occasions new ideas would come to us in a manner that cannot be believed unless one has seen or experienced it many times.[12]

Whereas at an earlier time men such as Abraham ben Eliezer ha-Levi had believed that the redemption would come of its own accord, independent of the cooperation of human beings, the Safed mystics were motivated by the belief that redemption would only come if the people Israel worked for it. Mystical devotion during prayer and fulfillment of the commandments (*miṣvot*), accompanied by the appropriate contemplative kabbalistic intentions, rigorous ascetic behavior, and ethical deeds, would lift the *Shekhinah* out of Her exile and restore the divine realm to its original state. What is more, the Safed pietists, following a tradition found in the classical work of thirteenth-century Spanish Kabbalah, the Zohar (Book of Splendor), which promised redemption if even one Jewish community would achieve complete repentance, regarded themselves as standing at the very center of the messianic drama. In this drama every single individual had a role to play and no action was devoid of redemptive significance. It is this as much as anything that defines the special nature of Safed spirituality. Safed appropriated a basic kabbalistic idea concerning the efficacious quality of human action and made it the cornerstone of the religious life by heightening the stakes, so to speak. It is one thing to be concerned about one's own personal spiritual condition, quite another to be responsible for the fate of one's people and even God. Under the pressures generated by

---

11. This translation is drawn from R. J. Z. Werblowsky, *Joseph Karo, Lawyer and Mystic* (Oxford, 1962), p. 52.

12. Ibid., p. 54.

INTRODUCTION

an intensified sense of sin and exile, and a deepened longing for redemption, these individuals possessed an unusually onerous notion of personal and collective responsibility.

The corporate, public efforts of this intensely single-minded community could, it was believed, reverse the flow of history, bringing about physical and spiritual redemption. Redemption would occur, not when Israel had sunk to the lowest possible depths, as some earlier rabbinic theories had proposed, but when it succeeded in restoring all things to their flawless primordial condition. It is to this monumental task that the Kabbalists of sixteenth-century Safed devoted themselves.

Organized Brotherhoods

Alongside of conventional synagogue congregations, which were divided according to ancestral origins (Sefardim, Ashkenazim, Musta'rabim, and so forth), a number of *havurot* or intentional brotherhoods developed in Safed. While membership in a congregation was usually based on the arbitrary factor of one's family background, devout fellowships brought together individuals interested in a greater degree of specialization when it came to the life of piety. Persons of like mind could organize to pursue a particular course that served their needs and their sense of how best to fulfill their spiritual vision.

It should be pointed out that while Kabbalism permeated the air of Safed in the sixteenth century in general, and few could have been left untouched by the powerful currents around them, there can be no doubt that some regarded themselves as especially devoted to the pursuit of the kabbalistic life. That is to say, even in a society that stressed the responsibility of every person, some naturally chose a greater degree of professionalization. Most of the individuals whose names appear with any frequency in the mystical literature are likely to have been associated with one or another of the several groups about which we know.

These *havurot* served, to a certain degree, to institutionalize kabbalistic devotion. They helped to define the proper direction that piety ought to take and to channel religious energy in a disciplined way. These fellowships thus constituted a vehicle by which the idea of collective obligation described here could find expression. From a psychological point of view they must have served as both a means of support and a source of peer pressure to live the correct life of mystical piety. As R. J. Z. Werblowsky observed, "The social habits and values of the Safed Kabbalists helped to integrate the individual mystic in an ideal, normative community which

10

gave him spiritual security and support, and which provided him with a fund of energy and discipline on which he could constantly draw."[13]

This is illustrated well by the ideal of mystical fellowship described by Hayyim Vital:

> When it comes to the love for one's associates who study Torah with one another, each and every person must bind himself to the others as if he were one limb within the body of this fellowship. This is particularly important when an individual possesses the knowledge and the mystical insight with which to understand and apprehend his friend's soul. And should there be one among them in distress, all must take it upon themselves to share his trouble, whether it has to do with some illness or with his children, God forbid. And they must all pray on his behalf. Likewise, in all one's prayers and petitions one should be mindful of his fellows. My teacher, of blessed memory, took great care to caution me about the love which we must bear towards our associates, the members of our brotherhood.[14]

Some of the fellowships were under the spiritual guidance of particular personalities, such as Moses Cordovero, Eleazar Azikri, Isaac Luria, and, following Luria's death, Hayyim Vital. Other groups, as evidenced by the rules of pious conduct (*Hanhagot*) presented in this volume, appear to have been devoted to highly specialized goals. Thus, the fellowship of penitents concerning whom Abraham Berukhim informs us directed its efforts at atonement through especially severe ascetic practices. Berukhim also provides a report about a group whose only purpose seems to have been rejoicing at the conclusion of every Sabbath. An anonymous Safed authority indicates that "there is a group which goes out on the night of Simḥat Torah for the purpose of singing and dancing in the presence of the Torah scroll in every synagogue."[15]

Ascetic Behavior

Sixteenth-century Safed religiosity was permeated by a strain of asceticism, in some cases of a rather severe nature. While ascetic tendencies

---

13. Ibid., p. 62.

14. *Sha'ar ha-Kavvanot* of the *Shemonah She'arim*, 2a-b. (All references to Hayyim Vital's version of Lurianic teachings, the *Shemonah She'arim*, are to the Yehuda Ashlag edition, Tel Aviv, 1962.) H. Vital, *Sefer ha-Ḥezyonot*, ed. A. Z. Aeshcoly (Jerusalem, 1954), pp. 156–157. For the full text, see Isaac Luria's customs, no. 5, this volume.

15. See "Additional Customs from Safed," no. 13, this volume.

are typically associated more with medieval Christian piety than with Jewish piety, the fact remains that ascetic behavior is hardly unknown in Judaism. Thus, for example, Bahya ibn Paquda's famous ethical work *Duties of the Heart* (eleventh century), influenced to a significant degree by Sufi mysticism, reveals a strong interest in certain types of ascetic behavior.[16] The most striking instance of a more extreme tendency within medieval Judaism is present in the writings of the *Ḥasidei Ashkenaz*, the German-Jewish pietists of the twelfth and thirteenth centuries. Thus, the Safed mystics were by no means the first medieval Jewish community to be attracted to the ascetic life. Nevertheless, the scale on which this kind of behavior took place and the motives underlying it serve to mark Safed as an unusual case.

Ascetic practices in which the Safed pietists engaged were of several types. We find repeated reference to the desirability of avoiding meat and wine, or at least to consuming these in a sparing way. According to Moses Cordovero, for example, wine is prohibited during the day, although diluted wine may be taken at night. He further cautions against eating more than a spare amount of meat during the weekdays "as these foods endow *Sama'el* [that is, Satan] with strength." Abraham Berukhim reports that "there are certain especially pious scholars of Torah who neither eat meat nor drink wine during the entire week." In addition to advising against eating too much meat or drinking wine, Joseph Karo's mentor-angel exhorts him to "take care not to enjoy your eating and drinking and marital relations. It should be as if demons were compelling you to eat that food."[17]

A second type of ascetic practice was fasting. Cordovero instructs his disciples to fast for three consecutive days during each of the four seasons, though it is praiseworthy to increase this amount. Fasting in penitence on the eve of the New Moon (*Rosh Ḥodesh*) was apparently a widespread custom, important enough to be done by women. One authority instructs individuals to "fast on Thursdays and pray the afternoon service with a quorum of ten people who are likewise fasting." Far more extreme regimens of fasting, including long periods of abstinence, were enjoined by Isaac Luria in order that his disciples might atone for specific transgressions.[18]

Additional kinds of self-mortification exercises were performed by particular groups. Concerning one group, Abraham Berukhim reports the

---

16. A. Lazaroff, "Bahya's Asceticism against Its Rabbinic and Islamic Background," *Journal of Jewish Studies* 21 (1970): 11–38.
17. L. Jacobs, *Jewish Mystical Testimonies* (New York, 1977), p. 105.
18. *Sha'ar Ruaḥ ha-Qodesh* of the *Shemonah She'arim*, 40b–74a.

practice of flagellation and the donning of sackcloth and ashes. For his disciples, Isaac Luria prescribed ritual immersions in the winter, sleeping on the ground, rolling naked in the snow and on thorns for especially egregious sins.

Mention should also be made in this connection of the extreme concern of the Safed pietists with proper sexual behavior. On the one hand, Jewish mystical practice reflects a fundamentally positive attitude toward sexual practice within the boundaries determined by rabbinic law. Even more, the Kabbalists regarded married sexual life as partaking in a sacred mystery. Not merely a vehicle for fulfilling the essential *miṣvah* (religious obligation) of procreation or an opportunity to avoid sinful thoughts and deeds, marriage enabled the mystic to realize the sefirotic reunification of *Tif'eret* and *Shekhinah*, and to mend the breach within God caused by human sin. Thus, for the Kabbalists, the sacramental and theurgic qualities of married sex took on great importance. This metaphysical understanding of sexuality did not represent a romantic notion of marriage. Rather, the focus of attention was transferred from one's partner to the sacred unification of male and female within God. As such, one's sexual life served an instrumental purpose of an exalted nature. In his *Sefer Ḥaredim* (Book of the Devout), Eleazar Azikri writes that while God has given man a wife of flesh and blood whom he is to love, his real love must be for the daughter of the King, that is, the *Shekhinah*.[19]

Just as the Kabbalists heightened the significance of married sexuality that was properly carried out, they correspondingly viewed sexual sin with the gravest anxiety. According to Isaac Luria, for example, sexual misconduct of any type—homosexuality, adultery, masturbation—called for the most rigorous self-mortification and repentance. Such sins were not merely injurious to an individual, or simply offenses against God's will. They were regarded in kabbalistic terms as inflicting still further damage on the realm of the *Sefirot*, the upper world.

Several considerations serve to explain such an outbreak of asceticism and austere behavior. First, the Safed mystics shared the generalized sense of deep guilt over the state of exile under which the Jewish people continued to live. Thus, Moses Cordovero explains that the midnight vigil that his circle practiced was for the purpose of mourning the destruction of the Temple and weeping on account of one's transgressions, which delay the redemption. Such traditionally motivated guilt was deepened, as we have already seen, by the related responsibility felt for the fate of the *Shekhinah*.

---

19. Concerning this whole question, see Werblowsky, *Karo*, pp. 133–138.

Every sin was believed to exacerbate the exiled condition of the *Shekhinah*, whereas every proper devotional act contributed to the reunification of the Holy One, blessed be He (*Tif'eret*), and the *Shekhinah*. Ascetic activities constituted means by which one could atone for sin and seek a life of purity.

For example, Joseph Karo's mentor-angel, whom he identified as the *Shekhinah*, expresses gratitude for the fact that Karo and his colleagues afflicted themselves by studying all night on the eve of the Feast of Weeks (*Shavu'ot*) in order to raise up the *Shekhinah* from Her miserable state:

> Happy are you in this world and happy in the next that you resolved to adorn Me on this night. For these many years had My head fallen with none to comfort Me. I was cast down to the ground to embrace the dunghills, but now you have restored the crown to its former place. . . . You are not like those who sleep on beds of ivory in sleep which is a sixtieth of death.[20]

Elijah de Vidas puts it this way: "It is appropriate for a person to arouse himself in repentance when he considers that the *Shekhinah* is exiled on his account, as it is written: 'And for your transgressions was your mother put away' (Is. 50:1). Her return from exile depends upon an individual's repentance."[21]

Safed asceticism was also bound up with the related notion that perfect purity was required of a person who desired to achieve the mystical state of *devequt* (cleaving to God), or to attain various other kinds of mystical inspiration. This is expressed with clarity by Hayyim Vital in explaining the moral prerequisites for mystical arousal.

> When the soul is pure and unblemished, then the supernal holy matters take shape in it, and when it dwells in rust and stain everything becomes bittersweet [i.e., evil appears as good]. This is similar to the sick person who, when he is ill, abhors the good things and loves things which aggravate his illness. The doctor, in order to restore his health, gives him spices including gall, by which his nature will return to what it originally was, and his health as before. So too, the sick soul, to remove the sickness from it, must receive the bitterness of medicine and "return" in the form of mortifications and fasts, sackcloth and ashes and stripes, ritual immersions, and purifications from filth and the stains of sins. This is in order

---

20. Jacobs, *Jewish Mystical Testimonies*, p. 100.
21. See *Beginning of Wisdom*, The Gate of Repentance, chap. 1, this volume.

to be able to attain and comprehend supernal matters, which are the mysteries of the world, hidden from the world from the days of Rabbi Shimon bar Yohai until now.[22]

Finally, notice should be taken in this connection with the particular needs of Marranos living in Safed. Having accepted baptism against their will, these penitents sought to atone for their sins by recourse to especially severe acts of self-mortification. There is no doubt that the presence of these individuals contributed to the emotional climate of atonement and penance in this community.[23]

The austerity that characterized Safed was not unmitigated. In the first place, the requirements of Jewish law served to compel restraint or temper what would have otherwise been ascetic behavior of an even more extreme sort. Safed Kabbalists, for example, may have been more preoccupied in pleasing the *Shekhinah* than in satisfying their wives, but Jewish tradition prevented an individual from renouncing marriage and sexual life altogether. Celibacy, even in the most severely ascetic settings, was never intentionally practiced among medieval Jews no matter how much some might have preferred it. In a similar way, no rabbinic Jew could, in good conscience, ignore the obligation to celebrate the Sabbath with the appropriate joyousness, and by wearing fine clothes and enjoying three festive meals. Likewise, the other joyful holidays afforded opportunity for a complete change of mood. More generally, the traditionally social character of Jewish life, with its insistence on involvement with the larger community,

---

22. *Sha'ar Ruah ha-Qodesh*, 39a–39b.

23. The problem of the Marranos was one of the factors behind the famous controversy over ordination that took place in Safed. Based on Moses Maimonides's opinion that "if all the Palestinian sages would unanimously agree to appoint and ordain judges, then these new ordinants would possess the full authority of the original ordained judges" [*Yad, Sanhedrin* 4:11], an effort was made in 1538 by Rabbi Jacob Berab of Safed to reinstitute the practice of rabbinic ordination. Even though rabbis continued to have judicial authority, official ordination as it had been granted in the days of the Sanhedrin came to an end sometime in late antiquity. Berab succeeded in convincing the rabbis of Safed to ordain him. When he sought to gain the acquiescence of the chief rabbi of Jerusalem, Levi ibn Habib—whose support he needed for his own ordination to be valid—he was rebuffed. Despite ibn Habib's objections, on various grounds, Berab went on to grant ordination to four other Safed sages, including his student Joseph Karo. Of concern to us is that one of the primary motivations behind Berab's effort was his hope to be able to enjoin the rabbinic punishment of lashes; such punishment was necessary in order for the Marranos to become fully cleansed of their sins. Lacking the authority to impose such punishment, Berab—who felt that the Messiah's appearance was nearing and that atonement had better be accomplished—sought to attain that prerogative. Concerning the controversy, see J. Katz, *Sion* 16 (1951): 28–45; M. Benayahu, "The Revival of Ordination in Safed," *Sefer Yovel le-Yiṣḥaq Baer* (Jerusalem, 1960), pp. 248–269; H. Z. Dimitrovsky, *Sefunot* 10 (Jerusalem, 1966): 113–192.

made it impossible for ascetically oriented Kabbalists to go off on their own to form truly private communities along the lines of a monastic sect.

In addition to these factors, joyfulness in the service of God was actually a spiritual *ideal* among the Safed pietists. While this was to become an important tenet of the Hasidic movement in the eighteenth century, it was also a feature of sixteenth-century piety. Thus, for example, Isaac Luria is reported to have discouraged sadness, calling it an impediment to the acquisition of mystical inspiration.[24] Elijah de Vidas devoted the entire tenth chapter of the "Gate of Love" from his *Reshit Hokhmah* (Beginning of Wisdom) to the role joy plays in the religious life: "A person ought to derive greater pleasure from the joy of serving God and fulfilling His commandments than from all the money in the world . . . no joy in the world may be compared with that of the commandments."

Finally, and perhaps most significantly, it should be noted that austerity and a profound sense of responsibility did not, in this case, lead to resignation and despair. Quite the opposite is true. The pietists of this community were *activists*, convinced that they held in their hands the power with which to alter history and heal the cosmos. They were devoted to setting things right and they appear to have lived in hopeful anticipation that they would soon reap the fruits of their labor. There were, in other words, *two* foci to the Safed world view: the bitterness of the *Shekhinah*'s exile and the dread of sin on the one hand, the anticipated redemption and the enthusiasm for serving God on the other. It is precisely this tension between death and rebirth, between exile and redemption, that stood at the heart of the creative forces at work in sixteenth-century Safed.

Ritual Innovation

With the prominent exception of the Sabbatian movement, which, in some of its forms, constituted heresy, the kabbalistic movement remained within the fold of rabbinic Judaism. This was especially evident in the sphere of law and ritual. The Kabbalists did not oppose traditional Jewish law in any way; they did, however, *transform* it by investing conventional ritual practice with a new level of meaning. The Kabbalists themselves, of course, believed that the esoteric meaning with which they endowed prayer, festival celebration, and life-cycle ritual was not new at all, but the

---

24. See Isaac Luria's customs, no. 2, this volume; for an analysis of the idea of joy in Hasidism and its Safed antecedents, see A. Schochat, "On Joy in Hasidism," *Sion* 16 (1951): 30–43 (Hebrew).

deepest and truest level of meaning. Rather than discard traditional liturgy and ritual observance, they "discovered" in the conventional rites hidden mystical truth.

Thus, for example, the Kabbalists of thirteenth-century Spain saw in the words of prayer symbols representing the ten *Sefirot*. Prayer became transformed into an elaborate vehicle for the contemplation of God and for cleaving with one's soul to the sefirotic world. In this manner, Kabbalah functioned in a way that was simultaneously conservative and radical. By retaining traditional forms of ritual it displayed a genuine conservatism. Yet revolutionary tendencies were at work to the extent that these older forms became the medium for radically new meaning.[25]

In their desire to achieve mystical goals, however, the Safed Kabbalists were not satisfied with merely endowing older forms with new meaning. Their need to give expression to novel ideas drove them to search for and create entirely innovative practices, although even here we find that they frequently drew on mythical motifs embedded in older Jewish tradition in the development of these rituals.

Let us take as an example the ritual of the midnight vigil, to which the texts presented in this volume make frequent reference. One of the most popular themes of the Zohar is the mystical importance attached to rising at night, especially midnight, in order to study the Torah. Midnight was considered to be a time of divine favor and arousal, during which the forces of strict judgment were quieted and the powers of mercy and compassion brought forth. According to this theme, God visits the righteous in Paradise at midnight and the pious arise to sing His praise. In addition, midnight was held to be the time at which the *Shekhinah* sings songs and hymns to Her Husband (*Tif'eret*), and according to some sources, the hour at which the two join one another in love.

Drawing their inspiration from these Zoharic themes—some of which themselves go back to still older rabbinic literature—the mystics of Safed fashioned a dramatic ritual in which pious adepts arose every night for the purpose of study, praising God, mourning the destruction of the Temple, and lamenting their sins. Although this practice is frequently mentioned in the earlier Safed sources, it was under the guidance of Isaac Luria that it assumed a far more elaborate form.[26] It consisted of three parts, the "rite for Rachel," the "rite for Leah," and the "rite for the soul." During the first

---

25. On this question, see G. Scholem, "Religious Authority and Mysticism," in his *On the Kabbalah and Its Symbolism* (New York, 1965), pp. 5–31.

26. This rite is described in Nathan Hannover's *Sha'arei Sion* (Prague, 1662) as well as in numerous other sources, including those prayer books that follow the Lurianic tradition.

part of the night, during which the rite for Rachel takes place, an individual laments the exile of the *Shekhinah* by engaging in acts of mourning: removal of shoes, weeping, placing ashes on one's forehead, and rubbing one's eyes in the dust on the ground in order to symbolize the *Shekhinah*, who lies in the dust Herself. The adept then recites Psalm 137, which recalls the Babylonian exile, Psalm 79, the final chapter of the book of Lamentations, and other songs of lament. This is followed by the rite for Leah, in which attention shifts to the theme of redemption. During this part of the ritual hymns that look forward to the coming of the Messiah are sung. Finally, the rite for the soul is celebrated, in which one contemplatively seeks to restore the unity of *Tif'eret* and *Shekhinah*.

In this remarkable ritual, then, an individual is called on to reenact, night after night, the "history of the world" so to speak. It is a history that recalls the fate of a dispersed people and the parallel suffering of God; yet it also looks forward to a future time when both will be restored to a state of unity and perfection. More than a rite of memory and hope, however, the midnight vigil served as a contemplative *action* whereby the adept actively contributed to the restitutive process.

As will be seen later, some rituals, such as those connected with the Sabbath, were celebrated by the Kabbalists as sacred marriage ceremonies. Still others were devised to establish control over the forces of evil. Together, the ritual innovations for which these individuals were responsible attest to the spiritual vitality of this community.

Contemplative Exercises

Other practices of a more contemplative character constitute a subject of major importance for our understanding of the religious life of Safed. These may be said to fall into two broad categories: (1) those exercises in which the primary emphasis was placed on the mystical experience itself, usually described as the act of cleaving or communing with God (*devequt*), and (2) those exercises that were mainly oriented toward the attainment of mystical knowledge.

Devequt

For many of the Safed Kabbalists, *devequt* was considered to be the highest form of spiritual achievement, the ultimate goal of religious life. Even though various authors took different approaches to the question of *devequt*, we find virtual consensus that, in addition to the presumed moral qualifications, *devequt* necessitated withdrawal from the material and physical world, from the realm of ordinary sensation, in one way or another. An extreme ascetic disposition led Joseph Karo to regard worldly activity in general, and physical pleasure in particular, as essentially repugnant. Moreover, the denial of such pleasure was an absolute prerequisite for attaching oneself to the *Shekhinah:*

> Be careful to perform worldly actions only so far as strictly necessary for life. If there is any pleasure connected with any such action, do not regard the pleasurable side of it but be perturbed, and strongly desire to be able to perform the action without feeling any pleasure. . . . Consider in your heart that you are standing before the King of all kings, the Holy One, blessed be He, whose *Shekhinah* is constantly above your head. . . wherefore all pleasures should be repulsive to you . . . and all your thoughts should be focused on me, my Torah, and my fear. . . . Unify your heart at all times and at every hour and minute to think of nothing but me, my Torah, and my worship. This is the mystery of union in which man is verily united with his Creator, for the soul adheres and unites itself to Him, while the body and the limbs become a true dwelling place for the *Shekhinah*.[27]

Eleazar Azikri proposes divesting oneself of this world through the practice of solitude:

> We find in the ascetic writings of the ancients that the pious used to practice ascetic solitude and *devequt*, which means that when they were alone they withdrew their minds from all worldly things and concentrated their thoughts on the Lord of all. . . . This is the meaning of the report in the Mishnah [Berakhot 5:1], "the early ḥasidim used to wait one hour before praying in order to concentrate their mind on God." The commentators explained this to mean that they cleared their minds from all worldly things, concentrating on the Lord of all with fear and love.[28]

Elijah de Vidas expresses the need to disavow normal reality for a deeper one in somewhat different terms:

> In order for a wife's love for her husband to be perfect, it is important that she see that he loves no other woman in the world besides her. She will then bind herself to him in a covenant of unrestricted love. In the same

---

27. Werblowsky, *Karo*, p. 156.
28. Ibid., pp. 63–64.

way, the *Shekhinah* will not bind Her love to a man who is devoted to worldly matters. Hence, the essential element in love consists in his not loving anything whatsoever in this world more than he does God, may He be blessed. His love for God ought to be greater than that which he bears for his wife and children and all other worldly things. For a man becomes separated from the love of the Holy One, blessed be He, while praying or studying the Torah, due to the evil, distracting thoughts which intrude upon his awareness. This happens because he is not totally immersed in the love of the Holy One, blessed be He. Instead, his love is greater for matters of this world, for this or that thing.[29]

Devequt, however, involves more than negative detachment or withdrawal from this world. Positively formulated, it has to do with the natural disposition of the soul, which, after all, derives from the divine realm, to cleave continuously to God. Thus, Eleazar Azikri writes:

At the appropriate times one should withdraw to a secluded place where one cannot be seen by others, lift up one's eyes on high to the one King, the Cause of all causes, like a mark for the arrow; "as in water face answereth to face, so the heart of man to man" [Proverbs 27:19], and similarly as man turns his face to his God so also will He turn to him and they will cleave together.[30]

Elijah de Vidas develops a three-stage process involving what he calls "cleaving," "longing," and "desiring" God.[31] Cleaving to God, for de Vidas, means concentrating all one's attention on uniting the *Shekhinah* with Her Husband, *Tif'eret*. In order to achieve this the contemplative adept must not only remove all distracting thoughts from his mind; he must also direct attention toward removing from the *Shekhinah* all evil dross through which She has become tainted. Longing consists primarily of attaching oneself to the *Shekhinah* by means of each and every commandment that one performs, carrying them out with virtually ecstatic enthusiasm and passionate love. Finally, desire for God is associated with, among other things, both the impassioned performance of the commandments and the intensive preoccupation with the study of Torah. Both activities, executed with the necessary love and zeal, will enable the soul to cleave to God.

In this connection, it is worth noting the strong erotic character of *dev-*

---

29. See *Beginning of Wisdom*, "The Gate of Love," chap. four, this volume.
30. Werblowsky, *Karo*, pp. 64–65.
31. See *Beginning of Wisdom*, "The Gate of Love," chap. four, this volume.

equt as described by some of the Safed Kabbalists. While the earlier Kabbalah was quite prepared to describe the relationship *within* the sefirotic realm in stark sexual terms, the older Kabbalists were generally more reticent to depict the relationship between an individual and God in explicitly erotic images.[32] Not so with Safed mystics, as illustrated by these words of Elijah de Vidas:

> A man would not delay making love to his wife when he feels passion for her, even if he were given all the money in the world. In a similar manner, it is proper that he feel passionate about carrying out the commandments since, through their performance, he makes love to the King's Daughter, that is, the *Shekhinah*.[33]

De Vidas goes so far as to argue that an individual who has never experienced love for a woman is unprepared to love God since "as a result of the feeling of longing for a woman, one learns to cultivate longing for God." Just as a person rises at night to love his wife out of his intense passion, so should one rise in the middle of the night out of his great love for God.

As these examples suggest, the Safed mystics did not pursue the goal of *unio mystica*, according to which an individual seeks utter abandonment of the self so as to be completely absorbed within the divine. Ever conscious of the ultimate transcendence of the Creator over against the finitude of being human, the Kabbalists, in the main, preferred the experience of cleaving or communion rather than union in the strict sense.

Mystical Knowledge

The desire to acquire esoteric or mystical knowledge of the Torah was a basic goal of the earlier Kabbalists. Although it is true that some of the important representatives of the older Spanish Kabbalah reported that they gained mystical knowledge by experiencing a direct, personal revelation of the prophet Elijah or of the Holy Spirit, most did so in more conventional ways. It was the study and interpretation of traditional texts such as Scripture and rabbinic homilies that yielded esoteric teachings. In

---

32. Concerning this question, see Scholem, *Major Trends*, pp. 225–28. While Scholem claims that the Zohar employs sexual imagery only in depicting the relationship between Moses and God, I. Tishby argues that there are many examples in which the Zohar utilizes erotic imagery to describe man's relationship to the Godhead. See his *Mishnat ha-Zohar* (Jerusalem, 1961), pp. 298ff.

33. See *Beginning of Wisdom*, "The Gate of Love," chap. four, this volume.

sixteenth-century Safed, however, the attempt to achieve mystical gnosis through direct, personal experience was widespread, and a variety of techniques existed for this purpose.

Mention has already been made of the *gerushin* or exiles of Moses Cordovero and Solomon Alkabez, during which they experienced the revelation of biblical interpretations by means of <u>automatic speech</u>. Along similar lines, Joseph Karo was the recipient of angelic revelations throughout the course of his adult life. The angel, or *maggid*, would come to Karo at different hours of the day and night, although the most propitious time was after midnight or in the early morning. The diligent study and repetition of passages from the Mishnah, along with ascetic exercises and austere practices, induced the revelations. These consisted of exhortations, spiritual advice, flattering praise of Karo, and the communication of kabbalistic explanations of biblical verses. The *maggid* spoke through Karo's own voice: "As I was reading the Mishnah the voice of the beloved knocked in my mouth and the lyre sang of itself."[34] Moreover, Karo identified the *maggid* with the Mishnah itself, as well as with the *Shekhinah*. This identification was based on the fact that in Kabbalah the Mishnah stands as the representative of the Oral Torah, and as such symbolizes the *Shekhinah*, the tenth *Sefirah*, *Malkhut*. In Her guise as Mishnah/Oral Torah, the *Shekhinah* is the "articulate" aspect of the Godhead, the manifestation of God's vocal revelation. In light of such symbolic associations, it is clear that Karo imagined the voice that spoke to him and through him to be divine communications.

For Isaac Luria as well, one of the means of achieving the Holy Spirit or the state of prophecy was by meriting angelic revelations in the form of a *maggid*. According to the Lurianic theory, *maggidim* are angelic creations whose existence is brought about by the sounds of a man's voice uttered in the course of religious devotion:

> When a man is righteous and pious, studies Torah and prays with kabbalistic intention, from those sounds which emerge from his mouth, angels and holy spirits are created. . . . And these angels which are created from that which a person utters are the secret of *maggidim*.[35]

---

34. Joseph Karo's kabbalistic activities form the subject of Werblowsky's *Joseph Karo—Lawyer and Mystic*.

35. *Sha'ar ha-Yihudim* (Jerusalem, 1970), 2a. For an analysis of this practice, see L. Fine "Maggidic Revelation in the Teachings of Isaac Luria," in *Mystics, Philosophers, and Politicians—Essays in Jewish Intellectual History in Honor of Alexander Altmann*, ed. J. Reinharz, D. Swetchinski, and K. Bland (Durham, 1982).

It was also possible, according to Luria, for the angelic voice to join with that of a departed *ṣaddiq* (righteous person) in the world above. Having merged, these two voices descend and speak through the voice of the adept.

A rather unusual meditative technique that Isaac Luria taught to his closest disciples was known as *yiḥudim* (unifications). The adept was instructed to begin by stretching himself out on the grave of a departed sage—one with whom he shared spiritual kinship—and concentrate on "arousing" the soul of that *ṣaddiq*. After successfully achieving this, the mystic was directed to focus attention on cleaving with his soul to that of the sage. This was followed by meditation on various letter combinations constituting esoteric names of God; these were intended to unify various aspects of the sefirotic realm as conceived according to Lurianic Kabbalah. Hayyim Vital preserved several descriptions of his own practice of such *yiḥudim*.[36] These exercises resulted in an experience of automatic speech in which the sage on whose grave one was lying revealed mysteries of the Torah.

Hayyim Vital, Isaac Luria's student, devised a contemplative technique of his own that drew on elements of the various practices already described. As in Karo's case, Vital utilized passages of Mishnah for meditative purposes; whereas Karo appears to have been concerned with the quantity of *mishnayot* recited, and the importance of doing it as often as possible, Vital instructed individuals to choose a *particular* passage of Mishnah. According to him, the adept was to concentrate on the communion of his soul with that of the sage whose teaching is mentioned in the text of the Mishnah. As with the other techniques, the resulting revelations were in the form of unreflected automatic speech in which the voice of the *ṣaddiq* became incarnate in the voice of the adept.[37]

The preoccupation on the part of the Safed Kabbalists with the revelation of new mystical knowledge had to do, in part, with the conviction that the disclosure of the hidden meaning of Torah constituted both a *sign* of the coming redemption and a means to *facilitate* the redemption. Con-

---

36. The *yiḥudim* were preserved in *Sha'ar Ruaḥ ha-Qodesh* and *Sha'ar ha-Yiḥudim*. Vital's experiences are described in *Sha'ar ha-Gilgulim* of the *Shemonah She'arim*, 140b–142a, and *Sefer ha-Hezyonot*, pp. 149–151, 170–173. For an English translation of some of the material from *Sefer ha-Hezyonot*, see Jacobs, *Jewish Mystical Testimonies*, pp. 130–133. For a detailed consideration of the *yiḥudim*, see L. Fine, "The Contemplative Practice of Yihudim in Lurianic Kabbalah," *History of Jewish Spirituality*, ed. A. Green (New York, forthcoming).

37. Concerning Vital's practice, see L. Fine, "Recitation of Mishnah as a Vehicle for Mystical Inspiration: A Contemplative Technique Taught by Hayyim Vital," *Revue des Études Juives* 141, no. 1–2 (1982): 183–99.

templative exercises such as those described here were vehicles through which mystical gnosis (i.e., salvational knowledge) could be disclosed. These practices suggest, as well, the intense interest the Safed Kabbalists had in communing and communicating with the souls of departed sages. The widespread belief in metempsychosis, the transmigration of souls (*gilgul*), led individuals to seek to commune with the souls of persons with whom they had a special spiritual kinship. The departed were believed to possess kabbalistic knowledge that was hidden from contemporary individuals. Techniques such as these were able to provide the properly qualified person with the opportunity to partake of such knowledge.

Rules of Mystical Piety

Introduction

That genre of Jewish ethical literature known as *Hanhagot*, referring to rules of behavior, is characterized by certain distinctive features. Whereas other kinds of ethical works systematically explore broad general ethical problems, the *Hanhagot* literature tends to focus on the most specific, practical details of daily religious life. Forsaking speculative, theoretical, and analytical concerns, the *Hanhagot* are usually composed of lists that, in a terse, systematic format, enumerate practical behavioral standards and expectations. In tone they are conspicuously directive and didactic. In this latter respect, the *Hanhagot* are very much like Hebrew ethical wills, letters written by a father to his children before his death, or by a scholar to his community.[1]

The six sets of texts presented here all derive from sixteenth-century Safed and were composed by Kabbalists interested in promoting the practice of mystical piety. They constitute a unique and invaluable source for our knowledge of the Safed community, providing us with concrete information concerning how powerful mystical ideologies led to devotional commitment and ritual innovation.

What is the relationship between these special practices and the traditional corpus of *miṣvot* to which virtually all medieval Jews felt themselves bound? Some of them represent an attempt to merely accentuate the importance of certain legal precepts. At the same time, they often add a new twist to such normative obligations. This is done either by a call for greater stringency of observance, stressing some particular aspect of a precept, or attaching new features to it altogether. On the other hand, a large number of these rules go beyond the usual realm of the *miṣvot* entirely by adding novel obligations that are intended to enrich the life of piety; at the same time, they serve to distinguish such piety from conventional patterns of observance. Thus, for example, the frequently mentioned practice of a midnight vigil to mourn the exile, the especially intensive preoccupation with studying the text of the Mishnah, and the indulgence in prolonged, regular fasting are rites that set off the Safed mystics from their brethren in other places whose piety was restricted to more typical rabbinic practice. Although such rites technically fall into the category of *minhag* (custom) over against what is strictly obligatory according to Jewish law, it is clear that for the Safed community many of these new "customs" acquired the status of obligation.

A great many of these and other Safed devotional practices found a prominent place in the religious life of subsequent generations, both among Near Eastern and European Jewry, especially from the middle of the seventeenth century forward. For example, *Kabbalat Shabbat* (Welcoming the Sabbath), the special service that ushers in the Sabbath, became a highly popular and enduring feature of Jewish ritual. Similarly, the practice of reciting the Song of Songs on Sabbath eve, as well as Proverbs 31:10–31 at the festive table, originated in Safed. Even today these Sabbath customs are popular, although in many communities they have been shorn of their kabbalistic associations.

The practice of holding a midnight vigil for the exile of the *Shekhinah* was especially common in Eastern Europe until relatively recent times. Likewise, the custom of assembling for study throughout the night on the Feast of Weeks, *Hoshannah Rabbah*, and the seventh night of Passover, became widespread. In fact, the dusk-to-dawn study session for the Feast of Weeks has experienced something of a renewed popularity in our own time. The celebration of the day before the new moon as a "minor Day of Atonement" also owes its conception to sixteenth-century Safed.[2]

A whole literature developed that served as a vehicle through which these practices found their way into homes and synagogues in the most diverse Jewish communities. It includes manuals called *Tiqqunim*, containing detailed instructions and texts related to a specific rite, such as *Tiqqun Leil Shavu'ot* for the Feast of Weeks.[3] It includes, as well, more general anthologies of kabbalistic customs, among the most important of which are *Seder ha-Yom* by Moses ibn Makhir, Jacob Semah's *Shulḥan 'Arukh ha-'Ari* and *Naggid u-Meṣaveh*, and *Sha'arei Ṣion* composed by Nathan Hannover.[4]

Two other extraordinarily influential books must be mentioned in this connection. *Shnei Luḥot ha-Brit*, by Isaiah Horowitz, is an encyclopedic volume that explores various dimensions of kabbalistic ethics and religious life. Taking its inspiration from the literature of Safed, it exerted wide influence, particularly among Ashkenazi, that is, European Jewry. *Ḥemdat Yamim*, a compendium of mystical rituals, also played an important role in the dissemination of such customs, most especially among

Near Eastern Jewish communities.[5] In addition, a considerable number of Sefardic and Hasidic prayer books preserved these rites, particularly those issuing from the Lurianic school. Such prayer books also include numerous kabbalistic variations on traditional liturgical texts.[6]

These practices, then, originating in a historical setting that at first glance seems far removed from our own, have never completely died out. What is more, to some contemporary Jews they represent an opportunity to recover an earlier spirituality that appears to be especially attractive by virtue of its mystical-mythical nature.[7]

Moses ben Jacob Cordovero

Introduction

Among the most prominent names in the history of kabbalistic literature is that of Moses Cordovero (1522–1570).[1] Though not known for certain, it is likely that he was born in Safed. From his name it is clear that his family was Spanish in origin. Although Cordovero was not particularly well known for his legal achievements, he did study rabbinic law with Safed's preeminent legal authority, Joseph Karo. Karo's respect for Cordovero's rabbinic prowess is evidenced by the endorsement Karo gave to a legal decision by Cordovero: "This case requires no further deliberation, the judge has penetrated to the heart of the matter. May all such good things be repeated in his name and concerning him may the verse be fulfilled: 'My son, if thy heart be wise, my heart will be glad, even mine' " [Prov. 23:15].[2]

But it is in the realm of Kabbalah, not rabbinic law, that Moses Cordovero achieved widespread fame as a scholar and teacher. His mentor in kabbalistic studies was Solomon Alkabez, Cordovero's brother-in-law, whose influence upon him was decisive. Cordovero's major literary contribution was his construction of a systematic synthesis of all kabbalistic thinking up to his day. His genius consisted in his ability to organize the vast corpus of earlier literature in a comprehensive and coherent fashion. At the same time he sought to creatively address the theoretical problems raised by kabbalistic theology and speculation. Thus, for example, he concerned himself with detailed analyses of such questions as the nature of the dialectical process through which the *Sefirot* pass in the course of their unfolding, or the precise relationship between the *'Ein-Sof* and the *Sefirot*. A prolific writer, Cordovero treated these problems in a variety of works, the most important being *Pardes Rimmonim* [Orchard of Pomegranates], which he completed at the age of twenty-six, *'Elimah Rabbati* [The Great 'Elim], and a massive commentary to the Zohar, *'Or Yaqar* [The Precious Light].[3]

While better known for his theoretical and speculative work, Cordovero's interest to us lies primarily in his more practically oriented activities and writings. One of his shortest but most influential books in this connection is entitled *Tomer Devorah* [The Palm Tree of Deborah]. It was among the very first attempts at synthesizing kabbalistic theology with traditional Jewish ethics. His method is to delineate the variety of ways in which individuals are able to bind themselves to the life of the divine by imitating God. A person can tie himself to God by modeling his activities on the spiritual qualities represented by the ten *Sefirot*. Thus, the opening words of this treatise:

> It is proper for man to imitate his Creator, resembling Him in both likeness and image according to the secret of the Supernal Form. Because the chief Supernal image and likeness is in deeds, a human resemblance merely in bodily appearance and not in deeds, abases that Form. Of the man who resembles the Form in body alone it is said: "A handsome form whose deeds are ugly." For what value can there be in man's resemblance to the Supernal Form in bodily limbs if his deeds have no resemblance to those of his Creator? Consequently, it is proper for man to imitate the acts of the Supernal Crown, which are the thirteen highest attributes of mercy.[4]

Widely quoted by later scholars and carefully studied by the pious, *Tomer Devorah* exerted considerable influence on later generations.[5]

That Cordovero also took an interest in the more esoteric forms of contemplation is evidenced by his use of the writings of Abraham Abulafia, a thirteenth-century Spanish mystic.[6] Further, his practice of *gerushin* (literally, "exiles"), to which we referred earlier, testifies to his own contemplative and visionary experiences. This, along with the other practices recorded in the *Hanhagot* that follow, makes it clear that Cordovero's mystical life was by no means restricted to the scholarly study of kabbalistic tradition.

Moses Cordovero's importance as an author is equaled, if not surpassed, by the incalculable influence he exerted as a teacher. His achievements in this regard are all the more remarkable given the fact that he died at the age of forty-eight. While, as mentioned, Cordovero began the study of Kabbalah under the tutelage of Solomon Alkabez, it appears that a reversal of roles took place in which pupil became teacher. Cordovero quickly succeeded in becoming the principal master of esoteric studies in Safed, at least until the appearance of Isaac Luria, not long before Cordovero's death. His disciples included most of the great Kabbalists of Safed: Elijah de Vidas, Abraham Galante, Hayyim Vital, Abraham ben Eliezer ha-Levi Berukhim, Eleazar Azikri. Samuel Gallico, another disciple, published a summary of his teacher's voluminous *Pardes Rimmonim* under the title '*Asis Rimmonim* [The Sweet Juice of Pomegranates].[7] Mordecai Dato studied with Cordovero for a short time while visiting Safed in the year 1560 from his native Italy. Dato is responsible for introducing Cordovero's teachings into Italy and for having preserved a description of his master's activities in his travel memoirs.[8]

The foremost exponent of Cordovero's system in Italy, however, was the prominent Italian Kabbalist Menahem Azariah Da Fano, who even helped to finance the publication of *Pardes Rimmonim*, and secured his other writings from Cordovero's wife following the master's death. Da Fano himself wrote a number of significant mystical treatises under the influence of Cordovero's teachings and subsequently under the influence of Lurianic Kabbalah.[9] Whereas in many places Cordovero's system was considerably eclipsed by the success of Lurianic mysticism, in seventeenth-century Italy Cordovero's teachings continued to be widely studied and revered.

The *Hanhagot* that follow were presumably compiled for the members of the brotherhood that assembled around Cordovero and Alkabez. It seems highly likely that these rules, ethical injunctions, and rituals represent the crystallization of practices current in this circle, rather than the creation of Cordovero alone. Moreover, there is no reason to believe that they were followed only by those directly associated with this group.

Of particular interest in this set of rules is the advice to "commune with one of the Associates each day for the purpose of talking about devotional concerns," and the injunction to reflect on the deeds of the past week with this same person just prior to ushering in the Sabbath. Noteworthy as well is the high degree of concern for the pursuit of pure and proper interpersonal relations. Thus, Cordovero stresses the avoidance of anger, enjoyment of the company of others, desisting from derogatory talk about another person, daily charity, and honesty in one's relationships.

Cordovero's *Hanhagot* were published in Hebrew in 1908 by Solomon Schechter on the basis of two different manuscripts, forming part of an appendix to Schechter's popular essay "Safed in the Sixteenth Century."[10] The first of these manuscripts is in the collection of the Columbia University Library, MS C812, X893. The second is found in the library of the Jewish Theological Seminary of America in New York. Schechter published the first thirty-six rules on the basis of the Columbia manuscript, and the last five (37–41) from the Seminary version since these are not present in the Columbia copy.

Following the *Hanhagot* we have provided a translation of Solomon Alkabez's *Lekhah Dodi* [Come, My Beloved], a poetic representation of the religious world view held by the Cordovero/Alkabez circle.[11] Like Cordovero, Alkabez was a prolific writer who composed in a wide variety of literary genres: biblical commentaries, prayers and poetry, sermons, a commentary to the Passover Haggadah, and independent kabbalistic treatises.[12] He is best known, however, for having authored the enormously popular Sabbath hymn *Lekhah Dodi*. This poem became the centerpiece of the *Kabbalat Shabbat* service, which appears to have come into being under the influence of Cordovero and Alkabez.

According to the rite of the Ashkenazi Jews, *Kabbalat Shabbat* begins with the recitation of Psalms 95 through 99 and Psalm 29. The Sefardic or Oriental rite has Psalm 29 only. Following *Lekhah Dodi*, Psalms 92 and 93 are recited. The refrain of the hymn, "Come, my Beloved, to meet the Bride," draws its inspiration from the following talmudic passage:

> R. Hanina robed himself and stood at sunset of Sabbath eve and exclaimed, "Come and let us go forth to welcome the queen Sabbath." R. Jannai donned his robes on Sabbath eve and exclaimed, "Come, O bride, Come, O bride!" [Shabbat 119a].

For Alkabez, of course, the image of the Sabbath as Queen/Bride assumed kabbalistic significance undreamed of by the talmudic rabbis. The feminine imagery indicates the kabbalistic identification of the Sabbath with the *Shekhinah*, or *Malkhut*, the last of the ten *Sefirot*. Thus, welcoming the Sabbath Bride became transformed into an act of ushering the female aspect of God into one's midst.

We know that the Kabbalists of Safed literally went out at sunset into a field to greet the Sabbath, designating it "the field of holy apple trees," as the *Shekhinah* is often called in the Zohar. When, eventually, the process of actually going out into the fields fell into desuetude, the congregation acted this out by going into the courtyard of the synagogue. A further attenuation of this ceremony took place when it became the custom simply to rise, open the door of the synagogue, and turn toward the West at the final verse of the hymn, while bowing to the approaching Bride. This is the custom today in most synagogues when *Lekhah Dodi* is sung.

For the Kabbalist, the Sabbath was more than an opportunity for an individual to welcome the *Shekhinah* into his midst. It was, simultaneously, a chance for the Sabbath Queen to unite with Her King, that is, *Tif'eret*, the Holy One, blessed be He. The traditional emphasis on having marital intercourse on the night of the Sabbath took on heightened significance. The earthly love between wife and husband was held to represent the supernal union between the *Shekhinah* and *Tif'eret*. Even more, it served to *facilitate* such unification within the sefirotic world. In such terms, the Sabbath experience as a whole assumed the character of a sacred marriage celebration.

The second, and related, theme of *Lekhah Dodi* is messianic striving. In the first place, the unification of King and Queen constitutes, at least temporarily, a redemptive moment. At the same time, it serves as a reminder of some future redemption, one more complete and more enduring. On an explicit level, the hymn evokes a variety of vivid messianic images: the restoration of Jerusalem, the coming of the Messiah, and the redemption of the people Israel. Thus, for example:

> Shake off your dust, arise! Put on your glorious garments, my
> people, and pray:
> "Be near to my soul, and redeem it through the son of Jesse, the
> Bethlehemite."

The two primary foci of the Safed experience, then, come together in this poem: longing for the restoration of the *Shekhinah* and the vision of redemption. No doubt, the powerful attractiveness of this song is rooted in its typically Safed synthesis of mystical sensibility and messianic yearning.

The Pious Customs of Moses Cordovero

These are the rules which the saintly Rabbi Moses Cordovero, may his memory be for an everlasting blessing, taught "which if a man practices, he shall live by them . . ." [Lev. 18:5]. They number thirty-six.[13]

1. A person should not turn his heart away from meditating upon words of Torah and holiness, so that his heart will not be empty and void of reflection upon the commandments, and in order that his heart may become a dwelling place for the *Shekhinah*.[14]

2. One should avoid anger altogether, because anger leads a person to commit a variety of transgressions. Come and learn from the example of

ix - 25

Moses, our Rabbi, may he rest in peace. You are already aware of the injury which is incurred through anger from what our Sages, of blessed memory, taught in the Zohar. This is alluded to in the verses "Cease ye from man, in whose nostrils is a breath; for how little is he to be accounted," and "Thou that tearest thyself in anger . . . " [Is. 2:22; Job 18:4].[15] And even if another person antagonizes him, he should act as one who is insulted yet refuses to insult others.

3. Let an individual always enjoy the company of others and behave toward them with a kindly spirit, even with respect to people who transgress the Torah.

4. One should drink no wine whatsoever during the daytime, but only at night, and even then diluted. Only on Sabbaths, Festivals, and the New Moon may one drink during the day.

5. One should be sparing with meat and wine during the weekdays, even at night, inasmuch as these foods endow *Sama'el* with strength.[16]

6. A person should not spend his time thinking about idle concerns during the hour of prayer, but only about Torah, the fulfillment of the commandments and sacred matters.

7. An individual ought to refrain from speaking derogatorily about any person; this holds true even with respect to animals.

8. One must never curse any fellow Jew, even in a moment of anger; on the contrary, let him bless him, and by doing so be blessed, as it is written: "I will bless those who bless you, and him who curses you I will curse" [Gen. 12:3].

9. A person should never speak anything but words of Torah in the synagogue.

10. A person ought to avoid speaking about worldly matters altogether, but should only discuss matters related to Torah.

11. Let an individual refrain from touching his body with his hand, and from lowering his hand below his navel.

12.   One should never swear any oath about something trivial. It is all the more important that one not do so concerning a serious matter, even regarding the truth.

13.   A person should never lie and ought to keep away from lies; he must not utter a false word in any manner whatsoever.

14.   Let a person commune with one of the Associates every day for the purpose of conversing about devotional concerns.

15.   A person ought to discuss with this same Associate, every Sabbath eve, what he did each day of that past week. From there he should go forth to welcome the Sabbath Queen.

16.   One ought to pray the *'Amidah* in a contemplative way to the degree that he is able; at very least he should concentrate meditatively during the three opening blessings, the four bows, as well as the four places where one stands erect again. For with respect to one who fails to concentrate upon these, the *Shekhinah* cries out: "The Lord hath delivered me into their hands against whom I am not able to stand" [Lam. 1:14].[17]

17.   An individual should take care to recite the afternoon prayer service while wearing a prayershawl and phylacteries; this includes the Reader's repetition of the *'Amidah*.[18]

18.   A man should recite the Grace after meals in a loud voice so that his children may repeat it after him, letter by letter and word by word.

19.   One should be careful never to eat meat on Sunday, nor any cooked dish, nor drink wine. He ought to take greater care not to indulge in levity on this day than on other days, unless it is a Festival, New Moon, or a feast connected with a religious celebration.[19]

20.   Every night one ought to sit on the ground, mourn the destruction of the Temple, and weep on account of one's transgressions which delay the redemption.

21.   A person should not prepare a secular banquet in his home, but only a feast which is connected with a religious celebration.[20]

22. Every weekday a person ought to recite the Psalm: "By the waters of Babylon" [Ps. 137], preceding the Grace after meals.

23. As far as possible a person must take care not to engage in idle conversation. This is one of the ten pious customs of Rav, who refrained from indulging in idle conversation throughout his life.[21]

24. Let a person be careful not to be counted among those four classes of people which do not merit the presence of the *Shekhinah*. They include the hypocrites, the liars, the scoffers, and those who engage in tale-bearing.[22]

25. A person should donate charity every day so as to effect atonement for his sins, as it says: "and break off thy sins with almsgiving" [Dan. 4:24].[23]

26. It is proper to concentrate meditatively during the recitation of the prayer "Hear, O Israel." These words ought to be upon one's heart in purity of thought.

27. One should listen attentively, as is proper, to the reading of the Torah without disturbing the Reader in any way.

28. A person must take care to fulfill a vow immediately and not delay doing so for thirty days.

29. An individual should be careful about confessing his transgressions prior to eating and before going to sleep.

30. During the three weeks of mourning[24] an individual should avoid reciting the benediction: "Blessed art Thou, Lord our God, King of the universe Who hast granted us life and sustenance and permitted us to reach this season." Nor should he eat meat or drink wine unless he is about to fast. He is permitted to do so on account of his fast.

31. A person should fast in accordance with his capacity.

32. A person ought to meditate upon matters of Torah with each and every bite he eats in order that his food may serve as a sacrifice and his drinking of water and wine as drink-offerings.[25]

33. Let an individual occupy himself each day with the study of Scripture, Mishnah, Talmud, Kabbalah, and legal judgments.[26]

34. One should study the entire Talmud three times in the course of every twelve months.

35. One should weep during each of the prayer services, or at least during one of them.

36. A person ought to fast for three consecutive days, four times each year, during each of the four seasons. Praiseworthy is the individual who adds to this.

37. A person ought to converse in Hebrew with the Associates at all times.

38. One should recite two chapters of Mishnah and one Psalm before the Grace following the meal.

39. A person should study Mishnah every Sabbath eve in accordance with his capacity.

40. Every week a person ought to review all the Mishnah that he knows.

41. An individual should learn at least two chapters of Mishnah by heart each week.[27]

Come, My Beloved

"Observe" and "Remember," in a single command, the One
    God announced to us.
The Lord is One, and His name is One, for fame, for glory and
    for praise.[28]

Come, my Beloved, to meet the Bride; let us welcome the
    Sabbath.[29]

38

RULES OF MYSTICAL PIETY

Come, let us go to meet the Sabbath, for it is a source of
blessing.

From the very beginning it was ordained; last in creation, first
in God's plan.

Come, my Beloved, to meet the Bride; let us welcome the
Sabbath.

Shrine of the King, royal city, arise! Come forth from your
ruins.
Long enough have you dwelt in the valley of tears! He will
show you abundant mercy.

Come, my Beloved, to meet the Bride; let us welcome the
Sabbath.

Shake off your dust, arise! Put on your glorious garments, my
people, and pray:
"Be near to my soul, and redeem it through the son of Jesse, the
Bethlehemite."[30]

Come, my Beloved, to meet the Bride; let us welcome the
Sabbath.

Bestir yourself, bestir yourself, for your light has come; arise
and shine!
Awake, awake, utter a song; the Lord's glory is revealed upon
you.[31]

Come, my Beloved, to meet the Bride; let us welcome the
Sabbath.

Be not ashamed nor confounded. Why are you downcast? Why
do you moan?
The afflicted of my people will be sheltered within you; the city
shall be rebuilt on its ancient site.

Come, my Beloved, to meet the Bride; let us welcome the
Sabbath.

Those who despoiled you shall become a spoil, and all who
would devour you shall be far away. Your God will rejoice
over you as a bridegroom rejoices over his bride.

Come, my Beloved, to meet the Bride; let us welcome the
Sabbath.

You shall extend to the right and to the left, and you shall
revere the Lord.
Through the advent of a descendant of Perez we shall rejoice
and exult. [32]

Come, my Beloved, to meet the Bride; let us welcome the
Sabbath.

Come in peace, crown of God, come with joy and cheerfulness;
amidst the faithful of the chosen people come, O Bride;
come, O Bride.
        Come, O Bride, O Queen Sabbath.

Come, my Beloved, to meet the Bride; let us welcome the
Sabbath.

Abraham ben Mordecai Galante

Introduction

Abraham Galante (second half of the sixteenth century) was one of Moses Cordovero's leading disciples. Galante employed the exegetical mode in which to express himself, writing a kabbalistic commentary on the Zohar entitled *Yareaḥ Yaqar* [The Precious Moon]. This book reflects Cordovero's influence and contains numerous references to Cordovero and his work.[1] In addition, he wrote mystical commentaries on the Book of Lamentations and the rabbinical treatise *Pirqei 'Avot* [Chapters of the Fathers].[2] Galante was influenced as well by Isaac Luria to some degree, although it does not appear as if he was ever among Luria's official disciples. In his several compositions he occasionally mentions Lurianic interpretations, relates stories about him, and in more than one instance indicates that he personally heard a teaching from Isaac Luria.[3]

Whereas the customs prescribed by Moses Cordovero appear to have been written for his circle of students and colleagues, Galante's text contains rules clearly pertaining to the Safed community as a whole. This is reflected in the primarily descriptive style in which these customs are stated, in contrast to the prescriptive format of Cordovero's list. It is apparent from these rules and customs that the community in general was expected to participate in the life of disciplined piety and special spiritual exercises.

Here we find one of the very earliest descriptions of the dramatic ritual surrounding the day preceding the New Moon, which became known as *Yom Kippur Qaṭan* [Minor Day of Atonement]. Galante also provides us with valuable information concerning an array of special rites associated with several holidays. Thus, for example, we learn of the practice of assembling at midday on the day before Passover for the purpose of study, as well as that of spending the entire seventh night of this holiday in study. Of particular interest is the report that on Passover there were some "who

41

fulfill the precepts of Gleanings, the Forgotten Sheaf, *Pe'ah*, Heave-Offering, Tithes and *Ḥalah*." These include obligations an individual had with respect to the Temple while it still stood. That there were some who practiced these in the sixteenth century suggests the air of expectation that prevailed in Safed for the time when these rituals might once again be relevant for one and all.

These *Hanhagot* were published by Solomon Schechter on the basis of the same Jewish Theological Seminary manuscript to which we have already referred.[4]

The Pious Customs of Abraham Galante

Holy and worthy customs practiced in the Land of Israel which were copied from a manuscript written by the perfect and righteous sage, our honored Rabbi and teacher, Abraham Galante, a resident of Safed, may it be rebuilt and reestablished speedily in our day.

These are the rules "which if a man practices, he shall live by them . . ." [Lev. 18:5]:

1.   On the eve of the New Moon all the people fast, including men, women, and students. And there is a place where they assemble on that day and remain the entire time, reciting penitential prayers, petitionary devotions, confession of sins and practicing flagellation. And some among them place a large stone on their stomach in order to simulate the punishment of stoning. There are some individuals who "strangle" themselves with their hands and perform other things of a like nature. There are some persons who place themselves into a sack while others drag them around the synagogue.[5]

2.   On the night of the New Moon there are men of action who rise at midnight and recite Psalms.[6]

3.   There are some individuals who wear a prayershawl and don phylacteries at every afternoon prayer service, just as is customarily done at the morning service; this practice is widespread among all the people.

4.   On the eve of Passover, at midday, there are those who assemble in the synagogues and houses of study in order to study the laws of the pas-

chal sacrifice as found in the RaMBaM. They pray the "great" afternoon service and depart to prepare the "guarded unleavened bread" [*mazzah*]. There are those who are in the habit of cutting the wheat for the unleavened bread with their own hands, and who fulfill the precepts of Gleanings, the Forgotten Sheaf, *Pe'ah*, Heave-Offering, Tithes, and *Halah*. They recite the blessing over the eating of the unleavened bread with that which has been subjected to ten ritual precepts.[7]

5.   On the intermediate days of the Festival of Passover, at midday, they assemble in the synagogues and recite the Song of Songs, translating it and commenting upon it each day.

6.   On the seventh night of Passover they rise at midnight and read until the "Song at the Sea" in *Midrash Vayosha*;[8] they sing songs of Torah until the dawn.[9] They then recite petitionary prayers at the conclusion of which they rise to their feet and sing the Psalm "When Israel went out of Egypt" [Ps. 114] in a sweet voice.

7.   Every night during the period of the '*Omer*, they concentrate upon a different word of the Psalm "The Lord will forgive us" [Ps. 67], which is composed of forty-nine words, as well as upon one letter from the verse: "Let the nations be glad and sing for joy . . ." [Ps. 67:5]. Each night on which they recite this Psalm following the counting of the '*Omer*, they raise their voices when they come to the particular letter designated for that night. There is a tradition among them that an individual who contemplates in this fashion will never spend a single night in prison, even if he should commit some capital offense.[10]

8.   On the eve of the Feast of Weeks there are those who sleep one or two hours after completely preparing for the festival. This is because, at night, following the meal, every congregation assembles in its own synagogue and those present do not sleep the whole night long. They read selected portions from the Torah, Prophets, and Hagiographa, the Mishnah, Zohar, and rabbinic Homilies until the break of dawn. And then all the people ritually immerse themselves prior to the morning service, as it indicates in portion '*Emor* of the Zohar [III, 97a–98b]. This is in addition to the immersion which they practice on the eve of the Feast of Weeks.

9.   Every Sabbath eve they go out into the field or to the courtyard of the synagogue and welcome the Sabbath. Everyone dresses in his Sabbath

garments. They recite the Psalm "Give to the Lord, O heavenly beings" [Ps. 29] and the Sabbath hymn, followed by the "Psalm for the Sabbath day" [Ps. 92].

10.   On the seventeenth day of *Tammuz*, at noon, they assemble in the synagogues, weeping, lamenting, and recounting that on that very day, at that very moment, the destruction of the Temple took place, on account of which we are dispersed throughout the lands of the nations.[11]

11.   On the eve of the Ninth of *'Av* an individual takes a pitcher of water and seats himself between the baking oven and the cooking stove, resembling one whose dead were lying before him.[12]

12.   On the Ninth of *'Av* they do not leave the synagogue whatsoever; there they study *Sefer Ben Gurion* and *Shevet Yehudah*. Also, they avoid eating meat on the evening of the Ninth of *'Av*.[13]

13.   On the night of the Day of Atonement they do not sleep at all, thus following the example set by the nobility of Jerusalem who stayed awake throughout the night; they spend it studying the laws of the Day of Atonement and its prohibitions, as well as by singing songs, praises of God, and liturgical hymns.[14]

14.   On the eve of the New Moon men, women, and students fast.

15.   Throughout the night of *Hoshannah Rabbah* they recite Psalms as well as penitential prayers, alternating between one and the other.[15]

16.   On the eve of the three pilgrimage festivals there are men of good deeds who purchase a lamb and divide it among the poor.[16]

17.   There are men of good deeds who prepare three measures of fine flour and bake "guarded unleavened bread," giving three pieces to each and every needy person.

18.   The pious are careful to pray with the congregation in the evening, morning, and afternoon.

19.   One ought to be among the first ten persons at the synagogue for worship in the morning as well as in the evening.[17]

20. It is proper to avoid conversation during the entire prayer service, as well as while the Torah scroll is open. This prohibition even includes conversation having to do with matters of Torah.

21. It is proper to establish regular times for the study of Torah, during the daytime as well as at night, and to refrain from sleeping before periods of study.[18]

22. There are men of action who recite the Psalm "By the waters of Babylon" [Ps. 137] at the table.

23. An individual ought to forgive transgressions and to pardon anyone who injures him, whether through speech or deed. It is all the more important never to take such a person to a [Gentile] court where they employ idolatrous practices.

24. A person should wash his hands when he rises from bed before touching anything whatsoever and before treading upon the ground. This is in order to drive away impure spirits.

25. When an individual leaves his house, it is fitting for him to place his hand upon the *mezuzah* so as to remind himself of God's unity and of His commandments.[19]

26. An individual ought to be careful with respect to taking false vows and oaths, for through the sin associated with doing so a man's children are stricken, as it says: "In vain have I smitten your children . . ." [Jer. 2:30]. Furthermore, it is written: "Thou shalt not take the name of the Lord thy God in vain; for the Lord will not hold him guiltless that taketh His name in vain" [Ex. 20:7]. These are the rules of the covenant which God established with Israel "which, if a man practices, he shall live by them . . ." [Lev. 18:5]. They constitute a "fence around the Torah" and correspond numerically to the sacred name *YHVH*. And the God of Jacob will support those who fulfill these obligations.[20]

27. There are certain especially pious individuals who fulfill the tithe obligation [to the poor] by doubling it, that is, with one-fifth of all their earnings. They set aside their money in a chest so that they have it available to them and can give generously in fulfillment of their pledge. Even among the poor themselves there are those who follow this custom.

28. There are some who practice the custom of welcoming the Sabbath following the afternoon service dressed in Sabbath garments. They recite the Song of Songs followed by the hymn for the *Kabbalat Shabbat*, "Come, my Beloved." And on the night of the Sabbath they recite eight chapters of Mishnah *Shabbat*, eight more in the morning and eight in the afternoon. It is for this reason that our holy teacher included twenty-four chapters in Mishnah *Shabbat*, corresponding to the twenty-four ornaments for the Sabbath Bride. "And now, I pray Thee, let the power of the Lord be great" [Num. 14:17] to enable us to serve our Creator, blessed be He, as in the injunction to "depart from evil and do good . . ." [Ps. 34:15]. Amen, may it be so.[21]

Abraham ben Eliezer ha-Levi Berukhim

Introduction

Even for a community such as Safed with its array of striking personalities, the figure of Abraham Berukhim (ca. 1515–ca. 1593) stands out.[1] Berukhim was born in Morocco and immigrated to Palestine probably before 1565. In Safed he associated himself with the Cordovero/Alkabez circle. With the arrival of Isaac Luria, Berukhim became one of his disciples.

In addition to his *Hanhagot*, Berukhim wrote a short but highly influential tract called *Tiqqunei Shabbat* [Rules for the Sabbath].[2] He is also responsible for having gathered Zoharic texts that had been circulating in Safed and had not been included in the first printed editions of the Zohar. These texts were subsequently published under the title *Zohar Hadash* [New Zohar].[3]

While we do not know much in the way of specific details about the life of this mystic (as is the case with the majority of Safed Kabbalists), there is a good deal of evidence concerning the particular character and style of Abraham Berukhim's piety, and the distinctive place he held in the Safed community. We know that he was among the few who were personally instructed by Isaac Luria regarding how to prepare for and practice the most esoteric forms of contemplation that Luria taught. Hayyim Vital reports that Berukhim told him that he was advised by Luria to avoid all idle conversation, to rise at midnight and weep on account of his generation's lack of mystical knowledge, and to study long sections of Zohar, all for the purpose of readying himself for mystical experience.[4] Berukhim also received detailed instructions for the practice of intricate meditative exercises known as *yihudim*.[5]

Accounts of some of Berukhim's own pietistic activities are preserved in the semi-legendary letters of Solomon Shlomiel of Dresnitz. Shlomiel informs us that Berukhim was in the habit of exhorting others to rise at midnight for purposes of study and lamentation. The deep sense of urgency and of communal obligation that characterized sixteenth-century Safed is perhaps nowhere better exemplified than in the zeal with which this ascetic figure is alleged to have promoted observance of the midnight vigil:

> There was a certain individual here in Safed, may it be rebuilt and reestablished speedily in our day, whose name was the honored Abraham ha-Levi, may the memory of the righteous be for a blessing, who composed *Tiqqunei Shabbat*, found at the end of *Reshit Hokhmah ha-Qasar*. Every midnight he would rise and make the round of all the streets, raising his voice and crying out bitterly: "Rise in order to honor God's name, for the *Shekhinah* is in exile, and our holy Sanctuary has been consumed by fire, and Israel is in great distress!" Many things of this nature would he proclaim; and he would summon each of the scholars by name and would not move away from the window until he saw that he had already arisen from his bed. And by the hour of one in the morning the entire city would be filled with the voices of those studying Mishnah, Zohar, the exegetical interpretations of our sages of blessed memory, as well as Psalms, the Prophets, hymns and supplicatory prayers.[6]

Abraham's urgent appeals were not limited to the midnight vigil; he was apparently as vigorously concerned about the proper observance of the Sabbath.[7] Known as the "great patron of the Sabbath," he is reported to have run about town on Friday mornings to the homes, markets, and streets to urge the homemakers and householders to hurry with their Sabbath preparations. He would exhort businessmen to close their shops in sufficient time to welcome the Sabbath Bride in the correct manner.

While Hayyim Vital identifies Abraham Berukhim's soul as deriving from that of the prophet Elijah, and in another instance as bound up with the patriarch Jacob,[8] Shlomiel's letters preserve a story in which we learn that Isaac Luria regarded Berukhim as an incarnation of the prophet Jeremiah. The following account, despite its obvious legendary qualities, suggests the general reputation Abraham Berukhim had among his colleagues as well as the consuming preoccupation of the mystics of Safed for the fate of the *Shekhinah*:

> The 'Ari, may the memory of the righteous be for a blessing, taught that he [i.e., Berukhim] was the incarnation of the prophet Jeremiah. He once said to him: "Now, know that your days are completed and that you have no longer to live unless you perform a certain act of restitution which I shall teach you. If you carry it out you may live another twenty-two

years. This is what you must do: Travel to Jerusalem and go to the Western Wall where you should pour out your prayers and your tears; and if you are acceptable before your Maker you will merit a vision of the *Shekhinah*. Then you may rest assured that you will live an additional twenty-two years."

As soon as he heard this, the honored Rabbi Abraham ben Eliezer ha-Levi sold all the possessions in his house in order to pay his expenses for the journey and went to Jerusalem. He immediately secluded himself without interruption for three days and nights which he spent in fasting, wearing sackcloth and in great weeping. After these three days he proceeded to the Western Wall where he began to pray and weep bitterly. While doing so he lifted up his eyes and saw upon the Wall the likeness of a woman with her back turned towards him. I do not wish to disclose the garments which she was wearing out of respect for our Maker. As soon as he saw her he fell upon his face, crying out and weeping: "Mother, mother, mother of Zion, woe is me that I have seen you thus!" And he continued to weep bitterly, afflicting himself, tearing hair out of his beard and head until he fainted and fell deeply asleep.

Then in a dream he saw the *Shekhinah* coming towards him and placing her hand upon his face, wipe away the tears from his eyes. She said to him: "Console yourself, Abraham my son, for 'there is hope for thy future, saith the Lord, and your children shall return to their own border' [Jer. 31:17] 'for I will cause their captivity to return, and will have compassion upon them' " [Jer. 33:26].

Our honored Rabbi Abraham awakened from his sleep and returned to Safed, joyful and in high spirits. The 'Ari, may the memory of the righteous be for a blessing, said to him: "I can readily see that you have been privileged a vision of the *Shekhinah*. From now on you may rest assured that you will live another twenty-two years." And so it came to pass. Following this incident he lived twenty-two years.[9]

Berukhim also stands out among his peers on account of his extreme ascetic behavior and acts of self-mortification. If the account provided by Shlomiel is even generally accurate, we have in Berukhim an ascetic whose zeal for self-affliction was matched only by some of the more excessive practices among the *Ḥasidei Ashkenaz* (medieval Jewish-German pietists).[10]

This pious one used to practice another custom. He would go out into the markets and the streets, calling for repentance. He would gather groups of penitents, lead them to the Ashkenazi synagogue and say to them: "Do as you see me do." Then he would crawl into a sack, ordering them to drag him the entire length of the synagogue in order to mortify his flesh and humiliate his spirit. After this he enjoined them to throw stones at him, each weighing a pound and a half, which they would do.

Following this, he would come out of the sack. A bed, covered with nettles which burn the flesh like fire, would be prepared for him, and he would remove his clothing, throw himself naked upon the thorns and roll around until his body was covered with blisters. In a similar way, he would simulate the four kinds of punishments meted out [in ancient times] by the rabbinic court.

Then he would say to those assembled: "My brethren, whosoever desires to save his soul from Hell must do as I have done." And immediately they all rushed at once and submitted themselves to all of the same torments, crying out in bitterness of soul and confessing their sins. They would not leave there until they had accomplished complete and permanent repentance.[11]

As for Berukhim's *Hanhagot*, they tend to accentuate some of the more stringent and ascetic practices of the community, reflecting his own penchant for such piety. Of particular interest in this regard is the description of a brotherhood of penitents whose members fast regularly and observe rites of mourning and self-affliction on an established basis. It is not unlikely that this group was constituted of Marranos whose goal was to atone, to the fullest extent possible, for the sins they had unwillingly committed. On the other hand, the severe picture he draws is tempered by references to the joyous celebration of the Sabbath, the existence of a fellowship dedicated to gladdening the hearts of bridegroom and bride at the conclusion of the Sabbath, and the joyful celebration of the day of the New Moon.

His account also provides us with some interesting information about social realities. Thus we note his mention of the very young age at which some parents saw to the marriage of their children, the daily collection of charity in the synagogues, the instruction of women and children by traveling teachers, and the practice of raising orphans. The following text was published on the basis of the Jewish Theological Seminary manuscript.[12]

The Pious Customs
of Abraham Berukhim

These are additional pious customs practiced in Safed, may it be rebuilt and reestablished speedily in our day. Some of these were recorded above as well. These rules are those of the exalted saint, the honored teacher,

Abraham ha-Levi, resident of Safed, may it be rebuilt and reestablished speedily in our day. May God protect and preserve him.

1.   It is a practice among most of the scholars of Torah, those who revere God, to pray the afternoon service while wearing a prayershawl and phylacteries. Some individuals wear them throughout the day, even while walking along the way.

2.   The majority of congregations, including nearly one thousand women, fast on the eve of the New Moon.

3.   There is a Fellowship of Penitents whose members fast regularly and who pray the afternoon service each day in weeping and in tears. They practice flagellation and wear sackcloth and ashes. Among them there are some who fast two days and nights every week. Some do so for three days and nights.

4.   Most of the scholars of Torah, when they rise in the middle of the night in order to study, sit upon the ground, wrap themselves in black, mourn and weep on account of the destruction of the Temple. Such also is the custom of the Fellowship of Penitents at the afternoon service of the eve of the New Moon.

5.   Most of the scholars of Torah learn Mishnah by heart; there are some among them who have memorized two Orders, others three and so on.[13]

6.   Some Torah scholars, those who revere God, practice ritual immersion in order to cleanse themselves of nocturnal pollution. Further, on Sabbath eve, they ritually immerse themselves so as to establish a distinction between the sacred and the profane. And they wear white clothes throughout the Sabbath.[14]

7.   A number of groups go out on the eve of the Sabbath [into an open field] while it is yet day, dressed in white clothes, and welcome the Sabbath. They recite the Psalm "Give to the Lord, O heavenly beings" [Ps. 29] and the hymn "Come, my Beloved," as well as the "Psalm for the Sabbath day" [Ps. 92]. Then they say: "Come, O Bride."

8.   During each of the three Sabbath meals, they sing and rejoice. They do likewise on the day of the New Moon and on Festivals. Furthermore,

they study eight chapters of the tractate *Shabbat* at each of the three Sabbath meals.

9.   The majority of townsfolk leave side-curls measuring one finger wide from above the ear. And there are some who leave a width of two fingers.

10.   There are certain individuals whose practice it is to go from courtyard to courtyard, and to all the stores, in order to warn people concerning the approach of the Sabbath and to welcome it while it is still daytime.[15]

11.   There are some individuals who eat "secular" food while in a state of ritual purity on two occasions: on the Sabbath preceding Passover and during the Ten Days of Penitence.[16]

12.   There are some who see that their sons and daughters are married at the age of thirteen or fourteen, in contrast to those who do not do so until the age of twenty-five or older because of financial considerations; by such time they will have committed a number of transgressions for which capital punishment is deserved.

13.   There exists a certain fellowship that goes out at the conclusion of every Sabbath to sing, dance, and gladden the Bridegroom and Bride.[17]

14.   Most of the scholars of Torah eat "guarded" unleavened bread on the night of Passover. Certain individuals do so on all seven nights and adhere to a number of rituals more strictly than do others.

15.   All of the Torah scholars study throughout the night of the Feast of Weeks until the break of dawn, as well as through the night of *Hoshannah Rabbah*. Likewise, a great many people rise on the night of *Hoshannah Rabbah* for penitential prayers.

16.   In every synagogue charity is collected prior to the main service, during the "Song of the Sea."

17.   There are teachers who travel throughout the region for the purpose of instructing women and young children in the prayers and blessings.

18. Certain Torah scholars spend the entire Sabbath night engaged in study.

19. There are certain especially pious scholars of Torah who neither eat meat nor drink wine during the entire week, because they mourn the destruction of the Temple and because of their own transgressions.

20. There are some people who celebrate the New Moon much as they do the Sabbath, by eating, drinking, and dressing well. So, too, as at the conclusion of the Sabbath, they have a lamp burning and a prepared table.

21. There are individuals who avoid swearing oaths altogether, even with respect to the truth; and they are careful always to speak the truth.

22. Some pietists fast for three days and nights, four times each year, during each of the four seasons.

23. There are those who raise orphans in their own homes, and attend to their marriages at the appropriate time.

24. On the New Moon of the month of *Nisan* the scholars assemble and occupy themselves with the laws having to do with the Sanctuary.[18]

25. On the New Moon of the month of *Nisan* a number of groups assemble and study all the laws connected with the vessels of the Sanctuary. And they recite the portion: "And it came to pass on the eighth day" until the verse "And when all the people saw it . . ." [Lev. 9]. Likewise, the passage: "And it came to pass on the day that Moses had made an end of setting up the tabernacle . . ." until the verse "This was the offering of Nahshon . . ." [Num. 7:1–17]. And each day they recite the portion describing the offerings of the princes [Num. 7].

Joseph Karo

Introduction

Joseph Karo (1488–1575), was born either in Spain or Portugal several years before the Expulsion from the Iberian Peninsula. In 1497 Karo's family left Portugal for Turkey, where he lived for approximately forty years. In Turkey, Karo may have come into contact with Solomon Molkho, an apocalyptically oriented visionary who died at the stake as a martyr in 1532. It was apparently this event that led Karo himself to aspire to fulfill his life through an act of martyrdom. Karo's *maggid*, for example, tells him that "I shall give you the merit of being burned for the sanctification of My name. All your sins and faults will be purged by fire so that you will rise from there like pure wool."[1]

In Turkey, Karo engaged not only in his important legal scholarship, but in kabbalistic matters as well. He came into the acquaintance of such prominent Kabbalists as Joseph Taitazak and Solomon Alkabez. In 1537 Karo went to Safed, where he became that community's leading legal authority and one of its most extraordinary visionaries. What makes Joseph Karo so unusual is that he combined in one personality the extreme rationalism of the talmudic legalist with the visionary gifts of a mystic. To be sure, Karo was by no means the only individual in the history of Judaism in whom we see these two tendencies joined. It is difficult to think, however, of another person who combined them in quite the way Karo did. On the one hand, Karo was a legalist of profound talent and is best known for his famous work the *Shulḥan 'Arukh*, still the authoritative code of Jewish law for traditional Jews. Thus Karo may be regarded as one of the several most important figures in the whole of Jewish law. And yet, as we have already seen, Karo was the recipient of mystical revelations, which he experienced on a regular basis.

The angelic voice or *maggid* he experienced appears to have functioned as a sort of alter ego for Karo, inspiring him to lead a morally pure and ascetic life, and reproving him when he failed to live up to the strictest standards of pious conduct. What we have in Karo is an individual who, in an extreme way, personalized and internalized the various concerns that characterized the community of which he was a part. The sense of responsibility for historical tragedy, as well as for the fate of the *Shekhinah*, clearly exhibited itself in Karo's unusually tortured self-doubts. The tension described earlier between exile and redemption seems, in Karo's case, to have given away to an emphasis on his sinfulness and the unredeemed nature of things. It is in these terms that we ought to understand the relatively severe life-style that Karo's *maggid* counsels.

The following text is the first part of a series of exhortations by Karo's *maggid* found in the published editions of his diary, *Maggid Mesharim*, that precedes the actual diary entries. The edition we have used is Vilna, 1865.

The Pious Customs of Joseph Karo As Taught by His Maggid

1. To begin with, take care never to think about anything, at any time whatsoever, other than the Mishnah, the Torah, and the commandments. And should some other thought occupy you, thrust it away.

2. Be careful to avoid thinking about anything at the hour of prayer besides the words of prayer themselves. This even includes avoiding thoughts of Torah and the commandments.[2]

3. Be careful never to indulge in idle conversation whatsoever, neither during the day nor at night.

4. Take care to avoid engaging in any kind of talk which may lead to frivolity. And if you should overhear conversation of this sort, do not indulge in laughter whatsoever. This extends to the complete avoidance of mockery.

5. Never become angry about anything at all having to do with material things.

6. Do not consume much meat; even on the Sabbath take care to eat meat sparingly.

7. Do not drink wine except for one drink only at the conclusion of the meal.

8. Be gentle in speech to all people.

9. Never act pridefully whatsoever; rather, be exceedingly humble.

10. Conduct yourself modestly, even in relationship to your wife.[3]

11. Be careful to avoid taking pleasure while eating meat and drinking, or while partaking of any other kind of enjoyment. Act as if a demon were forcing you to eat this food or indulge in the enjoyable activity. You should very much prefer it were it possible to exist without food and drink altogether, or were it possible to fulfill the obligation of procreation without enjoyment.

12. Always have your transgressions in mind and preoccupy yourself with them.

13. Never eat for dessert more than one measure, and not more than twenty of melon, grapes, and raisins. Do not eat more than a single kind of fruit at a meal, except on Sabbaths or Festivals. At the beginning of the meal cut three measures of bread and refrain from eating more than this at that meal. And when you drink water, avoid fully satisfying your thirst.

14. Acquire the habit of always keeping your eyes cast downward so that you do not chance to gaze upon a woman who is forbidden to you.

15. Occupy your mind with thoughts of the Mishnah during a meal; when you have finished eating, study a chapter of the Mishnah prior to the recitation of the Grace after meals.

16. Do not cease thinking about Me, even for the slightest moment, and limit your enjoyment. When you are eating and you desire to eat or drink still more, refrain from doing so. If you behave in this manner at every meal it will be tantamount to offering a sacrifice. Your table will serve as an actual altar upon which you slaughter the evil inclination.

17. Do not drink wine at a meal all at once and be careful when it comes to measuring it. Have no fear that this will diminish your eyesight. On the contrary, your eyesight will be strengthened as will your power.

18. Limit the pleasure which you receive from eating and drinking. And if you experience enjoyment while eating some particular food, refrain from eating it on a regular basis. Learn to eat something else from which you do not derive as much pleasure.

Additional Customs from Safed

Introduction

J. M. Toledano published in 1960 two additional lists of *Hanhagot* that were sent from Safed "to all the holy congregations outside the Land of Israel."[1] These manuscripts were discovered in Meknes, Morocco, and were copied about 1746 from older manuscripts. The first list was sent from Safed sometime before 1577, while the second was sent in 1577. The deliberate attempt on the part of the Safed pietists to disseminate their way of life to other Jewish communities substantiates the fact that Safed regarded itself as constituting the heart of the Jewish world, and as having responsibility for the spiritual guidance of all Jewry.

Inasmuch as these forty-eight rules contain many items that are present in the preceding lists, I have chosen to conflate the two lists and provide translation for only those items that are distinctive and offer new information.

* * *

1. Commune each and every day with a friend while in a state of reverence for God.

2. Fast on Thursdays and pray the afternoon service in the synagogue with a quorum of ten people who are likewise fasting.

3. Meditate upon the first three blessings of the *'Amidah* during the evening, morning, and afternoon services.

4. Neither eat meat nor drink wine on Sunday because on that day of the week the Sanctuary was destroyed.

5.   Never converse in the synagogue from the beginning of the service until the Sanctification [*Qaddish*] prayer. And read the Torah portion, word by word, in fear and trembling, as if you yourself stood at Mount Sinai.

6.   At a minimum, concentrate contemplatively on the passage "Hear, O Israel" as well as upon the passage "Blessed be His glorious name for ever and ever."

7.   Never allow a day to go by without offering charity, at very least, a small coin each day.[2]

8.   To the extent that you are able, avoid gazing upon women, even upon their clothes.

9.   An individual ought to converse with his Associates in Hebrew during the week; on the Sabbath he should do so with every scholar of Torah as well.

10.   One who has deliberately violated any of these rules ought to confess to having done so on the eve of the New Moon in the presence of the community of the pious, or before the majority of them. Any individual who fulfills these obligations will surely have a place in the world to come; however, he must perform them out of genuine love.

11.   There are pious individuals and men of good deeds who go to the houses of the poor in order to see if they have food to eat; they provide them with food without cost.

12.   Most of the synagogues practice the custom of carrying a wax candle in front of the scroll of the Torah [while it is being brought from the Ark to the Reader's table]. The person who carries the candle does so walking backwards[3] while members of the congregation accompany him until he reaches the table. When he returns, the sages of the congregation greet him with reverence.

13.   There is a group which goes out on the night of *Simḥat Torah* for the purpose of singing and dancing in the presence of the Torah scroll in every synagogue.[4]

14. It is the custom of Torah scholars and those who fear God never to begin their meal on the Sabbath, Festivals, or the New Moon, until there are young orphans or poor students of Torah present at their table.

15. It is the custom of the sages and pious ones only to deliver homilies to the congregation which bear upon the subject of repentance. This is especially true on Mondays and Thursdays, these being days of judgment. They are all the more careful to do so at the afternoon service of the eve of the New Moon. And there are some whose custom it is to preach about matters having to do with the Sabbath every Thursday and Friday, as well as on Sabbath eve, so as to encourage people to observe and honor the Sabbath in the correct manner.

16. There are pious individuals who refuse to speak about any worldly matter on the Sabbath, by virtue of which they merit divine wisdom.

Isaac Luria

Introduction

Isaac Luria (1534–1572) ranks among the several most influential religious personalities Jewry has ever produced. Regarded as the preeminent Kabbalist of Safed in the sixteenth century, Luria produced original mythological doctrines and ritual practices that were of fundamental importance to virtually all Jewish mystical creativity after him. By the middle of the seventeenth century Lurianic theology and ritual life had spread throughout the Jewish world and had established a supremacy that was virtually unchallenged. Indeed, it has been observed that Lurianism was the last theological system to enjoy nearly universal acceptance within Judaism.[1]

Luria was born in 1534 in Jerusalem, where his father had settled after having migrated from Germany or Poland. After his father's death his mother took him to Egypt, where he lived in the home of his uncle, Mordecai Frances, a wealthy tax farmer. In Egypt, Luria studied with two prominent rabbis, David ben Solomon Zimra and Bezalel Ashkenazi, collaborating with the latter on works of a legal character.[2] According to some accounts, Luria was still living in Egypt when he decided to seclude himself on the island Jazirat al-Rawda on the Nile. During this period he is reported to have immersed himself in the study of the Zohar and other kabbalistic texts.

In late 1569 or early 1570, Luria traveled to Safed and began studying with Moses Cordovero, to whom he refers as "our teacher whose light may be prolonged" and "my late teacher."[3] It is possible that even before Cordovero's passing in the fall of 1570, Luria may have begun teaching on his own to a small group of disciples. In any case, following Cordovero's death Luria attracted to himself a circle of students that included Hayyim Vital (1543–1620), who became his most important student.

Luria's circle, approximately thirty-five of whose names we know, was an elite—not to mention elitist—group that engaged in both normative rabbinic learning and kabbalistic studies. Besides Vital, his more illustrious disciples included Joseph Arzin, Gedaliah ha-Levi, Elijah de Vidas, Moses Jonah, Joseph ibn Tabul, Jonathan Sagis, Samuel Uzeda, Judah Mishan, and Elijah Falkon. That membership was highly restricted is evident from the apparent rejection of Moses Alsheikh, Vital's teacher in rabbinic studies, as a participant in Luria's most intimate group of associates.[4] Luria's activity in Safed was brief as he died at the age of thirty-eight in July 1572.

Besides the few legal writings to which I have referred, Luria composed a short commentary on the section of the Zohar known as Ṣifra de-Ṣeniuta.[5] This work, however, does not reflect his own original system, which he taught toward the end of his life, but suggests the distinct influence of Cordovero. Except for this commentary and some religious poetry, he committed to writing virtually nothing of his mystical thinking. Whereas Moses Cordovero possessed a natural talent for literary expression, the precise opposite was the case with Isaac Luria. He seems to have been unable to adequately express himself in writing, and is reported to have told the following to a disciple who asked him why he desisted from putting his teachings into written form:

> It is impossible, because all things are connected with one another. I can hardly open up my mouth to speak without feeling as though the sea burst its dams and overflowed. How then shall I express what my soul has received, and how can I put it down in a book?[6]

While we can appreciate such frustration, it is fortunate that Luria's students recorded their master's teachings. Our knowledge of his system is based entirely on the writings of several of his disciples who recognized the importance of preserving Luria's teachings.[7] Drawing on the basic themes of exile and redemption that permeated Safed even prior to Luria's activities there, he devised a complex and distinctive set of mythological doctrines. At the heart of this mythology stands the radically gnostic notion that sparks of divine light have, in the process of God's self-disclosure or emanation, accidentally and disastrously become embedded in all material things. According to Luria, these sparks of light yearn to be liberated from their imprisoned state and return to their source within the Godhead, thus restoring the original divine unity. The human task in the face of this catastrophic situation is to bring about such liberation through proper devotional means.[8]

Known as the process of *Tiqqun* (restoration or mending), this effort is essentially a *contemplative* one. Every religious action, regardless of the kind, requires contemplative concentration in order to "raise up the fallen sparks." The focus of contemplation is the inner dynamics of reorganization and restructuring that takes place within the Godhead through acts of devotional piety. The successful struggle on the part of the community, according to this theology, will result not only in the final separation of holiness from materiality, but also in a return of all divine reality to the original state of primordial unity that preceded the creation of the world. Capturing the imagination of a people preoccupied with the realities of exile and visions of redemption on an earthly, historical plane, Lurianic ideas exercised profound influence and had enduring appeal long after Safed itself ceased to be a prominent center of Jewish life.

Turning from issues of theological mythology to the sphere of mystical experience we face an important problem. When dealing with the sources having to do with Luria's devotional life, extreme care must be taken to isolate historical biographical data from the more abundant, but frequently less factual, hagiographical material. Not long after Luria's death, and for the succeeding decades, legendary accounts of the master's life began to emerge. Much of this literature bears only the most tenuous relationship to reality. Nevertheless, with caution, it is possible to reconstruct a fairly reliable picture of Isaac Luria's actual role as teacher and pietist.[9]

It is clear that Luria possessed the traits of a genuinely visionary personality. He quickly become known in Safed as a saintly person who had experienced the Holy Spirit and who had merited the revelation of esoteric wisdom from the prophet Elijah. He was known to have disclosed to his disciples, while on walks in the environs of Safed, the gravesites of departed saints and teachers with whose souls he was supposed to have communicated. Hayyim Vital's writings point to Luria's skills as a diagnostician of the soul, able to determine an individual's spiritual maladies and the sins for which he was responsible. Moreover, he was able to provide those in need with the specific penitential exercises by which they could effect atonement and restitution.[10]

Isaac Luria was a mystical master in the strict sense. To his formal disciples he imparted esoteric wisdom, vouchsafing to each of them mystical knowledge pertinent to their particular soul. Of special significance was his practice of telling every student the ancestry of that person's soul and the transmigrations through which it had gone.[11] As indicated, he instructed each of them personally in the performance of ethical and penitential exercises by means of which they were to purge their souls of all impurity; he also gave each one detailed instructions about meditation rituals whereby he could achieve visionary experiences of his own.

Thus, long before the phenomenon of charismatic leadership emerged in Eastern Europe among the Ḥasidim (as evidenced by that sect's impressive line of vivid religious personalities), Isaac Luria established himself as mystical master *par excellence*. Indeed, there is ample evidence that the figure of this sixteenth-century teacher served as a prototypical model among some of the Hasidic masters.[12]

The *Hanhagot* presented in this section include neither the intricate mythological theology of Lurianic Kabbalah, nor the highly esoteric forms of meditation to which we have made reference. Rather, they represent the day-to-day ethical, devotional, and ritual practices that Luria promulgated. These are likely to have been widely known in Safed beyond the confines of Luria's fellowship. While some of these customs reflect common practice in Safed as a whole, most of them provide us with information about Luria's distinctive habits. In this category belong, for example, the tradition concerning the importance of almost ritualistic study of the Zohar, intensive investigation of rabbinic law for the purpose of disclosing its inner holiness, and the high mystical significance attached to ritual immersion. Luria's characteristic flair for reshaping and redesigning elaborate ritual is attested by the detailed descriptions of Sabbath-eve prayers and devotional rites at the table.

While I have referred to the general dissemination throughout the Jewish world of rites developed in Safed, it is important to note that Luria's customs became especially popular. These practices are to be found in a great variety of Lurianic texts, although the primary source for most of them is Hayyim Vital's account of his master's teachings, the *Shemonah She 'arim* [Eight Gates]. In this multivolume collection we find an abundance of material bearing on Luria's personal customs, habits and practical teachings. As part of an appendix to his study of the hagiographical accounts surrounding the personality of Isaac Luria, *Sefer Toldot ha-'Ari*, Meir Benayahu brought together a series of such Lurianic customs from the works edited by Hayyim Vital; they are thus written from Vital's point of view. The texts that follow are based on the list assembled by Benayahu.[13]

Following the *Hanhagot* I have provided a translation of three brief invocations composed by Luria for the Sabbath meals. These invocations introduce the three different liturgical hymns that he wrote for the Sabbath, one of which (the hymn for Sabbath eve) is presented here in translation. Written in much the same Aramaic style as the Zohar, this song dramatically depicts the welcoming of the beautifully adorned Sabbath Bride. In rich mystical symbolism and vivid erotic imagery, Luria describes the love between Male and Female that occurs on the Sabbath and the joy that love creates.[14]

The Pious Customs of Isaac Luria

I. Ethics and Interpersonal Relations

1. The most important of all worthy traits consists in an individual's behaving with humility, modesty, and with the fear of sin to the greatest possible degree. He should also, to the utmost degree, keep his distance from pride, anger, fussiness, foolishness, and evil gossip; and even should he have a significant reason for behaving harshly, he ought to refrain from acting in this way. . . . He should also abstain from idle conversation . . . and not lose his temper, even with the members of his own household.

2. Melancholia is, by itself, an exceedingly unpleasant quality of personality, particularly in the case of an individual whose intention is to acquire esoteric knowledge and experience the Holy Spirit. There is nothing which impedes mystical inspiration—even for someone who is otherwise worthy of it—as much as the quality of sadness.

3. Additionally, the quality of anger, aside from serving as an obstacle to mystical inspiration altogether, [has other injurious repercussions]. My teacher, of blessed memory, used to be more exacting when it came to anger than with all other transgressions, even in a situation where a person loses his temper for the sake of some religious obligation. . . . This is because all other transgressions "injure" only a single limb of the body whereas the quality of anger "injures" the soul in its entirety, altering its character completely.[15] This is the issue: when an individual loses his temper, his holy soul deserts him altogether; in its place a spirit of an evil nature enters. And this is the esoteric meaning behind the verse: "Thou that tearest thyself in thine anger . . ." [Job 18:4]. For such a person actually tears his holy soul, rendering it unfit at the moment of his wrath and anger. . . .[16]

There is no restitution whatsoever for a wrathful person. Moreover, even when I was teaching my brother,[17] may God protect and preserve him, and he failed to learn as I wished, I became angry with him; on account of this my teacher, of blessed memory, cautioned me and reproached me vigorously.

4.   Once I was taking a walk with my teacher, may his memory be for an everlasting blessing, when a certain scholar came and deliberately walked in front of him. Upon seeing this, my teacher himself intentionally walked behind this individual, even after the latter had gone across to the other side. I said to him: "God forbid, it appears as if you are placing an obstacle in front of a blind man,"[18] inasmuch as this scholar failed to recognize my master's importance. He replied to me that seeing as how this person feels honored by behaving as he does, he [Luria] was obliged to grant him such honor and to serve him in this fashion. In this same manner, Hillel the Elder ran for three miles before a certain poor individual who was of a good family.[19]

5.   Before an individual begins to pray in the synagogue . . . he must take upon himself the precept ". . . and thou shalt love thy neighbor as thyself . . ." [Lev. 19:18]. And he should concentrate upon loving every member of the house of Israel as he loves himself, on account of which his prayer will ascend, bound up with all the prayers of Israel. By this means his soul will be able to rise above and effect *Tiqqun*.

And especially when it comes to the love for one's Associates who study Torah with one another, each and every person must bind himself to the others as if he were one limb within the body of this fellowship. This is particularly important when an individual possesses the knowledge and the mystical insight with which to understand and apprehend his friend's soul. And should there be one among them in distress, all must take it upon themselves to share his trouble, whether it has to do with some illness or with his children, God forbid. And they must all pray on his behalf. Likewise, in all one's prayers and petitions one should be mindful of his fellows. My teacher, of blessed memory, took great care to caution me about the love which we ought to bear toward our associates, the members of our brotherhood.

6.   My teacher, may his memory be for an everlasting blessing, also practiced recitation of the Confessional [for the Day of Atonement] in its entirety, even including confession for those sins which he had not personally committed. He used to say that every person must confess these sins, even though he was not responsible for them. It is for this reason that the Confessional is expressed in plural form. Thus, an individual must use the

plural expression and not the first person form: "We have sinned" rather than "I have sinned." This is because the people Israel constitutes a single body of which every Jew is an organic part. For this is the mystery of the unity of souls.

7. With respect to the wages owed a hired laborer, my teacher, may his memory be for an everlasting blessing, used to be exceedingly careful. He would sometimes delay in praying the afternoon service until he had paid someone his wages. And on occasion, he would not pray the afternoon service until after sundown when he did not have the money with which to pay what he owed; he would request money from this one and that one until he could pay what he owed to a hired laborer. Only afterwards would he pray the afternoon service. He would say: "How can I pray to God, may He be exalted, when I have an obligation such as this to fulfill and I have not yet done so? And how can I lift up my countenance to pray?"[20]

8. As regards the attribute of charitableness and generosity, I observed that my teacher, of blessed memory, was not concerned with his own vanity, as expressed [for example] in the wearing of especially fine clothes. In his eating, as well, he would consume very little. However, when it came to his wife's apparel, he was exceedingly careful to honor her, and to clothe her well. He used to satisfy her every desire, even if it was not within his means.[21]

9. When it came to giving charity and fulfilling the commandments, he was in no way a miser. With respect to the ceremony of *Havdalah* which is celebrated in the synagogue, he used to give four florins of gold to charity in order to personally provide for the wine to be used. Whenever he purchased something for the purpose of performing some religious obligation, such as buying phylacteries or an *'etrog*, he would not be concerned with finding out how much he was supposed to pay. Rather, he used to pay the amount which they asked of him the first time. He would say to the vendor: "Here is my money, take as much as you wish."[22]

10. My master, of blessed memory, also frequently used to request members of his household to bring him wild grass from the field, or thorns and thistles which some men are accustomed to eating. He would consume these in order to personally take upon himself the curse given to Adam, "Thorns and thistles shall it bring forth to thee; and thou shalt eat the herb of the field" [Gen. 3:18].

11.   My master, of blessed memory, used to be careful never to destroy any insect, even the smallest and least significant among them, such as fleas and gnats, bees and the like, even if they were annoying him.

12.   My teacher, may his memory be for an everlasting blessing, also used to teach that it is beneficial for an individual to reside in a house which has windows. This is in order to be able to gaze always at heaven, at every moment. It is especially good if he gazes upon God's wondrous creations of nature, as did King David, may he rest in peace: "When I behold Thy heavens, the work of Thy fingers, the moon and the stars which Thou hast established" [Ps. 8:4].

The *Midrash ha-Ne'elam* comments in a similar way concerning Nebuchadnezzar, about whom it is written, "And at the end of the days I, Nebuchadnezzar, lifted up mine eyes unto heaven, and mine understanding returned unto me, and I blessed the Most High, and I praised Him that liveth forever . . ." [Dan. 4:31]. Acting in this way imbues an individual with wisdom, endowing him with reverence for God and holiness. Therefore, it is good to gaze at all times at every moment upon heaven.[23]

13.   An individual must be careful not to reside in a place where others do not dwell. This is because a certain demon known as Tanya governs in such uninhabited places. My teacher [even] cautioned a certain individual not to travel on his own to the gravesites of Rabbi Shimon Bar Yohai and his son Rabbi Eliezer in order to study there. This being the case, how much more important is it to avoid traveling on one's own to other places where there are no people to be found.

II.   Mystical Inspiration and the Study of Torah

14.   My teacher, of blessed memory, used to tell me that the principal element of a person's contemplation—while studying Torah—which is directed at drawing upon himself mystical inspiration and supernal holiness consists in this: All his mental concentration must be directed towards binding and uniting his soul to its supernal source by means of the Torah. He should do so in order that the restoration of the supernal Adam might be accomplished. For this is God's purpose in creating human beings and His intention in enjoining them to occupy themselves with Torah.[24]

An individual must also be mindful never to forget about the fixed, daily study of Scripture, Mishnah, Talmud, and Kabbalah, accompanied by the proper devotional intentions, as will be explained in the appropriate place. One ought to be exceedingly careful about this.

15. In addition, Rabbi Abraham ha-Levi, may God protect and preserve him, related to me that my master, of blessed memory, gave him the following advice concerning the attainment of mystical inspiration: a person must not indulge in idle conversation; he must rise in the middle of the night and weep on account of our poverty of knowledge. He ought to study forty or fifty pages of Zohar each day with the exclusive goal of textual familiarity, without engaging in intensive investigation. He should read the Zohar frequently.

When I asked my teacher how he had merited all the esoteric wisdom in his possession, however, he told me that he had invested a great amount of effort studying. But I responded that Rabbi Moses Cordovero, of blessed memory, had also done the same. Even I, Hayyim, devoted a tremendous amount of effort in acquiring this wisdom. He then told me that while it is true that we applied ourselves extremely diligently, to an extent greater than any of our contemporaries, we did not do as he had done. For how many nights had he remained awake, poring over a single passage of the Zohar? Sometimes he would seclude himself, sit and study only a single passage during the course of six weekday nights. And usually, he would avoid sleeping altogether during these nights.

16. Rabbi Samuel Uzeda, of blessed memory, informed me that he heard from my teacher, may his memory be for an everlasting blessing, that an individual who spends forty consecutive days without uttering a mundane word will acquire esoteric wisdom and achieve mystical inspiration.

17. My teacher, of blessed memory, also informed me that the source of inspiration is the intensive study of the law [*halakha*]. This is so, he said, because intensive legal study consists in concentrating one's attention upon the fact that every nut possesses a shell [*qelippah*] which protects its inner core, the part constituting its holy element. This protective shell corresponds to the difficult problem [*qushia*] in need of resolution in the particular legal question; for the shell shields the law, preventing an individual from comprehending it. . . .

My master, of blessed memory, reported to me that he always used to interpret legal problems, in accordance with the exoteric meaning, in six different ways. The seventh interpretation would be in accordance with the esoteric meaning; this corresponds to the mystery of the six weekdays and the seventh day, the Sabbath.

He told me, however, that it is improper for a person for whom intensive study does not come easily, and who has to go to great lengths until he finds what he is looking for, to ignore the study of Torah for the sake of this kind of penetrating investigation. It is far better for him to concern himself with legal decisions or the homilies of our Sages, of blessed memory, and the like. But one for whom such intensive study is not difficult, and who does not need to exert a great deal of effort, must take an hour or two every day for purposes of this kind of study. Afterwards, he should spend the remainder of the day studying as described earlier. He should not, however, spend the whole day in intensive study.[25]

18.   I observed that whenever my teacher, may his memory be for an everlasting blessing, began to study Torah, that is, rabbinic law, in an intensive way, along with the Associates of our academy, even if they were studying in his house, he would recite this prayer beforehand: "May we not fail to understand a matter of law, and may we not declare something which is impure, pure, and something which is pure, impure."

19.   Additionally, in connection with the intensive study of rabbinic law with the Associates of our academy, I observed that my master, may his memory be for an everlasting blessing, used to gird up his strength like a lion to such an extent that he would become exhausted and break out in a great sweat. When I asked him why he exerted such tremendous effort, he replied that the purpose of such study was to destroy the evil, namely, those difficult problems connected with particular legal questions which are not easily understood. Therefore, an individual has to expend enormous effort and to exhaust his strength. Thus, the Torah may be called wisdom which exhausts the strength of one who engages in its study.

20.   Also, Rabbi Jonathan Sagis, of blessed memory, reported to me in the name of my master, of blessed memory, that he heard from him that there is nothing more imperative and critical for a person to do so as to achieve mystical illumination than to practice ritual immersion; for an individual must remain pure at all times. I observed, however, that my teacher did not ritually immerse himself for the better part of six months during the winter because of illness; he was afflicted with a hernia and his mother prohibited him from doing so. And I am certain that his mystical illumination did not take leave of him at all because of this.

21. In my humble opinion it seems that I heard from my master, may his memory be for an everlasting blessing, that an individual who sins causes the powers of mercy to depart and the powers of strictness to appear, thus warranting the imposition of the punishment of lashings. I observed that my master was not particularly exacting in this regard as he was concerning the punishment of fasting. The reason for this is that the current generation is lacking in rabbinic judges, properly ordained rabbis and experts, and lashes are not normally administered in our time. The acceptance of self-affliction alone remains to us.

22. Another kind of knowledge which my master, of blessed memory, possessed was the ability to understand the language of birds. This can be explained in the following way. Ever since the day upon which the Torah was burnt on account of our numerous sins, at the hands of the nations, the concealed mysteries of the Torah were delivered over to the realm of evil. Because of this, there are no creatures in the world, including all of the unclean animals—be they domestic or wild animals, foul or creeping animals—which do not have guardian angels accompanying them. These angels possess knowledge of the Torah and its inner secrets. Their chirping and the sounds of their voices contain deep mysteries of the Torah. Anyone who comprehends their language is capable of acquiring recondite knowledge of the Torah. There are generations in which there can be found saintly persons who have the ability to understand such mysteries, just as I have personally witnessed with respect to my teacher, of blessed memory.

III. Prayer and Synagogue

23. When a person is among the first ten to arrive at synagogue he must not leave until he completes his prayers there. He should not behave like those who are among the first ten in one synagogue and then leave and go to pray in a different synagogue where they were not of the first quorum. They are mistaken, and to do so should not be thought of as fulfilling a religious precept whatsoever.[26]

I observed that it was not the custom of my teacher, of blessed memory, to be among the first ten. He informed me that this was because he was sickly and needed to remain at home for a while in order to see to his personal needs. Another reason is that, after readying himself, he used to put on his prayer shawl and phylacteries in his home and walk dressed this way to synagogue. He had to do so while it was daytime, for at night one is not permitted to don phylacteries; however, those who comprised the first ten at the synagogue arrived in the dark before the break of dawn.

24. I heard it said in the name of my master, of blessed memory, that when one enters the synagogue he should bow in the direction of the Ark, after which he ought to recite the Psalm: "May God be gracious to us and bless us" [Ps. 67] which is composed of seven verses. Corresponding to the number of verses in the Psalm he should circle the Reader's table, which stands in the middle of the synagogue, seven times . . . . On the Sabbath, however, there is no need to circle it more than one time . . . . This is what I heard reported in my master's name. I observed, however, that he himself never actually practiced this upon entering the synagogue; perhaps this was due to the fact that he was not among the first ten to arrive there.

25. I observed also that my teacher, of blessed memory, was exceedingly careful never to speak at all in the synagogue, even when it was not time for prayer. He even disliked engaging in conversation about ethical matters, or speaking words of chastisement or repentance lest this draw him into talking about secular concerns.[27]

26. Further, he would never recite his prayers out loud—even during those prayers which are recited while seated—such as the Psalms and the like. He behaved this way in order to demonstrate his submission, reverence, and fear before God, may He be exalted. On the Sabbath, however, he used to raise his voice sweetly during these prayers, at least to an extent more than he did during the rest of the week. Even this he did only for the sake of the Sabbath's honor.

27. Once, on a Sabbath day, I experienced a terrible pain in my eyes which lasted for nearly two months. During this time I had no other symptoms of illness except for this terrible pain. I inquired of my teacher, of blessed memory, what the reason was for this pain. He provided me with two explanations. The first was that on weekdays when I take a walk, I take long strides; it is known that "long strides diminish a man's eyesight by a five-hundreth part" [Ber. 43b]. It is not restored except by partaking of the Sanctification wine on the eve of Sabbath. And inasmuch as I had failed to concentrate properly while reciting the Sanctification prayer I continued to be afflicted in this way.

72

The second explanation was as follows: I used to pray regularly at my master's study house and I would always sit to his right, gazing at him in order to learn his habits in every detail. During his prayer he used to employ great and wondrous meditations, on account of which celestial light would shine upon him. But I was not qualified at that time to gaze upon him. He said to me, "Seek to avoid staring at me while I am concentrating upon the prayer 'Hear, O Israel,' while I am bowing during the *modim* prayer, and while I am reciting the *Qedushah* prayer, 'Holy, Holy, Holy, is the Lord of Hosts.' For these three prayers require extraordinary contemplative concentration. If you act properly your eye pain will be relieved." The following day I refrained from gazing at him during these three moments of prayer and I was suddenly healed.

28.   It was the custom of my teacher, of blessed memory, to kiss the scroll of the Torah and to accompany it, walking behind it when it is brought from the Ark to the Reader's table in order to be read. After this, he would remain there next to the table until they opened the Torah scroll and showed it to the congregation, as is known. Then he would gaze upon the letters of the Torah. He used to say that a person could draw great light upon himself by looking at the Torah so closely that he was able to read the letters clearly. Following this, he would return to his original place and remain seated until the completion of the Torah reading, unlike those whose custom it is to remain standing. Often my master used to pray in his own home with a quorum of ten individuals, on weekdays as well as on the Sabbath, without worrying about whether there was a Torah scroll available from which to read.

29.   I observed that when we were praying in his study house, my teacher, of blessed memory, used to go up to the Torah on the Feast of Weeks and recite the Ten Commandments in a raised voice. This was the practice of the sages of the Spanish congregations.

Likewise, on that Sabbath when the section *Behukotai* is read from the Torah, I noticed that my master went up and recited the "curses" from this portion out loud, as do the sages of the Spanish congregations. I also observed that on Sabbath morning he was always the sixth to be called up to bless the Torah.[28]

30.   It was the practice of my master to offer charity at the afternoon service as well, before beginning to pray. He would donate three small coins

just as was his custom to do at the morning service. Also, he was exceedingly careful to recite the afternoon service while wearing his prayer shawl and phylacteries.

31.   My teacher, of blessed memory, never recited any hymn, liturgical poem, or prayer composed by the later Sages, such as Rabbi Solomon ibn Gabirol and the like. This is because these Sages were not familiar with Kabbalah, made mistakes and did not know what they were saying. He did recite, however, all the liturgical poetry and hymns composed by Rabbi Eleazar Kallir found in the prayerbook of the Ashkenazim, since all the early Sages wrote in accordance with Kabbalah.[29]

IV.   Sabbath and Festivals

32.   These were the practices of my teacher, of blessed memory: as soon as he had finished the morning service on Friday, he would walk to the synagogue or to his house of study. If there was a proper Torah scroll there, he would remove it from the Ark and read the portion for the coming Sabbath, twice in the Hebrew and once in Aramaic translation. He used to read the Hebrew from the Torah scroll and he had a certain student who would read the Aramaic translation after him from a book in which it was found. My teacher would recite the Aramaic aloud, following the student's reading. He would adopt this procedure, verse by verse, until he had completed the portion.[30] . . .

After having read the portion he would ritually immerse himself in preparation for the Sabbath. . . . He used to say that having read the portion an individual already possesses the power with which to receive the extra sanctity of the Sabbath. And therefore, he desisted from immersing himself before reading the portion, unless he did so unwittingly. . . .

Know that an individual must immerse himself twice in a row, first for the purpose of divesting his soul of its weekday "garments," and the second time in order to honor the Sabbath and receive its extra holiness.[31] . . . When you climb out of the ritual bath avoid drying yourself off with a towel so as to permit the body to absorb the Sabbath's waters.

33.   This is the order of *Kabbalat Shabbat:* Go out into an open field and recite: "Come and let us go into the field of holy apple trees[32] in order to welcome the Sabbath Queen. . . . Stand in one place in the field; it is pref-

erable if you are able to do so on a high spot, one which is clean as far as one can see in front of him, and for a distance of four cubits behind him. Turn your face towards the West where the sun sets, and at the very moment that it sets close your eyes and place your left hand upon your chest and your right hand upon your left. Direct your concentration—while in a state of awe and trembling as one who stands in the presence of the King— so as to receive the special holiness of the Sabbath.

Begin by reciting the Psalm: "Give to the Lord, O heavenly beings" [Ps. 29], singing it entirely in a sweet voice. Following this, recite three times: "Come, O Bride, Come O Bride, O Sabbath Queen." Next, recite: "A psalm, a song for the Sabbath day" [Ps. 92] in its entirety, followed by "The Lord is King; He is robed in majesty" until "for all time" [Ps. 93]. Then open your eyes and return home.

Enter and wrap yourself in a fringed prayer shawl. . . . Circle the table—prepared with the Sabbath loaves—walking around it several times until you have repeated everything which you had recited while in the field.

34. Upon returning home and entering the house sing out with great joy: "Sabbath peace!" For such an individual may be compared to a bridegroom who greets his bride with tremendous happiness and warmth. If your mother is still living, go and kiss her hands. Then circle the table. . . . Following this take two bundles of myrtle . . . and holding them between your hands, join them together and recite over them the blessing: "Blessed art Thou, Lord our God, King of the universe, who creates fragrant trees." After this, smell their fragrance.

Following this, walk around the table once again with the bundles of myrtle in silence. . . . The reason for taking two bundles is because one represents the obligation to "remember" the Sabbath while the other represents the obligation to "observe" the Sabbath.[33]

After the Grace following the meal, once again pick up the two bundles of myrtle and hold them together while concentrating upon the intention indicated above; recite the words "observe and remember in a single command." Then recite the blessing: ". . . who creates fragrant trees" and smell them.

Regarding devotional practices at the Sabbath table, I observed that my teacher, of blessed memory, used to take very great care to eat at a table which had four legs, after the pattern of the table which was used in the Sanctuary. Further, as to the bread with which the table is prepared, care must be taken to place twelve loaves upon the table at every meal, corresponding to the twelve loaves of show-bread.[34] Place them in the following manner: six loaves on the right side of the table and six on the left side. The six on the right side should be arranged in three pairs; the same with the six on the left side. The three bottom loaves on the right should be arranged in the form of the vowel *segol* with the upper three resting upon them, and so too with the loaves on the left.

This is their exact placement: on the extreme right side of the table there should be four loaves, two pair. Likewise, on the left side there should be four loaves. And in the middle there should be four other loaves, two pair. But the two middle pair are to be separated from each other by some distance between them, for one pair is closer to the two pair on the right and the other pair of middle loaves is closer to the two pair on the left.

When you are about to recite the blessing over the bread, take the two upper loaves from the four middle breads, bring them together in your hands, with the undersides of the breads joined together, so that they are facing one another and appear as a single loaf. They will thus look like the shew-bread in the Sanctuary.

Having finished the meal, my master, of blessed memory, would sing a certain hymn in a sweet melody. He composed three special hymns of an esoteric character which include all the detailed contemplative intentions associated with the Sabbath, one song for the evening meal, one for the morning meal, and one for the afternoon. . . .

Following the song a person ought to recite several chapters from Mishnah *Shabbat*. If you want, read the first eight on Sabbath eve, the eight middle chapters at the morning meal, and the final eight chapters in the afternoon. . . . Generally, however, my teacher, of blessed memory, used to recite the first four chapters in the evening, the second four in the morning, and the third four in the afternoon. . . . And sometimes, when he was preoccupied with conversation about Torah with other people at the table, he would recite only a single chapter at each meal.

35.   With respect to conversation on the Sabbath, my teacher, of blessed memory, was particularly careful never to speak in the vernacular, neither during the day nor night. The only exception to this was when he would deliver a homily to us and he was compelled to use the vernacular in order that the public which was listening could understand. He was also cautious about never engaging in idle conversation or weekday talk on the Sabbath, even in Hebrew. On all of the Festivals he would act as he did on the Sabbath when it came to this.[35]

36.   Know that my teacher, of blessed memory, cautioned me . . . that it is improper for a person to wear any of the clothes which he wore during the week on the Sabbath. It is wrong even to wear one's Sabbath cloak during the rest of the week.

Moreover, on the Sabbath a person must wear white garments, not colored ones. My master reported to me that the color of the garment which one will wear in the world to come, following his death, will be the same color of the clothes which he wears on the Sabbath in this world. He told me that once, during *Kabbalat Shabbat*, he envisioned the soul of a certain sage who had recently died, and he saw that he was dressed in black. My teacher told me that because this person used to wear black clothes in this world on the Sabbath, they were punishing him in the world to come.[36] . . .

37.   . . . My teacher, of blessed memory, used to remain awake the entire night of the Day of Atonement and engage in the study of Torah.[37]

38.   I observed that my teacher, of blessed memory, traveled to Meron once on the holiday of *Lag Be-'Omer*, he and his entire household, remaining there for the first three days of that week. This occurred soon after he arrived from Egypt; but I do not know if he was already expert in the wonderful esoteric wisdom which he attained subsequently. Rabbi Jonathan Sagis reported to me that during my master's first year in Safed—before I became his disciple—he brought his young son to Meron along with all of his household. And there they cut his hair in accordance with the well-known custom, and enjoyed a day of feasting and joyous celebration.[38]

Isaac Luria's Aramaic Invocations
for the Sabbath Meals

Sabbath Eve
>Prepare the meal of perfect faith
>To rejoice the heart of the holy King,
>Prepare the meal of the King.
>This is the meal of the Field of holy apples,
>And the Impatient and the Holy Ancient One.
>Behold, they come to share the meal with Her.[39]

Sabbath Morning

> Prepare the meal of perfect faith
> To rejoice the heart of the holy King
> Prepare the meal of the King.
> This is the meal of the Holy Ancient One,
> And the Impatient and the Field of holy apples.
> Behold, they come to share the meal with him.[40]

The Third Meal

> Prepare the meal of perfect faith
> To rejoice the heart of the holy King,
> Prepare the meal of the King.
> This is the meal of the Impatient,
> And the Holy Ancient One and the Field of holy apples.
> Behold, they come to share the meal with him.[41]

Isaac Luria's Hymn for Sabbath Eve

> I sing in hymns
> to enter the gates,
> of the Field
> of holy apples.
>
> A new table
> we prepare for Her,[42]
> a lovely candelabrum
> sheds its light upon us.
>
> Between right and left
> the Bride approaches,
> in holy jewels
> and festive garments.
>
> Her Husband embraces Her
> in Her foundation,[43]
> giving Her pleasure,
> squeezing out His strength.

RULES OF MYSTICAL PIETY

Torment and trouble
are ended.
Now there are joyous faces
and spirits and souls.[44]

He gives Her great joy
in twofold measure.
Light shines upon Her
and streams of blessing.

Bridesmen, go forth
and prepare the Bride's adornments,
food of various kinds
all manner of fish.

To beget souls
and new spirits
on the thirty-two paths
and three branches.[45]

She has seventy crowns
and the supernal King,
that all may be crowned
in the Holy of Holies.

All the worlds are engraved
and concealed within Her,
but all shine forth
from the "Old of Days."

May it be His will
that He dwell among His people,
who take joy for His sake
with sweets and honey.

In the south I set
the hidden candelabrum,
I make room in the north
for the table with the loaves.

SAFED SPIRITUALITY

With wine in beakers
and boughs of myrtle
to fortify the Betrothed,
to strengthen the weak.

We plait them wreaths
of precious words
for the crowning of the seventy
in fifty gates.

Let the *Shekhinah* be adorned
by six Sabbath loaves
connected on every side
with the Heavenly Sanctuary.[46]

Weakened and cast out
the impure powers,
the menacing demons
are now in fetters.[47]

Elijah de Vidas's
Beginning of Wisdom
as condensed by Jacob Poyetto

Introduction

The propagation and dissemination of Kabbalism on a popular scale to other parts of the Jewish world was achieved through a new type of literature that began to develop in Safed during the second half of the sixteenth century. This literature consisted of treatises that fully integrated Jewish ethics with Kabbalah. It represented a novel synthesis motivated by the powerful drive in the sixteenth century to popularize kabbalistic ideas and practices.

In the earlier period of the Spanish Kabbalah we find some works that were primarily ethical or moralistic in orientation and infused with an *overtone* of Kabbalism, such as Moses ben Nahman's *Sha'ar ha-Gemul*. On the other end of the spectrum, there were full-fledged kabbalistic works that displayed a relatively peripheral interest in ethical matters. The most important example of this latter tendency is the Zohar itself. While it is by no means devoid of ethical discussion, on the whole the Zohar takes up other matters: detailed descriptions of the sefirotic world and the intricate relationship among the *Sefirot*. The author of the Zohar is, to be sure, very much interested in the effect human actions have on the "upper world"— but the human actions with which he concerns himself are typically of a ritual rather than ethical nature.

The new impulses that manifested themselves in the sixteenth century, however, gave birth to the need for a more comprehensive mystical approach toward Jewish religious life. If the Kabbalist of the Spanish period was caught up, relatively speaking, in his own private world of mystical experience and speculation, the Kabbalists of Safed, as we have seen, were consumed by a far broader set of religious obligations. Under such circumstances the anchoring of human behavior to a kabbalistic metaphysic was extended beyond the sphere of ritual activity to that of ethical and moral behavior. The Safed mystics set out to systematically demonstrate how each and every ethical and religious deed exerted an effect on the sefirotic world and on the relationship between man and God.

The major works giving expression to these tendencies were: (a) *Tomer Devorah* [The Palm Tree of Deborah] by Moses Cordovero; (b) *Reshit Hokhmah* [Beginning of Wisdom] by Elijah de Vidas; (c) *Sefer Haredim* [Book of the Devout] by Eleazar Azikri; and (d) *Sha'arei Qedushah* [Gates of Holiness] by Hayyim Vital. To this list may be added two other popular books not composed in Safed: Isaiah Horowitz's *Shnei Luhot ha-Berit* [The Two Tablets of the Covenant], written in the early part of the seventeenth century, and Zvi Hirsch Koidonover's *Qav ha-Yashar* [The Straight Path], a work written in Eastern Europe toward the end of the seventeenth century.

While every one of these books occupies a distinctive and significant place within the history of kabbalistic literature, there is no question that among them de Vidas's *Reshit Hokhmah* is the crown jewel. It has justifiably been said that this exhaustive and voluminous treatise on morals is, along with Bahya ibn Paquda's famous *Duties of the Heart* (twelfth century) and Moses Hayyim Luzatto's *Mesilat Yesharim* [The Path of the Righteous, eighteenth century], among the several most influential Jewish ethical works ever written.

Although he was the author of one of the preeminent books in the whole of Jewish ethical literature, virtually nothing is known about the life of Elijah de Vidas (d. ca. 1593). From his name it appears that his family came from Spain, although de Vidas himself was probably born in Safed. De Vidas was an important disciple of Moses Cordovero, whom he refers to as "my teacher" throughout his book. More significantly, de Vidas's relationship to Cordovero is recognizable in his fundamental reliance on this sage's teachings, for *Reshit Hokhmah* is suffused with the spirit of Cordovero's kabbalistic approach.

While de Vidas was not a formal disciple of Isaac Luria, we do know that he was acquainted with Luria and with his teachings. De Vidas mentions him in five places in *Reshit Hokhmah*, even referring to him as "my teacher" on one occcasion. In another instance, he writes that he heard a particular teaching directly from Luria.[1] Moreover, according to Hayyim Vital's detailed account of the contemplative exercises known as *yihudim*, which Luria taught, the latter provided ten such personalized instructions to de Vidas. On the basis of this, it would appear that de Vidas was the only person to have been given such instructions who was not a formal disciple of that master Kabbalist.[2] Even though *Reshit Hokhmah* does not bear the distinctive stamp of Lurianic Kabbalah, then, it is clear that de Vidas knew Luria personally and was drawn to his teachings.

Most of *Reshit Hokhmah* was written following Cordovero's death in 1570. According to de Vidas himself, the work was completed on the eighteenth day of *Adar*, 1575.[3] Although it was sent immediately to Venice in that same year to be published, it was not until 1579 that it actually appeared in print. De Vidas reports, in the book's introduction, that the work contains errors due to the urgency with which it was sent to Italy. *Reshit Hokhmah* was the first of the ethical-kabbalistic treatises to be published; while Cordovero's *Tomer Devorah* was composed before *Reshit Hokhmah*, it was not printed until 1589.[4]

De Vidas's book is divided into five "Gates": "The Gate of Fear," "The Gate of Love," "The Gate of Repentance," "The Gate of Holiness," and "The Gate of Humility." Each of these is in and of itself virtually book-length and is further divided into a number of chapters.

Though the structure is not identical in every Gate, each one treats its subject in the same general way by engaging in several different levels of discussion.[5] Each Gate begins with an opening chapter or chapters that set the topic under discussion within the perspective of kabbalistic theory, and in which de Vidas explains the reason for the position of the Gate within the scheme of the book. In addition, the author seeks to establish the significance of the issue at hand. The middle chapters tend to categorize the various levels or dimensions of the ethical or spiritual quality being analyzed. The later chapters discuss in greater detail the practical means by which one acquires the quality of personality under discussion. The net effect is to immerse the reader in a comprehensive analysis of both conceptual and practical dimensions of the kabbalistic life as conceived by de Vidas.

De Vidas draws on an exceedingly wide array of literary sources in the composition of *Reshit Hokhmah*.[6] These may be grouped according to three major categories. First, he extensively quotes talmudic and midrashic texts. He is especially attracted to *Tanna de-Vei Eliyahu*, a midrashic work particularly well suited to his purposes given its distinctly moral and ethical subject matter.

Second, de Vidas utilizes a broad corpus of nonkabbalistic texts from the medieval period, extracting especially the ethical and practical elements from them. A partial sampling provides an idea of the range of sources the author incorporates into his work: (a) *Sha'arei Teshuvah*, by Jonah Gerondi, (b) the *Commentary to 'Avot* by Joseph Yabez, (c) *Ma'alot ha-Middot* by Yehiel of Rome, (d) the anonymously authored *'Orhot Saddiqim*, (e) *Ba'alei ha-Nefesh* by Abraham ibn Daud, (f) *Ta'amei ha-Misvot* attributed to Isaac ibn Farhi, (g) *Sefer Hasidim*, (h) *Sefer ha-Roqeah* of Eleazar of Worms,

(i) *Sefer ha-Yashar* attributed to Rabbenu Tam, (j) *Menorat ha-Ma'or* by Israel Alnaqawa, (k) *Menorat ha-Ma'or* by Isaac Aboab, and (l) *Hovot ha-Levavot* by Bahya ibn Paquda. By far the most influential of these is the last mentioned, *Hovot ha-Levavot*. Its impact is seen not merely in the extent to which it is quoted, but in the substantive way it is used to help shape discussion of various issues.

The third set of writings de Vidas draws on—and that provides *Reshit Hokhmah* with its distinctive character—is kabbalistic. He occasionally cites such early mystical books as *Sefer ha-Bahir*, the Hebrew works of Moses de Leon, Joseph Gikatilla's writing, and *Berit Menuhah*. The significance of these books for de Vidas, however, pales in comparison with the central place he accords the literature of the Zohar. Virtually every chapter of *Reshit Hokhmah* contains numerous and extended quotations from the Zohar. Out of his desire to demonstrate what he considered to be the ancient roots of kabbalistic ethics, de Vidas felt it necessary to focus his attention on this centerpiece of kabbalistic literature. Inasmuch as the Zohar is not primarily concerned with practical ethics, however, de Vidas was compelled to cite passages of the Zohar at length and then to interpret them in ways he thought illustrated ethical issues.[7] That is, de Vidas "read" the Zohar in such a way as to extract from it practical implications and directions for the religious life that were frequently far from the author's original intentions. De Vidas was guided in this process chiefly by the work of his teacher, Moses Cordovero, whose understanding of the Zohar underlies the interpretation of Zoharic texts in *Reshit Hokhmah*. The effect of treating the Zohar in this manner was to draw out and build on the practical implications of Cordovero's kabbalistic perspective in a way that went far beyond Cordovero's own attempt in his *Tomer Devorah*.

In the introduction to his book, Elijah de Vidas provides some of his reasons for having written *Reshit Hokhmah*.[8] In the first place, he suggests that his goal was to create an anthology of earlier sources to serve as a guide for an individual in the proper spiritual and ethical path: "Inasmuch as we have observed the importance of practical deeds, I decided to compose a book which includes matters of a practical nature found throughout the writings of our Sages and in their homiletical discourses, in the Gemara and the Zohar, as well as in the works of the commentators . . . for when such practical instructions are gathered together in a unified way, a person will remember to carry them out and not easily neglect them."

In addition, de Vidas informs us that he wishes to enable individuals to develop their ethical and spiritual life so as to *prepare* and qualify themselves for the study of Kabbalah. This is one of the reasons, writes the author, that he calls his work the *beginning* of wisdom; it constitutes a gateway to the study of the inner wisdom. In particular, de Vidas thought of his own work as a primer that would lead a student to the study of his teacher's *Pardes Rimmonim*, Cordovero's influential and systematic treatment of kabbalistic theology.

The most important theoretical intention of de Vidas's work, evident from the manner in which he uses his sources, is to impose a coherent and unified kabbalistic framework on Jewish ethics and behavior. De Vidas transforms his exceptionally diverse nonkabbalistic sources by providing a kabbalistic Weltanschauung for them. That is to say, he interprets his materials and integrates them with mystical texts in such a way as to create a unified point of view. For de Vidas, Kabbalism was not simply another level or stratum to be added to previous ones, but an all-encompassing mystical perspective through which to understand the religious life.

Among the surest signs of the popularity *Reshit Ḥokhmah* achieved is the fact that it was subjected to a number of adaptations and condensations.[9] Of these, the most influential was the version produced by an Italian scholar, Jacob ben Mordecai Poyetto. This condensation—which Poyetto called *The Abbreviated Beginning of Wisdom* [Reshit Hokhmah ha-Qaṣar]—was compiled in 1580, just one year after the original was published. It was not until the year 1600, however, that it was printed in Venice. It is evident that this version was, itself, highly popular, inasmuch as it has been reprinted more than twenty times. Indeed, the frequency with which it was printed and the varied geographical locations of these printings suggest the popularity Poyetto's version achieved among the folk.[10]

Poyetto rearranged the order of de Vidas's book by placing at the end of his version the two Gates (Fear and Love) that, in the original, were at the beginning. The new order is as follows: Repentance, Holiness, Humility, Fear, and Love. This reordering, as well as an analysis of the kind of material he chose to include, suggests that Poyetto was primarily interested in making available to readers the *practical* dimensions of de Vidas' work.[11] Nonetheless, it is important to note that Poyetto's version is not lacking in conceptual and theoretical discussion.[12]

Poyetto renders de Vidas's book more readable in several ways. He virtually eliminates de Vidas's frequent and sustained quotations from the Zohar, along with those from the other medieval sources. He usually prefers to refer the reader to the proper source or, sometimes, to paraphrase it. He also deletes a great amount of the author's own discussion; on occasion he conflates two chapters or provides the briefest amount of material from one of the original chapters.

On the other hand, Poyetto's condensation remains far more faithful to the original than do any of the other adaptations. While he sometimes introduces minor stylistic changes of his own, on the whole he preserves de Vidas's original language. In addition, Poyetto follows the order of chapters set down by de Vidas within each Gate, and reproduces material from nearly every chapter of the book. What is more, Poyetto's version, in contrast with most of the other condensations, does not attempt to divest *Reshit Hokhmah* of its distinctive kabbalistic character. His intention in omitting Zoharic passages and in vastly reducing the scope of the material was not to eliminate the esoteric dimension, but to make this voluminous, encyclopedic volume accessible to a wider audience.

The following indicates some of the themes included in the present translation of Poyetto's version:

1. "Gate of Repentance": The importance of acquiring fear and love of God in order to achieve perfect repentance; recognition of God's greatness and of the blemishes caused by sin; motivations for engaging in penitence and its beneficial consequences; God's relationship to the penitent.

2. "Gate of Holiness": The significance of holiness; the means by which to acquire holiness; the importance of rising at night for the purpose of repentance and study; the dangers of failing to do so. Perfection of the senses of hearing and smell; things to which one should avoid listening, and things to which one must pay attention; the sense of smell and how to use it properly. Fasting and prayer as a form of sacrifice; the sanctity associated with eating and drinking; the importance of abstaining from forbidden foods and of not eating more than necessary; the proper spiritual intentions that must accompany eating and drinking; constraints associated with eating for the penitent.

3. "Gate of Humility": Explanation of the term humility; God's humility; God's special love for the humble and lowly; imitation of His attributes of humility; the many dimensions of humility. The importance of compassion, kindness, and generosity; avoidance of evil gossip, anger, and harshness; the need to be satisfied with one's portion and the avoidance of envy, jealousy, and greed.

4. "Gate of Fear": Arousal of the inner fear of God; the nature of the fear of sin and its diverse aspects; the injurious consequences of failing to fear

God. The importance of subduing pride, obstinancy, and anger; the honor due to God and how to achieve it; honoring one's soul more than one's body; honor belonging to the synagogue and the house of study; the importance of association with other God-fearing persons.

5. "Gate of Love": The significance of performing devotion to God with love; serving God in order to make Him joyful; the importance of surrendering one's soul and body for the sanctification of God; serving God without seeking reward. The importance of concentrating all one's attention on the *Shekhinah* and cleaving to Her; the intensity of one's love for God; cleaving to God by rising at night; the denial of worldly pleasures; the various grades of love for God and the value of solitude. Means of acquiring the love of God; the power of prayer and deeds in unifying the *Shekhinah* and the Holy One, blessed be He; the significance of serving God with joy.

The Influence of *Reshit Ḥokhmah*

The considerable influence that de Vidas's book and its adaptations exerted on Jewish practice and literature in succeeding generations is well documented. It was extensively quoted and referred to as early as the end of the sixteenth century and the beginning of the seventeenth century, especially in Germany and Poland. The attitude toward piety on the part of European scholars of this period such as Abraham Horowitz, Isaiah Horowitz, Moses Mat and Joseph Yuspa Hahn was significantly shaped by *Reshit Ḥokhmah*.[13] In the opinion of Isaiah Horowitz, whose *Shnei Luḥot ha-Berit* is replete with material from *Reshit Ḥokhmah*,[14] de Vidas's treatise and *Duties of the Heart* are the quintessential works of Jewish morals. Meir Poppers (d. 1662), who was responsible for editing various Lurianic treatises, counseled the regular study of *Reshit Ḥokhmah*, as did Hayyim ha-Cohen of Aleppo (d. 1655), an important disciple of Hayyim Vital.[15] A great Polish moralist of a later period, Alexander Susskind (d. 1793), praises this book and stresses its importance in his famous ethical will to his son.[16]

One eighteenth-century Polish rabbi provides testimony of an unusual kind concerning the esteem in which *Reshit Ḥokhmah* was held. Jacob Shraga reports that when his son Menahem was dying, the latter requested his father to give him a copy of *Reshit Ḥokhmah*. Menahem opened the book to a certain passage in "The Gate of Holiness," which he had been studying before he fell ill, and placed it on his head. According to his father, Menahem wept and cried out, "Woe unto me that I am going to be separated from this holy book!"[17]

The influence of *Reshit Hokhmah* on the Sabbatian movement is reflected in the extensive use of it by the anonymous author of *Hemdat Yamim*.[18] Among the Hasidim of Eastern Europe de Vidas's work was also immensely popular and was regarded as essential reading. Hasidic masters of no less rank than Dov Baer, the Maggid of Mezritch, and Elimelech of Lizensk counseled their followers to set aside time to study *Reshit Hokhmah* on a daily basis.[19] De Vidas's book, then, exerted influence not only on rabbinic scholars, but on the folk as well, who found in it an essential guide to religious piety. Jacob Poyetto's condensation doubtlessly contributed in a significant way to this popularity.

A Note about the Translation

The translation presented here consists of selections from Poyetto's condensation. I have sought to provide substantial representation of Poyetto's work by drawing material from each of the five gates of the book. A greater amount of material is drawn from the "Gate of Holiness" and the "Gate of Love," reflecting the fact that Poyetto himself allotted more space to these sections. My own selection has been guided by a desire to provide texts I thought would be of interest to the contemporary reader.

While no attempt has been made to offer a critical edition of the texts translated, I consulted different printed versions of the abbreviation as well as de Vidas's original full text in an attempt to provide preferred readings. In some instances I added to Poyetto's text by reference to the original when I thought it helpful in order to understand the meaning of a passage. In quoting biblical texts, I sometimes took the liberty of offering a complete verse where the author cited only part of a verse. In places where I have omitted a section within a particular chapter, owing to either its repetitiousness or its technical nature, such omissions are indicated by ellipsis points.

When quoting or referring to passages from the literature of the Zohar, the Poyetto text usually provides a source reference. In many cases, however, these references are either inaccurate or may correspond to a version of the Zohar other than the standard printed ones. I have sought to provide the precise source wherever possible and have thus placed all of the Zohar references in brackets.

Editions of Elijah de Vidas's *Reshit Ḥokhmah*

1. Venice, 1579	18. Lvov, 1804
2. Venice, 1593	19. Zhitomir, 1804
3. Cracow, 1593	20. Lvov, 1811
4. Berlin, 1703	21. Dyhernfurth, 1811
5. Amsterdam, 1708	22. Shklov, 1816
6. Amsterdam, 1717	23. Dyhernfurth, 1818
7. Amsterdam, 1731	24. Sudlikov, 1825
8. Constantinople, 1736	25. Livorno, 1856
9. Amsterdam, 1737	26. Czernovitz, 1861
10. Zolkiew, 1740	27. Lvov, 1863
11. Fuerth, 1763	28. Josefow, 1866
12. Amsterdam, 1776	29. Warsaw, 1868
13. Koretz, 1781	30. Warsaw, 1875
14. Dyhernfurth, 1786	31. Lvov, 1877
15. Zolkiew, 1791	32. Warsaw, 1886
16. Slavuta, 1792	33. Muncas, 1895
17. Shklov, 1797	34. Vilna, 1900
	35. Warsaw, 1930

Editions of Jacob Poyetto's *Reshit Ḥokhmah ha-Qaṣar*

1. Venice, 1600	11. Lvov, 1798
2. Basle, 1603	12. Zolkiew, 1804
3. Venice, 1605	13. Zolkiew, 1806
4. Cracow, 1612	14. Ostrog, 1806
5. Cracow, 1667	15. Shklov, 1816
6. Wandsbeck, 1688	16. Vilna, 1817
7. Frankfort-On-Oder, 1702	17. Hruboshov, 1819
	18. Minkovitz, 1822
8. Amsterdam, 1725	19. Satmer, 1838
9. Zolkiew, 1772	20. Satmer, 1937
10. Zolkiew, 1796	

The Gate of Repentance

Introduction

A person who desires to achieve perfect repentance must begin by acquiring knowledge of the fear and love of God, of which there are two aspects. First, when an individual recognizes that the Creator, may He be blessed, is the Master who created all humankind, he will learn to appreciate God's greatness. He will realize that everything which the Holy One, blessed be He, created was for the sake of His glory only, and that all living things are subject to His will. No person may go beyond the parameters within which the Creator of all things has placed him, as exemplified in the case of the sea, concerning which it is said, "Thus far shalt thou come, but no further" [Job 38:11]. And thus, if a person strays beyond the boundaries of the Torah, it is proper for him to return to the place to which he belongs as the Creator has enjoined him, and not disobey His word.

The second aspect concerns the blemish which extends throughout all the upper regions, whether it be injury incurred by one's body, vital-soul, spirit, or super-soul.[1] This is the most important reason that a person should practice repentance and be completely remorseful; that is, when he clearly realizes the harm caused by his deeds, in addition to considering the punishment which he will receive in this world as well as in the next. Sin causes the body to be cut off from this world and the soul from the world to come.

Hence, it is proper for an individual to protect himself, for even animals flee from fire when they realize that they are in a life-threatening situation. How can a person fail to protect himself inasmuch as the Creator, blessed be He, endowed him with intelligence superior to that of all other animals? How much more is this true in the case of Israel, His chosen people, which is distinguished from the idolatrous nations on account of the Torah? It protects itself when it sees that it might fall into a deep pit, into a place from which it may be unable to climb out. Surely, Israel's very existence and eminence is due to to the Torah, as well as to the Sages in whom there dwelled the Holy Spirit. It is they who instructed us concerning the rewards of Paradise and the punishment of *Gehinnom*.[2]

When an individual repents because of his love for his Creator, having reflected upon God's mercy and His beneficence, it is proper for him to feel gratitude. Since "there is not a righteous man upon earth who doeth good and sinneth not" [Ecc. 7:20], a person must repent before he merits any reward whatsoever on account of his having studied Torah or having performed the commandments. Our Sages, of blessed memory, taught: "A man is told: Before you ask God's mercy to put words of Torah inside you, seek His mercy on account of the transgressions which you have done so that they may be forgiven you . . . thus you will come to understand and remember Torah" [*Tanna de-Vei Eliyahu*, chap. 13]. The reason for this is that the Torah, because of its spiritual character, does not rest upon a soul which is not pure and free of all dross and blemish. Therefore repentance is required of everybody.

Another reason for engaging in repentance is to help a person realize that when he sins he estranges himself from God and flees from holiness. Such an individual is called a rebellious servant. When he returns to God he must serve Him through holiness. Such was the case with Hagar who fled from Sarah: "And the angel of the Lord said unto her: 'Return to thy mistress, and submit thyself under her hands' " [Gen. 16:9]. In returning a person will repent of his rebelliousness. Consider the case of a son who fled from his father. The longer he delays in returning to his home, the more difficult will it appear to him to do so. For he will tell himself, "Father will not receive me." Understand the difference between one who returns immediately, one who returns after a month, or after a year. The anger of one's Father in heaven increases in proportion to the amount of time which he separates himself from Him, and his repentance will be all the more difficult to accomplish. The weight of his burden will correspond to the degree to which he has distanced himself from holiness and attached himself to sin. And it will be difficult to remove the evil which adheres to him except by means of a great effort.

Chapter One

Before we embark upon an explanation of the nature of repentance, we must set forth a number of observations in connection with this topic.

93

Upon reading the following passages of our Sages, may their memory be blessed, one will be inspired to repent.

1. Because the Holy One, blessed be He, is exceedingly compassionate and created the world out of His mercy—voluntarily and without any compulsion—and since it is His nature to do that which is beneficial, people will learn to appreciate His greatness. For this is the essential purpose of the creation of the world, namely, that God's greatness be acknowledged, as explained in the *Ra'aya Mehemna* [Zohar II, 42a]. The whole creation was only for Israel's sake, for Israel is called "beginning."

In His wisdom the Holy One, blessed be He, saw the need for creating the souls of men with both the good and evil inclinations so that a person might receive just rewards for his deeds. Had he been created without the evil inclination he would have been like the angels which had already been fashioned. Another explanation for his having been created with the evil impulse is found in the Zohar [I, 23a]. Since man was created possessing the evil inclination, it is impossible for him to avoid sin. Because of this, the idea of repentance preceded the creation of the world.[3]

The Holy One, blessed be He, enjoined us to repent in numerous places in His sacred Torah. He did so through Moses, our teacher, may he rest in peace, when he said: "When a man or woman shall commit any sin that men commit . . . then they shall confess their sin which they have done; and he shall make restitution for his guilt in full . . ." [Num. 5:6–7]; "In thy distress, when all these things are come upon thee, in the end of days, thou wilt return to the Lord thy God, and hearken unto His voice" [Deut. 4:30]; "And it shall come to pass, when all these things are come upon thee, the blessing and the curse, which I have set before thee, and thou shalt call them to mind . . ." [Deut. 30:1]; "And thou shalt return and obey the voice of the Eternal . . ." [Deut. 30:8]. And there are many instances such as these.

Our sacred Torah also rouses us to repent in the portion *Mishpatim* with this verse: "And if a man sell his daughter [that is, his soul] to be a handmaid she shall not go out as the menservants do" [Ex. 21:7]. That is, she shall not go out soiled and tainted by sin, as do menservants [Zohar II, 96b–97a]. This is to be understood according to a rational interpretation. The soul is the daughter of the King of the king of kings, the Holy One, blessed be He, and is given to a person in this world against her will, as is explained in the Zohar. Now a man makes use of the soul which is within his body; it was not brought into this world except for the purpose of fulfilling the Torah and its commandments, as is known. What the Holy

One, blessed be He, desires from a person is that he not render his trust [that is, soul] foul through the impurity of sin. If he does soil the soul, however, he must redeem it immediately from the grasp of evil, as Scripture says: "If she pleases not her master, who hath espoused her to himself, then shall he let her be redeemed; to sell her unto a foreign people he shall have no power . . ." [Ex. 21:8]. In this way a "foreign people" [that is, the realm of evil] shall not have dominion over her in *Gehinnom*.[4]

2. It follows from this that it is only fitting for a person to have compassion upon the pure pearl (that is, soul) with which the Creator endowed him. It is improper for a person to soil the soul, thus making it necessary for him to enter *Gehinnom* in order to be cleansed. Rather, "render it back to Him as He gave it to thee" [Shabbat 152b]. This means to avoid the taint of sin. But the soul ought not be returned to God without having been adorned with Torah and righteous deeds. For if you return the soul [exactly] the way you received it, what benefit will it have gained when it arrives at the next world?

3. It is appropriate for a person to arouse himself in repentance when he considers that the *Shekhinah* is exiled on his account, as it is written: "And for your transgressions was your mother put away" [Is. 50:1]. The return of the *Shekhinah* from exile is dependent upon our repentance. Ought not each and every person arouse himself to repent in order to lighten Her yoke of exile and to shed light on the ways in which She is blemished, how we injure Her and prolong the exile, as we explain in the "Gate of Fear"? This matter is taken up in the *Tiqqunim* [22a], where you will learn how important it is that we awaken repentance so as to love the *Shekhinah* and extricate Her from exile.[5] This should not be done for the sake of receiving reward. . . .

Further, Rabbi Simeon bar Yohai, may he rest in peace, taught in this passage that one who recites the words "inscribe us for life" and petitions for forgiveness and expiation of sins when New Year and the Day of Atonement arrive, without arousing feelings of repentance, is regarded as insolent. In the same way, each and every day that we make requests through our prayers, namely, the thirteen middle prayers of the Eighteen Benedictions,[6] the Holy One, blessed be He, inquires: "Inasmuch as you request that I do this and that on your behalf, what is the nature of your repentance?" For we find in the Torah, Prophets, and Writings that the Holy One, blessed be He, does not desire the praise of the wicked, as it is written: "But to the wicked God says: 'What right have you to recite my statutes . . .' " [Ps. 50:16]. Therefore, one must repent so that his prayer and his praise of God will not be turned away. And even though we recite the words "Turn thou us unto Thee, O Lord, and we shall be turned" [Lam. 5:21] as well as "Forgive us," arousal from below is necessary, as Scripture says: "Return unto Me and I will return unto You" [Mal. 3:7].

That is to say, when Israel requests that the Holy One, blessed be He, imbue them with thoughts of repentance—as, for example, by means of the angelic herald who calls for repentance—God responds. For actual repentance is necessary in order to bring about God's response. In this connection, our Sages, of blessed memory, taught: " 'Open to Me, My sister, My delight . . .' [Song of Songs 5:2]: The Holy One, blessed be He, said to Israel, 'Present to Me an opening of repentance no bigger than the eye of a needle, and I will widen it into openings through which wagons and carriages can pass' " [Song of Songs Rabbah 5:3]. Repentance may be compared to the sea, as it is written in Scripture: "Thou the confidence of all the ends of the earth, and of the far distant seas" [Ps. 65:6]. Just as the sea is always open, so the gates of repentance are forever open.

4. When an individual realizes that death can occur at any moment without warning, as Scripture says: "In a moment they die . . ." [Job 34:20], and is unaware of when he himself will be called to give account, it is fitting that he rise up and hasten to prepare provisions for his journey. For no individual is assured of continued life for even a single day, as it is said: "Repent one day before thy death" ['Avot 2:10]. Rabbi Eliezer said: "Let him repent today lest he die on the morrow; let him repent on the morrow lest he die the day after, and thus all his days will be spent in repentance" ['Avot de-Rabbi Nathan, chap. 15]. There is excellent testimony concerning this in Chapters of the Fathers: "If I am not for myself, who is for me" [1:14]? See as well the commentary to Chapters of the Fathers by the saintly Joseph Jabez.[7] Similarly, King David said, "Man is like unto a breath; his days are as a shadow that passeth away" [Ps. 144:4] as well as, "For we are strangers before Thee, and sojourners, as all our fathers were: our days on the earth are as a shadow, and there is no abiding" [I Ch. 29:15].

"This world is like a vestibule before the world to come: prepare thyself in the vestibule that thou mayest enter into the banqueting hall" ['Avot 4:16]. It is therefore fitting for a person to hasten to carry out acts of devotion, concerning which it is taught: "The day is short and the task is great" ['Avot 2:15]; "The provisions are scanty and the road is long" [Ketubot 67b]. For a year's journey one must prepare a month or two of meals; for a journey of several years following one's death, how much more does one need to prepare? "And thus R. Johanan said, What is meant by the verse, 'Among the dead [I am] free' [Ps. 88:6]? Once a man dies, he becomes free of the Torah and good deeds" [Shabbat 30a].[8]

Repentance is accepted when it is performed during one's youth, as it is written: "Remember then thy Creator in the days of thy youth, before the evil days come . . ." [Ecc. 12:1]. And our Sages, of blessed memory, taught: "Happy is he who repents whilst he is still a man. R. Joshua explained it: Happy is he who overrules his inclination *like* a man" [Avodah Zarah 19a]. [Rashi comments]: " 'Whilst he is still a man' means while he is still of youthful vitality. That is to say, one should hasten to acknowledge his Creator before he becomes old. '*Like* a man' means like a courageous individual" [Rashi's comment to Avodah Zarah 19a].[9] Even an older person who engages in repentance and overrules his inclination as a youthful man does, happy is he.

Another explanation for repenting during the days of one's youth is given in the *Ra'aya Mehemna* [III, 227a–b]. We are taught there that a delicate nut possesses a shell which, when moist, separates easily from the kernel. The shell corresponds to the evil impulse, concerning which King Solomon said: "He that delicately bringeth up his servant from a child shall have him become a master at the last" [Prov. 29:21]. The servant in this instance represents the evil inclination [that is, the shell], which is the servant's servant. And if during the servant's youth the master pampers him [that is, the evil inclination] with the luxuries of this world, the servant will later rule over him, and it will be difficult for the master to subdue him.

5. The following has to do with the heralding angel which calls out each day on high for repentance. This topic is discussed in a number of passages, including portion *Lekh Lekha* of the Zohar [I, 77a–b]:

When midnight arrives and the Holy One, blessed be He, enters the lower Garden of Eden [to visit the righteous] . . . a herald loudly announces: "To you we speak, exalted holy ones; who is there among you whose ears are quick to hear . . .?". . . Woe to those that sleep with eyes fast closed and do not know or consider how they will arise on the Day of Judgment; for reckoning is exacted when the body is defiled, and the soul flits over the face of the transparent ether, now up and now down, and if the gates are not opened it is tossed about like a stone in a sling. Woe to them! Who shall plead for them? For they shall not be admitted to this joyful place, among the delightful habitations of the righteous their place shall be missing, and they will be delivered into the hands of Duma, they shall descend and not ascend. Of them it is written: "As the cloud is consumed and vanisheth away, so he that goeth down to She'ol shall come up no more" [Job 7:9].[10]

We find in the Zohar [II, 131a] another comment in connection with repentance, on the verse: "The watchman said: 'The morning cometh, and also the night. If ye will inquire, inquire ye; return, come' " [Is. 21:12]. The watchman refers to the angel *Meṭaṭron* who calls out for repentance at the time of the morning prayer, saying, "The morning cometh, and also the night . . . return, come." Likewise, the Holy One, blessed be He and His *Shekhinah*, who are called "the rule of day" and "the rule of night" [referred to in our verse as "morning" and as "night"] also call out saying: "Return, come."

Further, we may infer from this passage that the essential part of our prayer consists in petitioning our Maker to forgive our sins and in our returning to Him completely. And this is the meaning of, "If ye will inquire, inquire ye; return, come." That is, if you wish to petition [that is, "inquire"] the Holy One, blessed be He, and to pray before Him, first return in repentance and pray afterwards. For concerning a person who prays without having repented first, Scripture says: "Who hath required this at your hand, to trample My courts?" [Is. 1:12].[11] We thus learn from the Zohar that a person should not approach his Maker except after having repented of his transgressions, after having divested himself of all his iniquities. This is the meaning of "return, come," that is, return in perfect repentance and immediately you will "come" and you will be near to Him.

From this we learn of God's mercy towards Israel, His treasured people, when He says to them, "come." This may be likened to the father who says to his son who left him: "Come close to me, for I am completely prepared to accept you." Who will be able to read these sentiments and refuse to subdue his obstinate heart and return to his Father in heaven, inasmuch as He is compassionate, desirous that His son draw close to Him? It is proper for a person never to separate himself from Him, God forbid, and never to act stubbornly. He should rise quickly from his bed and plead in the synagogue, in tears and prayer, in order that God might accept him—inasmuch as the morning prayer is a favored time.

R. Simeon bar Yohai also discusses *Meṭaṭron's* call for repentance in connection with the verse, "Who among you reveres the Lord, and heeds the voice of His servant?" [Is. 50:10]. We learn that when a person who usually arrives at the synagogue before anyone else is absent one day, the Holy One, blessed be He, asks about him saying: "Who among you reveres the Lord and heeds the voice of His servant?" The servant referred to in this verse is *Meṭaṭron* who stands and calls out each day, asking for repentance.[12]

6. When a person studies the books of the Prophets, he will discover that all of them call for repentance—Hosea, Isaiah, and Ezekial more than the rest. All of the prophets who prophesied before Israel did so only in order to return the people back to the righteous path.

These six observations through which we have elaborated upon the subject of repentance were drawn together in a brief passage in the Zohar by R. Simeon bar Yohai, may he rest in peace. In addition to these, there is yet another observation: the soul itself is witness to an individual every day insofar as a person experiences stirrings of repentance daily. For there is no Israelite so wicked that he does not incline towards penitence. Sometimes, however, the evil inclination rules over him and entices him, because of which the soul will occasionally inspire some bad dream in order to arouse him to repent.[13]

Another observation: it is proper to think about the number of individuals who we find repented and were accepted by God. First, there was Adam, concerning whom our Sages, of blessed memory, taught:

> On the first day of the week Adam went into the waters of the upper Gihon until the waters reached up to his neck, and he fasted seven weeks of days, until his body became like a species of seaweed. Adam said before the Holy One, blessed be He: "Sovereign of all worlds! Remove, I pray Thee, my sins from me and accept my repentance, and all the generations will learn that repentance is a reality and that You accept the repentance of those who return." What did the Holy One, blessed be He, do? He put forth His right hand, and accepted his repentance, and took away from him his sin, as it is said . . . "thou forgavest the iniquity of my sin. Selah" [Ps. 32:5]. Selah in this world and Selah in the world to come [*Pirke de-Rabbi Eliezer*, chap. 20].

Adam [also] sang the Song for the Sabbath day: "It is a good thing to give thanks unto the Lord" [Ps. 92:2].[14] Achab's repentance was accepted as was that of the people of Anathot, King Jochanaiah, and many, many more. In the Zohar [II, 106a–b] you will learn about the great value of repentance, for the sentiments expressed in this passage serve to subdue the heart. You will discover the importance of penitence and how much God takes pity upon His creatures endowing them with the means to repent in order to lift them up from darkness to light and from death to life. And in this way the penitent will arouse himself so that he will return to God in love. Inasmuch as the Holy One, blessed be He, infuses a person's heart with repentance due to His love, and then provides him with the means to repent, it is appropiate for him to love God in return and fulfill His will. Thus, the saintly author of the *Duties of the Heart*, Bahya ibn Paquda, wrote that love is aroused when a person reflects upon the compassion with which God treats him, overlooking his transgressions and forgiving him.[15] In the Talmud we read: "Resh Lakish said that repentance is so great that premeditated sins are accounted as though they were merits" [Yoma 86b].

Another of those individuals whose repentance found acceptance was Manasseh, the son of Hezekiah, who committed every possible wicked transgression. Nevertheless, when he called out to the God of his fathers with all his heart, he was answered, as Scripture says: "And he prayed unto Him; and He was entreated of him, and heard his supplication, and brought him back to Jerusalem into his kingdom . . ." [II Ch. 33:13]. At that hour Manasseh knew that "there is judgment and there is a Judge" [Gen. Rabbah, 26:14].

Further, the Sages taught:

"And this is the ritual of the guilt-offering" [Lev. 7:1]. Thus said the Holy One, blessed be He, to Israel: My children, I am the one who once said to you, I have no desire other than that you bless me [through your prayers], and commit no sins. I retracted what I had said [and resolved as follows]: Even if a man commits numerous sins, each one more heinous than the one preceding, but then turns about in repentance, abases himself, regards himself as one who is equally meritorious and guilty, and every day believes himself liable to bring a guilt-offering, then I will feel compassion for him. I will accept him in repentance, give him sons who engage in study of Torah and fulfill its commandments. I will make certain that the words of Torah he acquires will be securely stored in his mouth, as it says: "Yet it pleased the Lord to crush him by disease; to see if his soul would offer itself in restitution, that he might see his seed, prolong his days, and that the purpose of the Lord might prosper by his hand" [Is. 53:10]. [*Tanna de-Vei Eliyahu*, chap. 6]

It is wrong for an individual to neglect the duty to repent inasmuch as repentance is so important in order to atone for one's misdeeds. For God's right hand is outstretched to welcome those who return to Him, and the opening is always there. The punishment for one who does not repent will be great in the world to come. Our Sages drew a nice analogy to this in connection with the verse, "The eyes of the wicked shall fail and they shall have no way to flee, and their hope shall be the drooping of the soul" [Job 11:20]:

> It may be likened to a band of robbers which rebelled against a king. They were caught and shut up in a prison. What did they do? One of them made an opening and they all escaped, except for one who did not flee. In the morning the king found him and said: "There was an opening before you and you did not flee!" In like manner the Holy One, blessed be He, says: "Repentance was before you but you did not repent." Therefore it is said: ". . . and they shall have no way to flee" [Ecc. Rabbah, 7:15].

Be aware that this exit [that is, the exit through which to repent] is represented by the small opening in the letter *heb*[16] as our Sages, of blessed memory, taught: "And wherefore was this world created with the letter *heb*?—Because it is like an *exedra*[17] and whoever wishes to exit may do so" [Menaḥot 29b]. The reason why this heavenly opening is so narrow is to enable a person to hide from the powers of strict justice. Similarly, it is taught in the *Tiqqunim* [94b] that by means of repentance an individual can conceal himself from the powers of strictness. Similarly, our Sages, of blessed memory, taught:

> What is implied by the verse, "And they had the hands of a man under their wings" [Ezek. 1:8]? *Yado* [his hand] is written: this refers to the Hand of the Holy One, blessed be He, which is spread out under the wings of the *Hayyot*, in order to accept penitents and shield them from the Attribute of Justice [Pes. 119a].[18]

The Gate of Holiness

Chapter One

Holiness is the root underlying observance of the commandments; because of this it is mentioned with such frequency in the Torah. For when an individual acts in a holy manner and detaches himself from the alluring things of this world, he will earnestly seek to fulfill the will of his Maker. He will bind himself to God's love, may He be blessed, so as to carry out His precepts with strong passion and love. For what benefit does this world and all its good things hold for a person, inasmuch as they are worthless vanities, as will be explained with the help of God? Thus, the subject of holiness is mentioned so often in the Torah on account of the enormous benefit which the soul derives from it.

. . . At first we are sanctified through God, and draw down holiness upon us from Him in order that we may sanctify ourselves through fulfillment of the commandments. Afterwards, He is made holy through us by means of the arousal from below which ascends heavenward as a consequence of our righteous deeds. The reason for this is that everything requires arousal from below, as Scripture says: ". . . but there went up a mist from the earth, and watered the whole face of the ground" [Gen. 2:6]. . . .

We must divest ourselves of material concerns, all of which stem from the realm of evil. We will be able to cleave to God only when we sanctify ourselves. This is the meaning of the words: ". . . and be holy unto your God" [Num. 15:40]. That is, you shall be holy so that you will be able to cleave to your God and He will be able to dwell with you. No bond can exist between an individual and God unless an individual sanctifies himself, for God is holy and purely spiritual in nature and you are of a material nature. How can that which is spiritual bind itself to that which is material unless a person sanctifies himself and practices abstinence from worldly things?

There are two dimensions to the general principle of holiness. The first is abstinence from material things and the establishment of a boundary for oneself beyond which one should not stray. The word "sanctity" signifies abstinence, as in: "Set bounds about the mount, and sanctify it" [Ex. 19:23].[1] This is the meaning of the words, "Depart from evil . . ." [Ps. 34:15], an expression which alludes to the observance of the *negative* commandments.[2]

The second dimension consists in drawing down the light of holiness upon us so that we can clothe ourselves in it. This corresponds to the rest of the aforementioned verse, "and do good' [Ps. 34:15]. Through the *positive* commandments we invest ourselves with sanctity; this is the esoteric meaning of the "divine garment."[3] For fulfillment of the positive commandments becomes a garment of light for the soul, the same garment in which the soul is clothed at a subsequent time in the lower Paradise. Thus, as part of those blessings which accompany the performance of commandments, we recite the phrase, "Who hast *sanctified* us by His commandments." For through the fulfillment of the precepts one sanctifies the soul and clothes it in a new light. Likewise, in connection with the Sanctification prayer which we recite each day: "Holy, holy, holy . . .," R. Simeon bar Yohai, may he rest in peace, commented that its purpose is to enable each person to draw down upon himself holiness from on high.

Chapter Seven

. . . One must accustom himself to rising every night at midnight and studying Torah until dawn. How many marvelous things occur by virtue of rising at midnight for the purpose of studying Torah? Among these is the subjugation of the evil shells, a topic which is treated in the Zohar [I, 242a–b].[4]

We have already mentioned above that the confusion of mind which a person may experience while engaged in praying or in studying Torah is on account of his sins, insofar as he renders himself unqualified for unifying God. Sin functions as an evil accuser which comes between a person and God; but when an individual accustoms himself to rise in the middle of the night in order to study Torah, he throws off the Evil One and atones for his sins.[5] Through such means he purifies his thoughts, and his efforts to unify God are not hampered. The reason for this is that night normally nourishes the forces of strict judgment. The night is transformed from darkness into light, from the quality of judgment to the quality of compassion, however, by virtue of the study of Torah. And since the night becomes "sweetened," so too are all those who are bound up with it.[6]

In addition, inasmuch as the hardest shell of all is that of death—and since sleep is one-sixtieth of death—this hard shell is broken when an individual avoids sleep.[7] Certainly, all the residue of evil is destroyed and shattered, and the light of the eye's pupil shines by virtue of the light of the Torah. Thus, King David, may he rest in peace, did not sleep at night even sixty breaths due to the reason provided here.

Therefore, every penitent must deny himself sleep at night by means of study of the Torah and prayer so as to destroy the strength of the evil shells. To be sure, this will serve as an important aid to him in accomplishing repentance. Refer to what is written concerning this in the *Tiqqunim* [86b] where you will see that the Holy One, blessed be He, was restored to His proper place because King David remained awake at night. From the example of King David, each and every person ought to learn that when an individual's sinfulness causes the Holy One, blessed be He and His *Shekhinah* to be exiled from their proper place, it is only fitting that he repent and deny himself sleep in order to restore them to the place where they belong.[8]

Similarly, when a person realizes that after his death his eyes will cease to function, how remorseful will he then be with respect to his earlier habits? While he is still able to see he will say to himself: "Why have I not used my eyes for the purpose of studying Torah by abstaining from sleep?" Therefore, while the spirit of life is still within him, a person should flee from death and cleave to the Torah, the Tree of Life.

Furthermore, evidence may also be found in the Zohar [III, 12b] to the effect that rising at midnight assists one in purifying his thoughts. We are informed there that the Psalm "Behold, bless ye the Lord, all ye servants of the Lord, that stand in the house of the Lord in the night seasons" [Ps. 134:1] alludes to those who arise at midnight for the purpose of studying Torah. And inasmuch as it says in the Zohar that the supernal King is blessed on account of such an individual, it is certain that his thoughts are proper and pure.

Whenever a person is confused and befuddled, his recitation of blessings is invalid and his attempts at unifying God are without success. He will assuredly receive assistance from heaven, however, enabling him to become perfectly righteous and pure of thought. Such is the merit which is provided a person who arises at midnight in order to occupy himself with Torah, as it says in the Zohar [III, 23b]: "But if a man awakes at night in order to study the Torah, then the Torah makes known to him his sin." This is in order that he may be able to repent.

There is additional evidence concerning this from a passage in the Zohar [III, 13a] where we find a comment on the scriptural expression mentioned above, "Behold, bless ye the Lord, all ye servants of the Lord, that stand in the house of the Lord in the night seasons" [Ps. 134:1]. "Lift up your hands to holiness and bless ye the Lord" [Ps. 134:2]. According to the Zohar the word "holiness" in this subsequent verse refers to divine Thought [*Hokhmah*], which corresponds to Eden. Surely, if an individual's soul does not cleave to "holiness" [that is, to the *Sefirah Hokhmah*], he will be unable to draw down blessing from that place with which to bless God. He must assuredly sanctify himself first by attaching himself to that holy place. As a result of doing so, he will subsequently be able to draw down blessing from there. . . .

A person who awakens from his sleep at night and turns his attention to matters having nothing to do with devotion to God risks his life. This is because he is obligated to rise solely for the purpose of studying the Torah. And should he fail to rise from his bed, he makes a mockery of the King's reward. It is therefore proper to rise quickly without sitting lazily upon one's bed, thinking about what one has dreamt, lest sleep overcome him again. Besides, every dream which derives from the realm of holiness will not be forgotten. There are some individuals who fail to rise in the middle of the night. This is on account of the meager degree of arousal stimulated by the paucity of their deeds and Torah study.

When the soul returns to its supernal dwelling place at night, the *Shekhinah* is aroused and is adorned [in preparation for Her unification with *Tif'eret*], through the study of Torah and the good deeds which this individual engaged in during the day.[9] In this connection, see the Zohar [II, 213b]. The Zohar also reports here that the angel Suria is in charge of raising up the souls of the righteous each night as a sacrifice to the Holy One, blessed be He. Suria inhales the scent of every one of these souls. That is, he "smells" their deeds and determines whether or not they are qualified to ascend still further.

We read elsewhere in the Zohar [II, 119b] that a person must elevate his soul each night by means of the study of Torah and the observance of the commandments in which he engaged during the day. Hence, an individual must take care to study a certain amount of Torah before praying the evening service, as it is taught:

> The Sages made a fence for their words so that a man, on returning home from the field in the evening, should not say: I shall go home, eat a little, drink a little, sleep a little, and then I shall recite the *Shema‘* and the *Tefillah*, and meanwhile, sleep may overpower him, and as a result he will sleep the whole night. Rather should a man, when returning home from the field in the evening, go to the synagogue. If he is used to reading the Bible, let him read the Bible and if he is used to repeating the Mishnah, let him repeat the Mishnah, and *then* let him recite the *Shema‘* and say the *Tefillah*. . . .[Berakhot 4b]

Any person who ignores the teaching of the Sages may be liable to the punishment of death.

The pattern for the midnight vigil is as follows [Zohar III, 178a]: Before lying down [in the early evening to sleep], one should examine his deeds for that day and commit them to writing so that he does not forget them. This is so as to fulfill the verse: ". . . and my sin is always before me" [Ps. 51:5]. Thus, let a person confess his sins. Additional details are provided with respect to the matter of confession in portion *Ṣav* of the Zohar [III, 33a].

It is also exceedingly beneficial to weep on account of one's sins, for when one's soul ascends because of his tears, it assuredly does so in a state of holiness. For all the heavenly gates are locked except the gates of tears. Following this a person should recite the prayer: "By the great power of the right hand, Oh, set the captive free," in which the forty-two-letter name of God is contained.[10] The *Tiqqunim* comments that by means of the forty-two-letter name of God a person can elevate his soul on high and conceal it from all the angels of destruction.

Following the confession of one's sins a person ought to concentrate upon offering up his soul as a sacrifice to God; he should do so in order that his soul might stimulate the "female waters" within the *Shekhinah* until the hour of midnight. And at midnight [when he rises from his sleep], the *Shekhinah* restores his soul to him. This is the meaning of the verse: "Into Thy hand I commit my spirit . . ." [Ps. 31:6].[11] It is also proper for a person to have a rooster for the purpose of arousing him at midnight, as in the case of Rabbi Akiba, who used to walk along with a rooster on the road.[12] The Sages did not rely upon their wisdom and their piety to ensure that they would awaken at midnight [Zohar I, 92a–b]. And if they were in need of assistance, how much more are we in need of help in awakening? I thus advise that anyone who does not own a rooster ought to seek a friend who does not go to sleep until the midnight hour so that he may arouse him at the precise time. Such a friend will be rewarded for doing so. . . .

One who wishes to sanctify himself when he arises at midnight ought to feel the distress of the *Shekhinah*, weep and mourn over the destruction of the Sanctuary; he should weep on account of God's desecrated name, as well as on account of his sins, which prolong the exile of the *Shekhinah*. For, at midnight, the Holy One, blessed be He, remembers Israel which is in exile, and the destruction of His Sanctuary. At that hour the souls of the righteous are restored to their bodies. Midnight is the hour of divine favor, as explained in the Zohar [III, 136b], and it is thus a fitting time for worship. The Holy One, blessed be He, forgives those who return to Him in repentance at midnight.

After all this, he should rise to study Torah, clothe himself, and ready himself to call out to God. When he rises he should study Oral Torah or Mishnah as well as the Aramaic version of the verse, "Arise, cry out in the night . . ." [Lam. 2:19].[13] And it is especially good if one stands during this time to the extent possible in order to ensure that he avoids falling asleep. This is what King David did, as Scripture says: "At midnight I will stand up to praise Thee . . ." [Ps. 119:62], as explained in the Zohar [I, 82b]. . . .

Chapter Nine

The present chapter will discuss the proper use of the senses of hearing and smell. The author of the *Duties of the Heart* wrote as follows in "The Gate of Abstinence":

> You should try to pay no attention to things which are no concern of yours, and abstain from listening to needless conversation. Do not hearken to lying, slander, and evil gossip. Avoid anything which may lead you to disobey God and neglect your duties to Him, such as all kinds of music, song, and amusement, all of which distract you from fulfilling the commandments and from the performance of good deeds. You should rather pay attention to the words of sages, as it is said : "Incline thine ear, and hear the words of the wise, and apply thy heart unto my knowledge"; "The ear that hearkeneth to the reproof of life abideth among the wise." [Prov. 22:17; 15:31][14]

It is necessary to elaborate upon this subject inasmuch as Bahya ibn Paquda's comments, may he rest in peace, are brief. An individual must avoid listening to the sound of a woman singing, it being sexually inciting.[15] Nor should "a man let his ears hear idle things, because they are burnt first of all the organs" [Ketubot 5b].[16] "Why are the fingers pointed like pegs? The reason is that if a man hears an unworthy thing he shall plug his fingers into his ears. . . . Why is the whole ear hard and the ear-lap soft? So that if a man hears an unworthy thing he shall bend the ear-lap into it" [Ketubot 5b].

One must never callously disregard the cry of the needy. A person must take care never to listen to evil gossip nor should he welcome it; for one who welcomes it is more blameworthy than the one who uttered it. An individual ought to be careful so as never to remain silent upon hearing deprecating remarks about a scholar. Testimony to this effect may be found in connection with the wife of R. Eleazar, son of R. Simeon bar Yohai.[17]

A person must take care to pay attention to a discussion of law or to a homily, even if he has heard it previously. He ought not declare that he has already heard it. For in connection with this, Scripture teaches: "He that turneth away his ear from hearing the law, even his prayer is an abomination . . ." [Prov. 28:9].

One must be careful never to allow his prayer to be overheard by another person while praying the Eighteen Benedictions. An individual who does so is known as one who is lacking in faith and his prayers are not accepted. The negative effects of allowing one's prayer to be overheard by others are explained in the Zohar [II, 202a].[18] Also, an individual must be careful to preserve a secret which he has heard. These are all commandments formulated in the *negative*.

One is obligated to pay attention to the repetition of the Eighteen Benedictions by the Reader of prayer and to respond "Amen" at the end of each blessing. And there are many additional *positive* precepts dependent upon the sense of hearing, such as listening to the sound of the Shofar, the recitation of the prayer "Hear, O Israel," the reading of the Torah by the Reader, and paying attention to the opinion of one's associate concerning a matter of law. It is not even permitted to study Torah while attending to the chanting of the Torah or while listening to the repetition of the Eighteen Benedictions, because it is wrong to combine the perfection of one sense with that of another. Each must be done at its own proper time. How much more injurious is it to join the profane realm to that of the sacred?

There is no doubt that anger and wrathfulness is the blemish associated with the nose, that is, with the sense of smell.[19] A person should derive no enjoyment from the smell connected with idolatrous practices and from the scent of forbidden foods.[20] Likewise, he ought to avoid the scent of a married woman's clothing, lest it arouse in him unchaste desires. Proper use of the sense of smell also consists in the "scent" of the "sacrifice" of our lips' utterance, which ascends on high in place of actual scent. For the scent of the ancient sacrifices used to provide pleasure on high.[21]

If an individual transgresses by losing his temper and by wrathfulness, he establishes room for the forces of strict judgment to spread and flourish. But when he studies Torah these forces are "sweetened" and restored to their proper place; the forces of supernal compassion will reveal themselves and render everything "sweet."[22]

How much better it is if a person engages in fasting while studying, for the scent which ascends from the utterances of one who fasts serves as a substitute for actual sacrifice. By means of the "breath" of the words of Torah, uttered in the course of study, the scent of his words ascends on high, unifying and "sweetening" the forces of strict judgment. For each "breath" of the Torah is a ladder by means of which prayer and the soul ascend above. . . .

Prayer constitutes a substitute for actual physical sacrifice; it rises on high to the "nose" of Ze'ir 'Anpin, providing a fragrant smell when an individual prays with appropriate awe and reverence.[23] And if he fails to pray in this manner, God forbid, on account of the quality of strict judgment within him, he arouses divine strictness, as it says in Scripture: ". . . but then the anger of the Lord and His jealousy shall be kindled against that man . . ." [Deut. 29:19].

It is all the more efficacious if one studies those sections of the Torah having to do with sacrifice, inasmuch as this provides a fragrant scent on high and "mends" the forces of strictness. In the same way, the incense used in the ancient sacrifices would ascend for the purpose of "sweetening" divine judgment. And if an individual recites that section of the Torah concerned with the incense, with appropriate contemplation, his words will ascend and accomplish the same thing. The rewards merited by one who does so are detailed in the Zohar [II, 218b–219b].[24]

Chapter Fifteen

This chapter will elaborate upon the sanctity associated with the activity of eating. Concerning this subject, King Solomon, may he rest in peace, taught: "Whoever keepeth his mouth and his tongue keepeth his soul from troubles" [Prov. 21:23]. The meaning of this is that a person should guard against eating impure foods and ought to sanctify himself through eating. For even with respect to the subject of foods our sacred Torah applies the term "holy." In portion *Shemini* of the Torah,[25] following the enumeration of those foods which are permitted and those which are forbidden, it reads: "For I am the Lord your God; sanctify yourselves therefore, and be ye holy; for I am holy; neither shall ye defile yourselves . . ." [Lev. 11:44]. In connection with this matter the Zohar comments that an evil and impure spirit rests upon the unclean foods about which the Torah cautions us. Therefore, an Israelite who eats of these foods defiles his soul, signifying that he has no share in holiness nor in the God of Israel. For the unclean food becomes an organic and intrinsic part of such an individual, and his soul becomes enclothed in it. From this we may conclude that a person who eats prohibited foods taints his soul.

On the contrary, an individual must partake only of those foods which are permitted to us by the Torah and ought to make certain that his eating is done for the sake of Heaven, as it is said: "The righteous eateth to the satisfying of his soul . . ." [Prov. 13:25]. If this verse is interpreted in the literal sense it is difficult to understand the expression "the satisfying of his soul." For the soul is immaterial and holy and cannot be satisfied through actual eating. Rather, the verse refers to the "consumption" [that is, the study] of Torah. Thus, the Zohar [II, 62b] explains that the expression "satisfying of his soul" refers to eating in a spiritual sense, the ingestion, so to speak, of Torah. We also read there that it is not fitting for a person to begin eating until he prays for his food. Here too "satisfaction" is understood in its deeper meaning, namely, the spiritual satisfaction which the soul experiences.[26]

There is also a holy element to eating itself; it is by virtue of this holy element that the soul becomes satisfied. Thus, it is proper for an individual to be exceedingly strict concerning what he consumes to ensure that he eats nothing prohibited whatsoever. Ezekial used to pride himself for not having eaten even of an animal "which a sage pronounced to be permitted" [Hullin 37b] in a situation where any doubt at all prevailed as to its permissibility.[27] This being so, it is all the more important to abstain from the forbidden portion [of otherwise permitted animals].[28] There are a number of foods concerning which difference of opinion arose among the later rabbinic judges.[29] Which opinion does the law follow? One authority prohibits a certain food while another permits it. To be sure, the prophet Ezekial did not partake of anything about which there was uncertainty.

The author of *Duties of the Heart* wrote that "some pious men used to abstain from seventy different kinds of permissible things, fearing that they might take one kind that was forbidden" ["The Gate of Repentance," Chap. 5]. An individual ought to exercise care not to purchase items concerning which there is question about their permissibility, except from Jews whose observance of the dietary laws is known to be meticulous. For a person's word is not credible if there is some suspicion concerning his observance.[30] This is particularly true in the case of bread, wine, meat, cheese, honey, and grapes, as well as any food which has been prepared by a non-Jew, except if it has been permitted by the rabbinic judges.[31]

"The righteous eateth to the satisfying of his desire; but the belly of the wicked shall want" [Prov. 13:25]. It appears from this verse that the reward merited by the righteous consists in their being satisfied with a small amount of food, whereas the wicked fail to be sated in this way. The reason why "the belly of the wicked shall want" is because the whole world would not suffice to satisfy their gluttony. From their point of view, it seems as if their stomachs are never full.

When an individual realizes that increasing the amount of food which he consumes merely increases the amount of flesh available to the worm— for this is one's final destiny—he will surely acknowledge that it is preferable for him to guard against eating too much.[32] The only exceptions to this rule are Sabbaths and Festivals, when it is proper to satisfy oneself. For the person who eats and drinks during the weekdays more than is necessary for the sustenance of his body and soul merits punishment. Concerning such people, Scripture says: "Behold, I will rebuke the seed for your hurt, and I will spread dung upon your faces, even the dung of your sacrifices . . ." [Mal. 2:3]. Our Sages, of blessed memory, taught: "This refers to people who abandon study and spend all their days at feasts" [Shabbat 151b]. We further read in the Zohar [II, 199b] concerning such people: "Three days after his death a man's belly ejects the dung onto his face, saying: 'Take back what thou gavest to me; thou didst eat and drink all day and never didst thou give anything to the poor; all thy days were like feasts and holidays.' "

We read further in the Zohar [II, 141a–b] that following death the spirit of impurity holds no power over the bodies of the righteous. For the righteous were not attracted during their lifetime to pleasures and festivities deriving from the hard shell of evil.[33] This is so because they enjoyed their pleasures only on Sabbaths and Festivals. For anyone who derives pleasure from feasts unrelated to Sabbaths and Festivals derives his enjoyment from the realm of evil. In such instances, the evil husk, that is, the husk of the hard shell, rules over him in death. The reason why these improper pleasures are associated with this hard shell is because all the food a man consumes which is unnecessary for actual sustenance constitutes needless enjoyment. Such unnecessary consumption increases the amount of flesh for the worm. . . .

Concerning the proper intentions which ought to accompany eating and drinking, the author of the *Candelabrum of Light* wrote that a person ought to be satisfied with what he has, and trust that his Maker will provide a living for him and not allow him to be reduced to a state of oppressive poverty.[34] Nor should a person eat gluttonously, as this will induce him to rob and steal in order to satisfy his cravings. An individual who consumes but small amounts of food so as to satisfy his soul, and whose intention is not physical pleasure, is a person who acknowledges his Creator. For when a person is very hungry he learns to appreciate his own limitations as well as the insignificance of human beings in general. For when someone is in need of bread to eat and water to drink, his power and the strength of all of his limbs diminishes, his eyes grow dim, and he lacks the strength with which to stand upon his feet. In such circumstances, he will acknowledge the perfection of the Holy One, blessed be He, who possesses need for neither eating nor drinking. When he is exceedingly hungry he will lift up his eyes to God, may He be blessed, in order to seek sustenance. Then he will realize that it is God, may His name be blessed, who provides bread for all people, sustenance for each and every human being, and gives "to every single person that which he needs" [Jerusalem Talmud, Berakhot 4:4].

Such a person will thereby have compassion upon the poor and avoid behaving in a haughty manner, for it is gluttony which lures an individual towards the commission of sin and transgression. When it comes to eating, a man is praiseworthy on account of three things:

1.   He should be completely satisfied with his portion; even if it is meager he ought not to seek more.

2.   He should eat at the correct time, before he becomes too hungry, thus weakening his body and becoming sick so that he lacks the strength with which to serve the Holy One, blessed be He, properly, as it says in Scripture: ". . . and thy princes eat in due season" [Ecc. 10:17].

3.   He ought not concern himself with his own physical gratification when he eats, but only with his sustenance. And he should desist from fol-

lowing his gluttonous instinct to eat everything which his palate desires of unhealthful foods, inasmuch as they can be harmful.

R. Moses ben Nahman wrote: "A person should always decrease his consumption of food by one-third."[35] Our Sages, of blessed memory, taught: "In a meal which you enjoy, indulge not too freely" [Gittin 70a]. The saintly Bahya ibn Paquda wrote as follows in the *Duties of the Heart* with respect to the subject of abstaining from eating too much food:

> Therefore, it is proper for you my brother to practice asceticism in enjoyment of those things which are lawful, so much so that you come to regard them as being in the same category with unlawful pleasures. For otherwise you will abandon your Torah. . . . Strive to discipline your sense of taste. Take only enough food and drink as you require for your sustenance, and abstain from anything beyond this. The subtle tactic to adopt in this regard is to diminish the number of different prepared courses and limit yourself to one course only, if you are able to do so. Accustom yourself to do occasionally without such food so as to control your appetite, and learn to be contented when it is withheld from you. If, however, you are able to forgo such prepared food entirely, which entails labor and effort in its preparation, and can rely upon that food which requires no exertion whatsoever, such as olives and grapes and the like, do so.
>
> If it is your custom to have two meals each day, let your meal during the day be lighter than the one you eat at night, so that your bodily movements will be easier by day and your religious and worldly occupations lighter. At a later time, train yourself to fast if your constitution is strong, even if it be only one day each week. And if you can train your soul to be insensitive to what you eat or drink, do so for the sake of disciplining it. Regard what you eat as being for your health rather than as a food. Your drink should consist of water only, unless your purpose in taking wine is to improve your physical health or to dispel anxiety from your heart. Be careful not to drink wine often, or to excess, and desist from taking up with drinking parties, since such behavior is a great detriment to the practice of Torah and religious devotion. ["The Gate of Abstinence," chap. 5]

This path, propounded by the saint Bahya ibn Paquda, of blessed memory, is one of abstention from pleasurable things for scholars whose primary activity is the study of Torah. For if a Torah scholar wants to spend his money in eating meat or poultry, and in similar kinds of pleasures, he diminishes himself through such worldly pursuits. Having behaved in this way, he will seek out food which is altogether unfit and neglect the study of Torah. At the point that he fails to obtain what he desires, he will be unable to tolerate it and will become sick. It is therefore preferable for every scholar of Torah to practice the kind of abstinence described above. In this connection, there is a variety of teachings of our Sages, of blessed memory, which can assist a person in avoiding worldly pleasures.

When a person becomes accustomed to eating little he will soothe his soul, sanctify himself through the Torah, and avoid flatulating while engaged in its study. The prudent individual will pay attention to this matter, curb his craving for food and refrain from eating gluttonously. A person's craving for food resembles that of an animal, for "Who is mighty? He that subdues his evil impulse" ['Avot 4:1].[36] And should his evil impulse seek to seduce him so that he overeat, he ought to overwhelm it and suppress his longings. As a result, reverence for God as well as holiness will rest upon him, as it is written in Scripture: "Oh, fear the Lord, ye His holy ones; for there is no want to them that fear Him. The young lions do lack and suffer hunger; but they that seek the Lord want not any good thing . . ." [Ps. 34:10–11].

A person should not long for pleasures, for the study of Torah succeeds only in the case of those who avoid excessive enjoyment, as it says in the Zohar [III, 247a–b] concerning the verse: ". . . fine flour for a meal-offering, mingled with . . . beaten oil" [Num. 28:5]. This refers to one who fulfills the teaching ". . . thou shalt eat bread with salt" ['Avot 6:4]. This means that one should "crush" that which is material in order to illuminate the Torah and the soul within oneself.[37] This is the means by which to attain knowledge of the Torah, for even though a man may be wealthy, he should not indulge himself with luxuries. Testimony to this effect is found in what King David, may he rest in peace, said: "It is good for me that I have been afflicted, in order that I might learn Thy statutes" [Ps. 119:71]. Similarly, R. Simeon bar Yohai and his son dwelt in a cave for thirteen years. During this time [of affliction] they experienced visions of the future and the depths of wisdom were revealed to them. In particular, one who has sinned must suffer affliction on account of his transgressions. For a sinful individual will not merit the supernal light—this being the oil concerning which King David said: "Thou hast annointed my head with oil . . ." [Ps. 23:5], unless he "beats" [that is, afflicts] himself.

We find another reference in the Zohar [III, 247b] concerning the verse: ". . . fine flour mingled with . . . beaten oil." Scripture says, "But he was wounded because of our transgressions, he was crushed because of our iniquities . . ." [Is. 53:5]. The meaning of this is that since the Messiah suffers because of our sins, causing him to be crushed, one who desires that he not suffer must himself suffer and experience affliction. A story is told about a certain pious individual who used to undergo various afflictions because of his transgressions; he did so in order to prevent the suffering of the Messiah. . . .

When an individual shares his meal with someone who is in need, his meal is regarded as fulfillment of a religious precept. "This is how R. Tanhum son of R. Hiyya was wont to act. When his mother went to buy him a pound of meat from the market she would buy him two pounds, one for himself and one for the poor, bearing in mind that the Holy One, blessed be He, '. . . hath made even the one as well as the other' [Ecc. 7:14], poor as well as rich, in order that they might benefit each other" [Lev. Rabbah, chap. 34].[38] . . .

The Gate of Humility

Introduction

Since we were concerned in the previous Gate with matters having to do with holiness—through which one acquires the power of repentance—we decided to juxtapose to it the subject of humility. For humility is required of a penitent as King David, may he rest in peace, said: "The sacrifices of God are a broken spirit; a broken and a contrite heart, O God, Thou wilt not despise" [Ps. 51:19].[1] The penitent ought to be humble and contrite, mindful of his shame, and must not return to his former ways so that his sins will find atonement, as will be explained. There are a number of stages and levels through which one must pass in order to acquire the trait of humility, as the interested reader will discover in the following chapters.

Chapter One

In explanation of the word humility: The term humility ['anavah] is derived from the words poor ['oni] and suffering ['inui], for the meaning of humility is submissiveness—which is what the word "poor" denotes. Similarly, the words suffering, affliction [ta'anit], and the like are associated with submissiveness.

Now the attributes of submissiveness and humility also characterize the Creator, blessed be He. Even though God is exalted above all things, and higher in majesty than all else, as it is written: "The Lord reigneth; He is clothed in majesty" [Ps. 93:1], He is nevertheless humble, as King David, may he rest in peace, said: "And Thy condescension hath made me great" [Ps. 18:36]. Thus, our Sages, of blessed memory, taught:

Is there anyone more humble than the Holy One, blessed be He, Himself? A man says to his fellow, "Come, adorn the bride, visit the sick,

116

bury the dead, comfort the mourners." And he replies to him: "I am powerful and wealthy, should I do these things?" But the Holy One, blessed be He, "fashioned the rib; The Lord appeared to him by the terebinths of Mamre; He buried him [Moses] in the valley; God appeared again to Jacob."[1] [Gen. 2:22; Gen. 18:1; Deut. 34:6; Gen. 35:9][2]

The Sages taught further: "Whenever you find mentioned in the Scriptures the power of the Holy One, blessed be He, you also find His gentleness mentioned . . ." [Meg. 31a]. Our Sages also taught as follows:

> R. Joseph said: Man should always learn from the mind of his Creator; for behold, the Holy One, blessed be He, ignored all the mountains and heights and caused His *Shekhinah* to abide upon Mount Sinai, and ignored all the beautiful trees and caused His *Shekhinah* to abide in a bush [Sotah 5a].[3]

From the various passages dealing with the topic of humility that are found scattered throughout the *Gemara*, especially in the tractates *Megillah* and *Sotah*, we find that the quality of humility in the supernal world is located within the first three *Sefirot*, as well as within the Holy One, blessed be He [that is, *Tif'eret*] and the *Shekhinah*, as will be explained.[4] Thus, the *Ra'aya Mehemna* [III, 223a] explains that the supernal place in which humility is located is the upper three *Sefirot*: "When he [King David] reached the uppermost three *Sefirot* he proclaimed, 'Lord my heart is not haughty, nor mine eyes lofty; Neither do I exercise myself in things too great or in things too wonderful for me' " [Ps. 131:1]. Furthermore, just as it is written in tractate *Sotah* that "man should always learn from the mind of his Creator . . . ," so humility itself is located within the Holy One, blessed be He.

One can find humility to an even greater degree residing within the lowest of the *Sefirot*, that is, the *Shekhinah* of the Holy One, blessed be He. She is called by the name "moon" and is exiled from time to time inasmuch as Her light has been diminished.[5] We learn in tractate Hullin [60b] that the Holy One, blessed be He, said to the moon: "The righteous shall be named after thee as we find, Jacob the Small, Samuel the Small, David the Small."[6] David is mentioned in this connection because he used to embody the quality of humility and would humble himself saying: "I am small and despised . . ." [Ps. 119:141], just as is the moon from time to time. And occasionally he would exalt himself: "The saying of David the son of Jesse, and the saying of the man raised on high . . ." [II Sam. 23:1].

In the Zohar [II, 233a] you will learn that the poor are called vessels of the Holy One, blessed be He, in whom God finds delight, as it is written: "I shall dwell in the high and holy place, with him also that is of a contrite and humble spirit . . ." [Is. 57:15]. Thus, the poor whose hearts are broken and contrite are characterized by this trait, as is explained in Zohar III, 9a. Similarly, the Midrash comments as follows on the verse: "The sacrifices of God are a broken spirit; a broken and a contrite heart, O God, Thou wilt not despise" [Ps. 51:19]:

> Whatever the Holy One, blessed be He, declared unfit in the case of an animal, He declared fit in the case of man. In animals He declared unfit the "blind, or broken, or maimed, or having a wen, etc." [Lev. 22:22], whereas in man He declared fit ". . . a broken and contrite heart." R. Alexandri said: If an ordinary person makes use of broken vessels, it is a disgrace for him, but the vessels used by the Holy One, blessed be He, are deliberately broken ones, as it is said, "The Lord is nigh unto them that are of a broken heart [Ps. 34:19]; Who healeth the broken in heart . . . [Ps. 147:3]; I dwell in the high and holy place, with him also that is of a contrite and humble spirit [Is. 57:15]; The sacrifices of God are a broken spirit; a broken and contrite heart, O God, Thou wilt not despise" [Lev. Rabbah 7:2].

It is a general principle that the quality of humility may be found at every stage of divine emanation; at each stage it manifests itself in a particular way. Refer to the *Tiqqunim* [5b], where you will see that the *Shekhinah* is associated with the quality of humility. The quality of humility is associated even with the *Sefirah Keter;* for the attribute of modesty enables a person to act with forbearance and to show mercy and the like, these being the thirteen attributes of God which we recite: "The Lord, the Lord, God, merciful and gracious, long-suffering . . ." [Ex. 34:6–7].[7] Likewise: "Who is a God like unto Thee, that pardoneth the iniquity, and passeth by the transgression of the remnant of His heritage? He retaineth not His anger forever, because he delighteth in mercy. He will again have compassion upon us; He will subdue our iniquities; and Thou wilt cast all their sins into the depths of the sea. Thou wilt show faithfulness to Jacob, mercy to Abraham, as Thou hast sworn unto our fathers from the days of old" [Micah 7: 18–20]. R. Simeon bar Yohai commented that these constitute the thirteen attributes of mercy belonging to *'Arikh 'Anpin* [*Keter*].

Behold, every place in which you find a manifestation of God's greatness, even in the supernal world above, which is the site of His glorious majesty, there you will discover humility. Therefore, an individual must imitate his Creator so as to behave with forbearance towards others, as well as with the other qualities which are associated with the Holy One, blessed be He, as indicated in His thirteen attributes of mercy. Just as God is gracious, so you too must be gracious; just as God is merciful, so you too must be merciful; and so on with the other qualities of spirit.

In the name of the *Geonim*[8] I have heard the meaning of that which is taught in tractate Rosh Hashanah [17b] with respect to the verse, "And the Lord passed by before him, and proclaimed 'The Lord, the Lord, God, merciful and gracious . . .' " [Ex. 34:6]:

> R. Jochanan said: Were it not written in the text, it would be impossible for us to say such a thing; this verse teaches us that the Holy One, blessed be He, drew His robe round Him like the reader of a congregation and showed Moses the order of prayer. He said to him: Whenever Israel sins, let them carry out this service before Me, and I will forgive them.

This is a difficult matter to understand, for we sometimes find that even though we recite the thirteen attributes we are nevertheless not forgiven by God. But the *Geonim* teach that the expression "let them carry out this service" refers not only to wearing a prayershawl [and reciting the thirteen attributes], but also to *practicing* the thirteen attributes which God taught to Moses. For He is a merciful and gracious God. That is, just as He is merciful, you too must be merciful, and so on with the rest of the thirteen attributes.[9]

The sage Moses Cordovero wrote that not only do the thirteen attributes of mercy—being the thirteen perfections of the beard of *'Arikh 'Anpin*—teach us about the quality of humility.[10] Each of the other aspects of *'Arikh 'Anpin* instruct us about humility as well, known as the head, forehead, eye, nose, mouth, and so on. All of these bear upon the great humility with which we must treat others. Thus, for example, humility derives from the divine head. Just as a man bows his head before one who is greater than himself, so *Keter* humbles itself before the Cause of causes and goes by the name "Nothing."[11] This is because it regards itself as nothing in comparison to God ['*Ein-Sof*] who brings forth everything. *Keter* also lowers its head in order to provide for and nourish the lower worlds, all of which turn in its direction to suckle from it.

In the same way, it is good for an individual to regard himself as nought in comparison to the exaltedness of God, may He be blessed, inasmuch as He has neither end nor limit. Concerning this Moses, our teacher, may he rest in peace, said: ". . . and what are we?" [Ex. 16:7].

Similarly, it is correct to say that for this same reason the *Sefirah Ḥokhmah* is called "what" [in relationship to that quality of God above it]. Thus it is explained in the Zohar that "what" is His name [Zohar II, 198b]. . . .

Also, with respect to one's mind, a person should turn his thoughts away from everything that is foul and loathsome. He ought to cleave to the Torah in the same way that divine Thought[12] cleaves above [to the *Sefirah Keter*] in order to draw down nourishment. In this connection, R. Simeon bar Yohai, may he rest in peace, and his colleagues used to be careful never to separate their thought from God for even an instant, as is known.

Further, with regard to the forehead [*meṣaḥ*], a person must avoid acting in an insolent manner, as it is said: "Yet thou hadst a harlot's forehead, thou refusedst to be ashamed" [Jer. 3:3]. Instead, one should be gracious to all people. Just as the supernal Forehead is known as "gracious" [*meṣaḥ ra-ṣon*], by virtue of which all the evil forces in the lower worlds are placated, so too a person should not engage in strife and contention in any of his relationships, neither with one who is lowly nor one who is powerful. Rather, he ought to be gracious and accepting of everybody, even non-Jews.

Also, when it comes to the eyes, one should be certain that his eyes are ever vigilant to show compassion to the poor and to care for them, just as the supernal Eye does, concerning which Scripture says: "Behold, the eye of the Lord is toward them that fear Him, toward them that wait for His mercy" [Ps. 33:18]. Similarly we read: "Behold, He that keepeth Israel doth neither slumber nor sleep" [Ps. 121:4]. For God ceaselessly preserves Israel, protects her and acts compassionately toward her. And even if those in the world below should transgress, God's protecting compassion will not take leave of them.

A person must also be charitable and generous with his money, giving wholeheartedly and sympathetically; for concerning the supernal Eye in the world above it is said: "He that hath a bountiful eye shall be blessed; for he giveth of his bread to the poor" [Prov. 22:9]. The individual who acquires this quality of spirit will merit length of days, as our Sages, of blessed memory, taught: "R. Nehunia ben ha-Kanah was asked by his disciples: By virtue of what have you reached such a good old age? He replied: . . . I have been generous with my money" [Meg. 28a]. A generous person displays compassion inasmuch as he provides for others voluntarily and his generosity extends even to one who is undeserving.

All of the qualities of spirit associated with '*Arikh 'Anpin* signify perfect compassion and completely unqualified generosity. Inasmuch as the location in the supernal world where such compassion resides is called "length of days," an individual prolongs his own days in proportion to his deeds. Thus, one's eyes ought to be downcast as is the supernal Eye for the purpose of nourishing the lower world. Concerning this subject, refer to what is found in the eighth chapter of the "Gate of Holiness."

With regard to one's ears, they must be alert in order to hearken to the sound of Torah and prayer, as well as to the voice of the poor so as to show them compassion. But the ears should pay no attention to the sounds of evil gossip and other such things which blemish an individual, as is explained in the "Gate of Holiness." If a person should hear such talk, however, he ought not reproach the speaker. For even the Holy One, blessed be He, pays no attention to the [moral] debts which men incur, and does not compensate them strictly according to their just rewards. By virtue of this, the Holy One, blessed be He, is called a King who bears humiliation.

As for his nose, a person should imitate the quality of patience as it manifests itself in the supernal Nose, concerning which Scripture says: "For My name's sake will I defer Mine anger, and for My praise will I refrain for thee, that I cut thee not off" [Is. 48:9], for God is forbearing.[13] From Him flow divine abundance, the foundation of life, and nourishment to all that exist. An individual ought to resemble this quality of God's, and display no anger towards any human being.

With respect to the face, one should imitate those supernal qualities which are called Countenance, concerning which Scripture teaches: "The Lord lift up His countenance upon thee . . ." [Num. 6:26]. A person ought to greet every individual with kindness; he should refrain from acting disrespectfully towards any person, God forbid. The punishment for one who does not act properly will be explained.

As for his mouth, a person ought to resemble the supernal Mouth, uttering neither a curse nor words of ostracism, condemnation, impudence, or harshness. R. Joshua ben Levi used to take pride in the fact that in the course of his entire life he had never excommunicated any person from the community, as reported in the Jerusalem Talmud.[14] From this example a person ought to learn never to speak derisively or in a ridiculing way of others. On the contrary, his manner of speaking should be gentle to each and every human being, be it someone great or lowly. An individual who avoids speaking much about worldly matters prolongs his days, inasmuch as his mouth thereby resembles the supernal Mouth. Concerning this subject, refer to the tenth chapter of the "Gate of Holiness."

Even though we have explained that an individual must imitate the behavior of his Creator with respect to humility, he must sometimes also practice the quality of strict justice in dealing with those who do evil, as

King David said: "Do not I hate them, O Lord, that hate Thee? And do I not strive with those that rise up against Thee? I hate them with utmost hatred . . ." [Ps. 139:21–22]. It is forbidden to have compassion upon those who are wicked, as Scripture says: ". . . the tender mercies of [that is, toward] the wicked are cruel" [Prov. 12:10]. Thus, occasionally one must rebuke an individual who deserves reprimand, as King Solomon said: "A rebuke entereth deeper into a man of understanding than a hundred stripes into a fool" [Prov. 17:10]. Similarly, a person must treat his son or student in the same fashion, as King Solomon said: "He that spareth his rod hateth his son; but he that loveth him chasteneth him betimes" [Prov. 13:24]. He must do so, however, in a calm manner without losing his temper. He must look upon the strike which he gives his son or student as constituting an act of lovingkindness which is intended to draw him near to holiness and to eliminate all evil from him. Thus, the Sages taught:

> R. Johanan ben Nuri said: I call heaven and earth to witness for myself that often was Akiba punished through me because I used to complain against him before our Rabban, Gamaliel Beribbi, and all the more he showered love upon me, to make true what has been said: ". . . reprove a wise man and he will love thee" [Prov. 9:8]. [Arakhin 16b]

In a similar manner, if a person becomes angry with his friend for having treated him unjustly, he [that is, the injured party] ought to remind himself of some good thing which his friend has done for him, so that his own anger will be assuaged. Let him learn this from the example of his Maker. This is one of the thirteen attributes of mercy which the prophet Micah mentioned in the passage, "Who is like unto Thee?" For one of these attributes is that God subdues [that is, overlooks] our iniquities, meaning that even though it is justifiable for a plaintiff to avenge someone who has injured him, the Holy One, blessed be He, subdues iniquities and reminds Himself of some virtuous thing which an individual has done. This is the way in which a person should behave towards his friend, recalling some good thing which his friend has done and ignoring the injury which he did to him.

Other dimensions of the attribute of humility include three things which we are taught in the tractate 'Avot [5:19]: "He in whom these three things are found is of the disciples of Abraham our father, may he rest in peace. A good eye and a humble spirit and a lowly soul." The majority of commentators agree that "a good eye" refers to satisfaction with one's portion. Even if one's neighbor possesses greater wealth than himself, such an individual harbors no jealousy. On the contrary, the little which he does have is, in his view, a great deal, and that which others possess is inconsequential as far as he is concerned. He even desires that others have more than himself. The opposite of this is the case of "a bad eye," where a person envies his neighbor on account of what he possesses; and even if he himself owns a great deal, he regards it as being too little, whereas even if his neighbor has little wealth, he considers it to be a large amount. Such is the jealousy which some individuals feel towards that which their fellows have; he begrudges another what he possesses and does not mind if he himself has little, provided that his neighbor has even less.

"A humble spirit" signifies great modesty; its opposite is a haughty spirit. We find that pride is called *ruaḥ* [nothing], as Scripture says: ". . . and that which cometh into your mind [*ruḥacham*] shall not be at all . . ." [Ezek. 20:32]. [15] The expression "lowly soul" refers to an individual who puts distance between himself and excessive passions, and who does not rush to satisfy his every appetite for food and lust. The opposite is a person who is greedy, who pursues his desires, as it says in Scripture: "All the labor of man is for his mouth, and yet the appetite is not filled" [Ecc. 6:7]. And one who pursues his desires for food and other things becomes arrogant, as it is written: "Beware lest thou forget the Lord thy God, in not keeping His commandments, and His ordinances, and His statutes, which I command thee this day; lest when thou hast eaten and art satisfied . . . then thy heart be lifted up, and thou forget the Lord thy God . . ." [Deut. 8:11–14]. . . .

Chapter Two

. . . Among those things which will draw a person towards humility is his consideration of the greatness of our Creator, the Creator of all things, the King of the king of kings, the Holy One, blessed be He, whose greatness is unsearchable and without limits. Recognition of this will lead one to humility. Thus, King David said: "When I behold Thy heavens, the work of Thy fingers . . . what is man, that Thou art mindful of him" [Ps. 8:4–5]. For even the whole world below the dome of heaven is like a grain of mustard in God's eyes. If this is the case, then human beings—who constitute only part of this world—are certainly as naught. And thus it is written in Scripture: "And all the inhabitants of the earth are reputed as nothing . . ." [Dan. 4:32].

Should an individual act in a conceited manner on account of his own knowledge, let him reflect upon the wisdom of the ancient Sages; by doing so he will realize that the totality of our knowledge is tantamount to outer shells and is insignificant when compared to the knowledge which they possessed. Further, let a person realize that his reverence for God, as well as his deeds, should correspond to his degree of knowledge, as our Sages taught: "R. Judah said: Be heedful in study, for an unwitting error in study is accounted wanton transgression" ['Avot 4:13]. Likewise, "For in much wisdom is much vexation; and he that increases knowledge increases sorrow" [Ecc. 1:18]. This is because the stain of one who stumbles while dressed in a silken garment is not the same as that of one who stumbles while dressed in a plain garment. For the difficulty of cleansing it will correspond to its value.

Should a man grow arrogant on account of his wealth, let him concern himself with the financial well-being of his friend, or worry about whether he is fulfilling his obligations with regard to what God obliges us to give to the poor.

Among the things which will lead a man towards modesty is reading what we have written in the "Gate of Fear" about the various ways in which sin blemishes the soul and harms the supernal worlds, causing the exile of the *Shekhinah*. He will become introspective, telling himself that it would have been better had he not been born since he causes so much evil. Therefore, it is proper for a man to flee from arrogance and domineering behavior, for arrogance is the root of all evil qualities and leads a person towards the commission of a variety of transgressions. In connection with this matter the Zohar [III, 8b] teaches:

> We have learned that famine comes to the world by virtue of three sins which are only found among the rich, because they are arrogant on account of their wealth, but these sins are not found among the poor.

And thus it is fitting for a person to desist from assuming airs of authority and from domineering behavior so that he does not become haughty and thereby sin.

Vanity is among those things which drive a person from this world as well as from the world to come. Haughtiness deprived Jeroboam ben Nebat of the world to come, as recorded in chapter eleven of the tractate Sanhedrin.[16] What is more, if a scholar behaves in a conceited manner on account of his knowledge, his learning will take leave of him and he will forget what he has learned. And if he is a prophet, his prophecy will depart from him. If one begins to study and becomes conceited, announcing that he is a great scholar, his punishment will be severe, as our Sages, of blessed memory, taught: "Anyone who is not a scholar, and parades in the scholar's cloak, is not admitted within the circle of the Holy One, blessed be He" [Baba Batra 98a].

It seems to me that this is a case of measure for measure; just as such an individual drives the *Shekhinah* from his house,[17] so those in the world above who are responsible for his soul will force him out of the circle of the Holy One, blessed be He. For the *Shekhinah* does not reside except in a heart which is contrite. This is what is taught in the *Tiqqunim*, namely, that a person must prepare a lovely dwelling place in his heart for the *Shekhinah*. This means that an individual has to act humbly and avoid losing his temper. For when he behaves in an arrogant manner, the *Shekhinah* takes flight and a handmaiden rules in her mistress' place. She will not abide with an individual who is not pleasing to the Holy One, blessed be He, and She will not glorify his soul in the world to come. Among those things for which the redemption is delayed is arrogant behavior, as our Sages, of blessed memory, taught: "The son of David[18] will not come until there are no conceited men in Israel" [San. 98a].

Having spoken of haughtiness and the punishment which accompanies it, we now want to consider the punishment for one who indulges in anger. For anger derives only from arrogance; were an individual of contrite spirit and broken-hearted, surely he would not lose his temper, nor would he act reproachfully. The relationship between haughtiness and angry speech is expressed in the words found at the end of the Eighteen Benedictions:[19] "My God, guard my tongue from evil, and my lips from speaking falsehood. May my soul be silent to those who insult me; be my soul lowly to all as the dust."

Thus, in many respects the punishment which results from anger is similar to that which results from arrogance, as in the case of one who is given to anger and forgets all that he has learned. Thus, we see that our Sages, of blessed memory, taught: "He who loses his temper is exposed to all the torments of *Gehenna*" [Ned. 22a], forgets his learning, and "even the Divine Presence is unimportant in his eyes" [Ned. 22b]. The Sages also said: "Fall not into a passion and thou wilt not sin" [Ber. 29b]. The reason for this is that "a wrathful man abounds in transgression" [Prov. 29:22].

. . .

The Gate of Fear

Chapter Two

Among those things which arouse the inner fear of God is consideration by an individual of the deeds of the Holy One, blessed be He. For we stand in awe of God on account of the greatness of His deeds, as King David, may he rest in peace, said: "Say unto God: 'How tremendous is Thy work' " [Ps. 66:3]. And when a person reflects upon God's actions, may He be blessed, he will learn to revere Him and to submit to Him by reason of His exaltedness; he will humble himself before God and refrain from transgressing His commandments.

Another way for a person to arouse reverence for God is to meditate upon the miracles and wonders which continually manifest themselves in the world, as it is said: "And Israel saw the great work which the Lord did upon the Egyptians, and the people feared the Lord . . ." [Ex. 14:31]. An individual must also revere Him when he beholds the numerous benevolent and compassionate things which the Creator continuously does on his behalf. For God is similar to a merciful father who takes good care of his son, showing compassion towards him. A person ought to revere his father lest he be responsible for evoking his father's harsh side, thereby causing him to withhold his goodness.

The primary locus for fear within the Godhead is the supernal Wisdom [*Hokhmah*] which is symbolized by the letter *yud* in the name *YHVH*.[1] This is the esoteric mystery of divine Thought [that is, *Hokhmah*] which disperses vital-life throughout all the worlds. That is the meaning of the verse: "The fear of the Lord is a fountain of life . . ." [Prov. 14:27], as it is well-known that fear is the wellspring for all the worlds.

Chapter Four

This chapter will elucidate various dimensions of the fear of sin. First, a person must be fearful lest he fall prey to any sin whatsoever, even unintentionally. The reason for this is that the divine soul is delicate and pure, deriving from an exalted place.[2] Anything which injures an individual, even inadvertently, harms the soul. He may be compared to one who pours a pitcher of oil or ink on his spotless, white clothes, even accidentally; the stain discolors the garment. Concerning this King Solomon, may he rest in peace, said: "Let thy garments be always white; and let thy head lack no oil" [Ecc. 9:8]. What is the meaning of the verse: "If anyone shall sin through error in any of the things which the Lord hath commanded not to be done . . . [Lev. 4:2]? This is to teach you that anyone who sins, even inadvertently, is like one who deliberately transgressed God's commandments.

A person who sins is punished on two accounts. First, because his soul is of a spiritual character, inasmuch as he is the son of a King, it is proper for him to take into account the supernal King's honor. Even if he sins unintentionally, he is punished as if he did so deliberately, since "an unwitting error in study amounts to presumption" ['Avot 4:13]. And with respect to a person who transgresses even a single commandment, it is as if he violated all 248 affirmative precepts, since all of them are bound up with one another.[3] That is the meaning of: "And when ye shall err, and not observe all these commandments . . ." [Num. 15:22].

If an individual is virtuous in his actions, he cleaves to the realm of goodness—which corresponds to the name *YHVH*, the Tree of Life, the side of mercy and compassion.[4] That is the meaning of, "The Lord [*YHVH*] is good to all, His tender mercies are over all His works" [Ps. 145:9]. Thus, the numerical value of the name *YHVH* equals that of the word *tov* [good] in "small" numbers.[5] And if an individual does not act virtuously, he cleaves to the realm of evil, the Tree of Death, the exterior husks.[6] After a person's death, his soul cleaves to one realm or another in accordance with his actions in this world. For a man is composed of both good and evil, that is, the good inclination and the evil inclination. If he subdues his evil inclination, he subjugates the forces of strictness and evil, and enables goodness to descend upon him. An individual must strengthen the good inclination so that it prevails over the evil inclination. And if, heaven forbid, he does the reverse, he injures the supernal roots and prevents blessing and divine abundance from flowing into this world. Therefore, he must always stand in awe of heaven lest he injure himself, that is, his soul, depriving it of its supernal light.

The husk, deriving from the realm of evil, is like the shell of a nut. The good element—which is concealed—is the kernel of the nut. Therefore, in order to achieve the fear of God—which is the good that is concealed—one must break and destroy one's evil obstinacy and distance himself from this quality to such a degree that he will be loathe to draw near to it again. Just as one must crack the shell of the nut in order to consume the wholesome kernel, and just as the nut possesses three layers of shells, so must one distance himself from three husks. The first of these is pride, for this is the root of all evil qualities. Second, corresponding to the nut's hard shell, is a man's stubbornness. The third is an angry person's fury and harsh words which make him seethe with the fire of the evil impulse and lead him to sin. When a man separates himself from the pleasures of this world, all of which derive from the husks, the serpent's skin, and the evil inclination, this realm is subdued. The same holds true when he is careful to avoid transgressing the Torah's negative commandments. For anyone who violates the negative commandments enables the evil serpent to penetrate the realm of holiness.

Chapter Eleven

There are a number of additional details associated with reverence for God having to do with God's judgment. An individual must fear God on account of the different witnesses who testify about him each day, as our Sages, of blessed memory, taught:

> Who testifies against me? The stones of a man's home and the beams of his house testify against him, for it is said: "For the stone shall cry out of the wall, and the beam out of the timber shall answer it" [Hab. 2:11]. But the Sages say: A man's soul testifies against him, for it is said: "Keep the doors of thy mouth from her that lieth in thy bosom" [Micah 7:5]. What is it that lies in a man's bosom? You must say it is the soul. R. Zerika said: Two ministering angels that accompany him testify against him, for it is said: "For He will give His angels charge over thee, to keep thee in all thy ways" [Ps. 91:11]. [Hag. 16a]

The Torah itself also testifies concerning a person, as Scripture says: "Take this book of the law, and put it by the side of the ark of the covenant of the Lord your God, that it may be there for a witness against thee" [Deut. 31:26]. The *Tiqqunim* comments that the *Shekhinah* is witness to the deeds which a person performs in private.

Furthermore, one must fear God on account of the judgment which hangs over him every day and every hour, as our Sages, of blessed memory, taught in connection with the verse, "And that Thou shouldest remember him every morning, and try him every moment" [Job 7:18]. "R. Jose says: Man is judged every day, as it says, 'And thou dost visit him every morning.' R. Nathan says: Man is judged every moment, as it says, 'Thou dost try him every moment' " [Rosh Hashanah 16a].

Chapter Fifteen

. . . In what ways should Sages be honored? A person ought to show them great esteem and reverence, similar to that shown to God, fearing them as one fears the countenance of God, that is to say, as one fears viewing the face of a king, his judges and officers.

In what way should sacred books be treated? A person ought to place his books in the most choice location in his home and cover them with a prayershawl. Just as we construct high shelves upon which to place food—in order to keep it from mice and cats—so one should also guard the honor belonging to God.[7] When an individual transfers his books from one place to another, he should not treat them as he does other objects. Rather, he must move them in a dignified and respectful manner as one would carry the garments of a king in his presence. He should not touch them unless his hands are clean. These are acts of piety which are known only to oneself; a person who stands in awe of God will observe all of them.

Our Sages, of blessed memory, taught that "it is forbidden for a scholar to stand in a place of filth, because he must not stand still without meditating on the Torah. . . . In every place it is permitted to meditate on words of Torah except in the bath and in a privy" [Ber. 24b]. The *Book of the Pious* reports that in the privy an individual should preoccupy himself with his expenses and his household finances.[8]

Furthermore, an individual must be careful to honor the name of God to ensure that it will not be desecrated on his account, as our Sages, of blessed memory, have taught:

> If someone studies Scripture and Mishnah, and attends on the disciples of the wise, and speaks pleasantly to people, is honest in business, what do people then say concerning him? "Happy is the person who has studied Torah, happy the father who taught him Torah; woe unto people who have not studied Torah—look how fine his ways are, how righteous his deeds!" Of him Scripture says: "And He said unto me: Thou art My servant, Israel in whom I will be glorified" [Is. 49:3]. But if someone studies

Scripture and Mishnah, but is discourteous in his relations with people, people say the opposite about him. [Yoma 86a]

Therefore, an individual has to avoid doing anything which involves the profanation of God's name; for repentance does not atone for this transgression. Death alone serves as expiation for such sin. The Zohar teaches [III, 231a] that on the New Year, judgment is initially passed on those who are not careful about honoring God's name. Our Sages taught: "We find that the Holy One, blessed be He, showed indulgence towards idolatry, but never condoned profanation of the Divine Name" [Lev. Rabbah, 22:6].

Further, the second aspect of God's honor is that one must be mindful never to pay respect to any man or woman before showing honor to the Holy One, blessed be He. This is similar to what our Sages, of blessed memory, taught, namely, that it is forbidden to "greet one's fellow before praying. . . . R. Abba explains the dictum as referring to one who rises early in order to visit another" [Ber. 14a]. Moreover, an individual should take care never to honor any person to a greater degree than he does God. One should honor God in the manner that he honors those human beings to whom one is obligated to pay respect, such as kings and distinguished individuals.

A person ought to be conscientious about honoring his soul to a greater extent than he does his body, since we find that the soul is called "Glory" [*Kavod*].[9] For inasmuch as the soul is a part of God, may He be blessed, one who honors it by means of the study of Torah, performance of the commandments, and deeds of lovingkindness honors the Holy One, blessed be He, at the same time.

The body, which is created from a fetid drop, is a part of this world; its ultimate destiny is destruction, just as every good thing belonging to this world winds up diminished and ruined. This is so because the body derives from the serpent's skin and its evil shell.[10] An individual who pays greater homage to his physical body than he does to his soul is like one who shows greater respect to human beings than he does the Holy One, blessed be He. Therefore, a person ought take more care to honor his soul than he does his body; before attending to the needs of his body he is required to attend to his soul's honor. For this reason our Sages, of blessed memory, taught that it is forbidden to eat before praying. Likewise, prior to eating, a person should occupy himself with Torah; for by virtue of the merit attained by doing so he will succeed in his endeavors and in his work.

Similarly, a person should learn to pay respect to his soul before partaking of *any* of the pleasurable things of this world. If a man who pays homage to his body, chasing after silver and gold, was to be told: "Go to such and such a place where you will acquire such and such amount of money," he would seek to do it with great diligence and enthusiasm; so too, a person must be conscientious and zealous with respect to honoring the Torah, insofar as this is the same as honoring one's soul. For there is no honor for a person in the world to come except through Torah, as it says in Scripture: "The wise shall inherit honor . . ." [Prov. 3:35].

Likewise, just as a human being displays respect for his body by wearing lovely clothing, so should he adorn his soul with the performance of lovely commandments, such as through the wearing of a beautiful prayershawl and phylacteries. Moreover, just as the body is honored by individuals when they adorn it with lovely clothes, free of any stain and the like, so too with regard to the soul. We do not adorn the soul in the world to come except by means of the soul's "garment." This heavenly garment is "woven" by the body's limbs in the course of their carrying out the commandments. Such garments are lovely, free of the stains of sins and free of all imperfection. In this way, a person draws honor upon his soul. If he is lacking in any one of the commandments, however, his soul experiences no honor.

Furthermore, a person ought not think of himself in a place of God's honor, such as in the synagogue or house of study. The synagogue is the place in which the *Shekhinah*—who is called "Glory"—abides. It is known that the synagogue is called a "substitute for the Temple."[11] We have, therefore, to remove and sweep away every bit of soil and dirt and the like from it, just as we would do in the palace of a king in order to demonstrate our respect. The *Book of the Pious* relates that Rashi's grandfather was in the habit of using his beard to sweep in front of the Ark containing the scroll of the Torah.[12] There is something else associated with the synagogue's honor. Upon leaving the synagogue, it is proper to take care not to exit with one's back turned towards the Ark in which the Torah scroll is contained; rather, one should face the Ark while leaving. The same holds true when one steps down from before the Ark. . . .

Still another aspect of the esteem which a person should have for the synagogue consists in not raising his voice there to call out to anyone, nor for any reason whatsoever. For it is the practice of those who reside in a king's palace never to raise their voices in his presence, but to speak softly. The synagogue is filled with the light of the "Glory" [*Kavod*] of God; and even though we see nothing, we are obligated to believe this with perfect faith.

It is proper that we argue from the lesser to the greater. We can learn about the honor with which we must treat the synagogue from the respect with which we are obliged to treat elderly people. For homage is owed to elderly persons, as it is taught in the Zohar: "Who can gaze upon the Holy Beard on high and not be abashed in its presence?" [III, 132a].[13] If we are to treat older people with honor, how much more important is it to honor the *Shekhinah* in the synagogue, as in: "Who can gaze upon the beauty of the *Shekhinah* which goes by the name "Glory," and not be abashed?"[14] Should you respond that the *Shekhinah* is not visible, you are lacking in faith. Similarly, with respect to the sin of imperfect faith, the Zohar teaches that an individual who open his eyes while praying the Eighteen Benedictions displays contempt for the *Shekhinah*. This is because he does not stand in awe of Her. On the basis of this we can learn about other aspects of sanctity associated with the synagogue.

Just as a person is obligated to conduct himself in a respectful manner in the synagogue because of its holiness, it is also appropriate to behave in a sanctified way in the house of study. It is only proper that the sanctity with which we treat the house of study exceed that of the synagogue. In a similar way, it is fitting to act respectfully towards the *mezuzah* on account of the sanctity of God's name inscribed therein. A person, for example, should not pour out filthy water in front of the *mezuzah*. . . .

Further, one must be conscientious about maintaining his reverence for God throughout the day, as it is said: "But be in the fear of the Lord all day" [Prov. 23:17]. Wearing phylacteries all day long, if at all possible, serves to remind an individual to stand in awe of God. Minimally, a person should wear them while studying Torah, a time during which he is free from the preoccupations of the world. Let a person learn from that which the Holy One, blessed be He, enjoins a king: "And it shall be with him, and he shall read therein all the days of his life; that he may learn to fear the Lord his God . . ." [Deut. 17:19]. The meaning of this, according to the Sages, of blessed memory, is that a Torah scroll was always by a king's side; thus he was continually reminded to revere God.[15] Since it is not possible for others [who are not similarly obligated] to keep a Torah scroll with them at all times—it behooves them to fulfill the obligation of wearing phylacteries at all times. Hence, the ancient pietists used to be exceedingly diligent about wearing their phylacteries throughout the day.

Now, assuredly, the study of Torah also serves to remind a man to stand in awe of God, as our Sages, of blessed memory, taught: "An uncultured person is not sin-fearing" ['Avot 2:6]. This teaches us how important is our responsibility to occupy ourselves with Torah; for it is a means by which to awaken our reverence for God. All of these, the scroll of the Torah and the phylacteries, are intended to prompt us to continually occupy ourselves with the study of Torah, as Scripture says: "And it shall be for a sign unto thee upon thy hand, and for a memorial between thine eyes, that the law of the Lord may be in thy mouth . . ." [Ex. 13:9].[16]

In addition, to the extent possible, a person must attend the synagogue regularly, whether in order to pray or to study the Torah. For one who attends the synagogue is regarded as an individual who fears the Lord, as Scripture says: "Who is among you that feareth the Lord, that obeyeth the voice of His servant? Though he walketh in darkness, and hath no light, let him trust in the name of the Lord, and stay upon his God" [Is. 50:10]. This verse is also understood to refer to a man who normally attends the synagogue on a regular basis, and fails to attend one day:

> If a man is accustomed to attend synagogue daily and one day does not go, the Holy One, blessed be He, makes inquiry about him. For it is said: "Who among you that feareth the Lord, that obeyeth the voice of His servant, and now walketh in darkness and hath no light?" [Ber. 6b].[17]

The reason that a person who frequents the synagogue is regarded as one who fears God is that the synagogue constitutes a substitute for the Temple concerning which Scripture teaches: "You shall . . . *revere* My sanctuary . . ." [Lev. 26:2]. The synagogue is also a place of awe because a shining light from above rests upon the people there. A person should associate with all those who revere God, and keep his distance from those who do not. One should even avoid speaking with such a person as one speaks to a friend.

The prophet Isaiah, may he rest in peace, taught: "And their fear of Me is a commandment of men learned by rote" [Is. 29:13].[18] From this we learn that a person must investigate and determine with inner certainty who it is that he worships and who it is that he reveres, just as King David commanded his son Solomon: ". . . know thou the God of thy father, and serve Him with a whole heart and with a willing mind . . ." [I Ch. 28:9]. The reason for doing so is that a person who serves God as "a commandment of men learned by rote" will worship Him off and on. Such an individual lacks complete faith. Should a heathen come along, or another such as himself, and contradict his faith by the use of proofs and contrived arguments, it is possible that he may become convinced. However, a person who serves God with knowledge of the heart will resist being overwhelmed whatsoever. The punishment for an individual who serves God out of mere habit is indicated by Isaiah in the verse which follows the one

133

quoted above: "Therefore, behold, I will again do a marvelous work among this people, even a marvelous work and a wonder; and the wisdom of their wise men shall perish, and the prudence of their prudent men shall be hid" [Is. 29:14].

A person shall also be conscientious when reciting his prayers and blessings to make certain that they are spoken with genuine devotion of the heart, that they not be uttered merely out of habit. For Scripture teaches: "And the Lord said: Forasmuch as this people draw near, and with their mouth and with their lips do honor Me, but have removed their heart far from me . . ." [Is. 29:13]. The *Book of the Pious* reports the story of "a certain individual who died quite prematurely. After many years he appeared in a dream to one of his relatives. His relative asked him, 'How are you faring in the world where you are?' He replied, 'Each day I am judged harshly because I was not conscientious with respect to reciting the blessing over bread, the blessings for fruit and the Grace after meals with wholehearted devotion.' And they say to me, 'You concentrated only upon your own enjoyment.' "[19]

Some of the rewards for revering God are enjoyed in the world to come: "Oh how abundant is Thy goodness, which Thou hast hid up for them that fear Thee . . ." [Ps. 31:20]. As far as this world is concerned, an individual who stands in awe of God will be provided for by a "watchful eye," the eye of *'Arikh 'Anpin*, as it is written in Scripture: "Behold, the eye of the Lord is toward them that fear Him, toward them that wait for His mercy" [Ps. 33:18]. Reverence for God serves to overcome the forces of strict judgment and to prolong life.

And with this the chapter and gate are completed.

The Gate of Love

Chapter One

Our devotion to God, may He be blessed, must be performed with love, as Scripture says: "And thou shalt love the Lord thy God with all thy heart, and with all thy soul, and with all thy might" [Deut. 6:5]. This passage is the gateway to our reverence for God, for it expresses the unity of the Creator and bears the reminder to love Him with all one's heart, with all one's soul, and with all one's might. The entire Torah is contained in this passage, for every thought of an individual who loves the King is directed toward doing what is good and proper in His eyes. Thus, the Holy One, blessed be He, enjoined us to remember Him each day in five ways: By reciting this passage upon retiring and upon rising, recalling it when we don phylacteries of the arm and head, as well as by writing it "upon the doorposts of thy house . . ." [Deut. 6:9]. Furthermore, we read in *Tanna de-Vei Eliyahu*:

> What is the difference between love and reverence? Consider a parable by which the difference may be understood. A king had two servants. The first loved the king and stood in awe of him; and the second stood in awe of him but did not love him. The king journeyed to a distant country across the sea. The one who loved the king and was in awe of him proceeded to plant gardens and orchards of every kind of choice fruit; but the one who did not love the king sat and did nothing. When the king returned from the country across the sea, he beheld gardens and orchards and every kind of fine fruit prepared for him as designed by the servant who loved him. And when this servant appeared before the king, and saw that the king had prepared all kinds of fine fruits for him, he was satisfied because of the king's happiness. But when the king entered the house of the servant who was in awe of him but did not love him, he saw all sorts of dried-up stuff laid out before him, as arranged by this second servant. This servant who only feared him subsequently appeared before the king

135

and saw that all sorts of dried-up stuff were arranged [by the king as a demonstration of his displeasure]. He became very anxious upon recognizing the king's anger, as it says: "He hath given food unto them that fear Him" [Ps. 111:5]. This verse refers to this world only, teaching you that the reward given to a person who loves God and fears Him consists of two portions, whereas the reward given to a person who only fears Him consists of one portion. Accordingly, the wicked have the merit of enjoying only this world, whereas Israel has the merit of enjoying two worlds. [Chap. 26]

The general principle that we may derive from this parable is that the essence of love consists in fulfilling the King's will so as to make Him joyful. And even though a person is aware that from the very trees which he plants, the King will provide him with all kinds of fruits as a reward, nevertheless, his sole intention is to assure himself that the King is happy—that He is pleased to see gardens, orchards, and trees planted for Him. It is clear that the one who only fears the king in our parable represents the idolatrous nations, all of which stand in awe of Him, as it says: "Who would not fear Thee, O King of the nations" [Jer. 10:7]? *All* acknowledge that there is none like Thee, but they do not all observe the commandments. Those who both fear and love Him, however, are the ones who fulfill the precepts of the Torah. Performance of the commandments and study of Torah constitute the planting of trees which sow supernal sparks above; by such acts the King is made joyful. For everything depends upon arousal in the world below, as explained many times.

By virtue of the supernal light which people draw down through the performance of the commandments, their souls enjoy satisfaction in the world to come, as in: "He who took trouble to prepare on the eve of the Sabbath can eat on the Sabbath" [Avodah Zarah 3a]. However, an individual must neither study nor perform the precepts for the sake of receiving a reward, nor for any worldly purposes, as is recorded in portion *Ve'ethanan* of the Zohar (III, 263b, 267a]. See also, in this connection, the "Gate of Trust" and the "Gate of Love" in *Duties of the Heart*.

The essence of love consists in surrendering one's soul and body for the sanctification of God. Refer to what R. Simeon bar Yohai, may he rest in peace, recorded in the Zohar [I, 11b], where you will learn that the essence of love involves incorporating divine Mercy [*Hesed*] within the severity of divine Judgment [*Din*].[1] That is, the scriptural phrase "with all your soul" means to surrender your soul for the sanctification of God's name. For when the Holy One, blessed be He, tests a person, showering him with Judgment—whether he be an ordinary or a great individual—so that he reaches the point of surrendering his soul out of his great love for God, he should do so as did Hanania, Mishael, and Azariah.[2] In this way an individual can incorporate Mercy within Judgment. Likewise, a person must include Judgment within Mercy, for an individual loves the Holy One, blessed be He, on account of His mercy and the many beneficial things which He does for him, all of which derive from Mercy. One should not rely upon his good deeds, however, but must also fear Judgment, telling himself that "sin might cause [God's promise of reward not to be fulfilled]" [Ber. 4a].

This constitutes perfect love of God, for Mercy is incomplete without being bound to Judgment, while Judgment is incomplete without being bound to Mercy. [The esoteric meaning of the name *YHVH* is *Elohim*].[3] Abraham our father, may he rest in peace, merited Mercy inasmuch as he displayed concern for neither his physical needs nor wealth.[4] For by nature it is difficult for an individual to surrender his body and soul for the sake of sanctifying God's name. It is contrary to human nature to do so. This is also true when it comes to giving of one's money to charity, especially if one gives a great amount, and behaves in a way which is contrary to human nature. A person must do such things out of love so as to merit Mercy.

Chapter Two

Genuine love means to serve God without seeking a reward; one who behaves in this way merits Mercy. The reason for this is that an individual who serves God with the intention of receiving a reward is inevitably bound to the quality of divine Judgment; for one receives divine blessing exactly in accordance with the kind of devotion he performs. However, it is different in the case of a person who serves God selflessly; just as his devotion to God is limitless, so is he blessed without measure from the quality of Mercy which flows freely. In such a way he binds himself to God in love. Since he serves God without seeking reward, but rather out of pure love, he causes the crown of Judgment to be subsumed under the crown of Mercy. As a result, the *Hasadim* spread out in all directions;[5] for Mercy is that aspect of the Godhead which permeates the world, and upon which the whole structure of the universe is constructed. It is in the nature of Mercy to love, to provide for and to satisfy; human beings are infused with Mercy by virtue of the love which Mercy bears toward all creatures.

Mercy functions in this way without even requiring arousal from below beforehand. In a like manner, a person who loves the King will act mercifully towards Him. This means serving Him without anticipating any reward, just as Mercy gives of itself selflessly.

The reward of an individual who serves God out of love consists in experiencing celestial joy of a wonderous character. I learned from my teacher, may he rest in peace, a clearer explanation concerning the rewards of those who devote themselves to God out of love. One who serves the King of the universe out of love, without expectation of reward in this world or the next—but out of love alone—will be compensated by the Holy One, blessed be He, Himself. If he serves Him for the sake of some earthly reward, for the purpose of acquiring wealth or having children, he receives his reward entirely in this world. Just as this world is transitory, so too is his reward. And if he serves God for the sake of securing a place in Paradise, his reward will be administered by the angels who tend there. But, if he devotes himself to God out of pure love, his soul cleaves to the "Infinite One"[6] as well as to His *Sefirot*, thereby uniting them in the proper manner.

Thus his reward from above is "to behold the graciousness of the Lord" [Ps. 27:4], as explained earlier in greater detail. For every person merits reward in the future in proportion to his earthly deeds. If he merits reward on the level of vital-soul [*nefesh*] alone, his resting place will be in the location where the vital-souls reside following death. And if he merits reward on the level of spirit [*ruah*], he will enjoy Paradise. If he merits reward on the level of super-soul [*neshamah*], he will be privileged to ascend to the upper realm of Paradise.[7] Those who attain the grade of super-soul are called God's lovers.

Chapter Three

See portion *Vayehi* of the Zohar [I, 245a] where you will discover that one of the signs of love is jealousy. The meaning of this is that a man who is jealous on account of his wife—because of his deep love for her—hopes that nothing will come between them that might estrange them from one another. On the contrary, he desires that his wife's love be his forever. So too, on account of his deep love for the *Shekhinah*, a righteous person must bind himself to Her love, so much so that he will be jealous lest She separate from him and dwell with another. This is the meaning of the Zohar's comment, "a man cleaves to God with the love of his vital-soul and spirit"

[III, 68a]. Such a love involves rising at night in order to study Torah.

This kind of love may be compared to that of a man for his wife. For at night when he awakens with strong feelings of love, he will hasten to satisfy his longing with deep affection, particularly when he knows that she whom he loves, loves him as well. So it is with Torah scholars who are separated from their wives all week long because of their "marital" duty to the King's daughter, that is, the Torah. It is proper for them to make haste in their desire for the Torah; for through its study they cleave to the life of the upper realm as well as to the *Shekhinah*. She comes and pours forth divine abundance upon them from the Holy Spirit.[8] The love which the *Shekhinah* bears for us requires no proof, for She says: "The companions hearken for thy voice: Cause Me to hear it" (Song of Songs 8:13). That is what it means when the prophet calls out to the *Shekhinah*: "With my soul have I desired Thee in the night" [Is. 26:9]. He longs for Her, since it is the Holy Spirit which comes and rests upon him [as a result of such longing].

In a passage from the Zohar [III, 68a] which precedes the one quoted above, it says further: "I will rise early to cleave to Thee in great love." This may be understood by reference to what R. Simeon bar Yohai explained in portion *Beshallah* of the Zohar [II, 46a]. Upon those who remain with the *Shekhinah* throughout the night until the break of dawn, as well as upon the *Shekhinah* Herself, the Holy One, blessed be He, spreads out a thread of Mercy so that in the morning they cleave to the King in great love, that is, with Mercy. This will cause a person's love for God to grow even greater, for until this moment he had cleaved to the lesser light, which is the level of vital-soul, a lower grade of love. But in the morning he cleaves to a great love. It says there in the Zohar [II, 46a]: "When the dawn is about to break the sky darkens . . . ," for a person must study Torah until daybreak so as to join the quality of night to the daytime. This is the meaning of the expression "I will rise early" which contains the word "daybreak" [*shaḥar*]. For it is at this time [that is, at daybreak] that the light of divine Mercy is aroused and one receives gifts from the King. And even though this love depends upon the study of Torah at night, it is appropriate for it to take place at all times, even during the day. The fact is that the desire of one who loves God is already awakened during the day, but at night the intensity of his love increases. And he asks himself: "When will nighttime arrive so that I may rise to perform my Maker's will, and so that I may fulfill my obligations on account of my love for God, may He be blessed?"

A person who rises at midnight for the purpose of study is regarded as one who serves God out of love. For you will find no greater lover of the

Holy One, blessed be He, than such an individual. He rids himself of the body's longing for sleep and pleasure because of his love for God, the object of his soul's affection. And even though he may be discomforted, he bears it for the sake of his love for God. He thus fulfills the biblical precept: "And thou shalt love the Lord thy God with all they heart . . ." [Deut. 6:5] with both of his inclinations, with the good impulse and the evil impulse. For subjugation of the evil inclination constitutes perfect love; and it is fitting that he be called God's servant inasmuch as he serves God rather than the needs of his own body. But an individual who does not rise at night because of his desire to sleep and provide his body with rest serves his evil impulse and his body rather than his soul and his Maker. This general principle applies to all devotion which is based upon love: When a person subdues his evil desire and suffers discomfort for the sake of God's devotion, he is called a lover of God rather than a devotee of his evil desire. If he fails to subdue his evil desire, however, he is called the evil desire's servant. Love prepares the way for the fulfillment of the entire Torah.

A person also acquires the attribute of love for God when he rises at midnight and meditates upon the great mercy with which the Creator treats him. For God restores his soul to his body and revives him from sleep, sleep being one-sixtieth of death. And if a person realizes that he will die one day, how much more will he feel obliged to love the Creator who provides for him so well, and how will he be able to sleep without rising at midnight? When he awakens from sleep his soul will be enflamed with love for the Creator who restored his soul to him. He will awaken with love for the Creator who revived him; he will ponder the fact that God will do so once again in the future when the dead are resurrected.[9]

Further, our sacred Torah teaches us how to acquire love in the verse: "And thou shalt love the Lord thy God with all thy heart, with all thy soul and with all thy might" [Deut. 6:5]. These correspond to three aspects of love which, when they are joined together as one in an individual, will bind him to God in love. See portion *Terumah* of the Zohar [II, 162b–163a] where these three aspects of love are discussed.[10] It is impossible for a person to achieve the grade of love for God—which constitutes cleaving to Him and the highest possible spiritual level—if it is not preceded by reverence for God. Such reverence entails abstinence from the pleasures of this world.

The love which different human beings bear for God, may He be blessed, is unequal. The degree of their devotion to God corresponds to the level which their soul achieves. For the love of one who achieves the grade of super-soul is greater than the love of one who achieves the grade of spirit or vital-soul. To the degree that a person ascends the [contemplative] ladder are his soul and body purified. And the love of one who attains the grade of super-soul will be continuous, preventing him from separating himself from the Creator on account of his great desire for Him. The reason for this is that the vital-soul, which is fashioned after the angel Sandalfon [who resides in the world of "making"], is close by the evil shells.[11] And the evil shells serve as a curtain separating one's vital-soul from God. Therefore, such a person's love for God will not be constant, but of short duration only. When a person merits the grade of spirit, that is, Meṭaṭron, which is somewhat removed from the evil shells, his love will be sustained longer.[12] But when an individual merits the grade of super-soul, which derives from the divine Throne to which no evil whatsoever clings [this being the King's garment for Sabbaths and Festivals], he will cleave to God in love continuously.

Scorn the needs of the body in this world, the body being governed by means of the six weekdays;[13] divest yourself of love for this world which is clothed in the skin of the serpent, and clothe yourself with the love for that world where the super-souls reside. There they are bound up in the bond of eternal life, cleaving to their Maker.[14] An individual should cleave to that which will be his at the end of his life. "For who is wise? One who can foresee events" [Tamid 32a], and contemplates the fact that a person is like a stranger passing by in this world. Thus, he will divest his heart of love for this world and concentrate upon cleaving to the world in which the super-souls reside; there he will continuously cling to *YHVH*.

We may infer from this that the love of solitude is a primary means for attaining the love of God. For during the time that a person draws near to his fellowmen in love, it is impossible for him to cleave to God. Thus, R. Isaac of Acco, may he rest in peace, wrote:

The practitioner of solitude who wishes to acquire the solitary state so that tranquility will rest upon him during his life, must adhere to the following three things and distance himself from their antitheses. As a consequence, peace will rest upon him not only in this life, but also afterwards. These are that he find satisfaction with his portion, that he love solitude, and that he flee from arrogance and self-importance. To do so constitutes subjugation of the heart. The opposite of these feelings involve not being satisfied with what he possesses [for the person who loves money is not satisfied by it], and being bored when he is by himself. Instead, such a person delights in the companionship of other people and their chatter; he enjoys indulging in idle conversation and the pursuit of self-glorification and haughtiness.

The individual who desires to serve God out of love must begin with three things: "cleaving" to God, "longing" for Him, and "desiring" Him.[15]

Chapter Four

"Cleaving" to God consists in a person's attaching himself with his soul to the *Shekhinah* and concentrating all his attention upon Her unification, as well as upon the separation from Her of all the evil shells. Similarly, a person ought to remove from his mind all impure thoughts, as R. Simeon bar Yohai, may he rest in peace, explained. For at the moment of unification he must contemplatively unite the *Shekhinah* without allowing any extraneous thoughts to distract him.[16] This is what our Sages, of blessed memory, meant when they taught: "One may not drink out of one goblet and think of another" [Ned. 20b]. This is also what is known as a child born of "a woman mistaken for another" [Ned. 20b].[17] A person must concentrate exclusively on the *Shekhinah* and recognize that his impure thoughts are distractions from without which can separate him from Her, God forbid. Instead, one should cleave to the *Shekhinah* in the proper manner, and divest Her of all evil.

Further, in the case of an individual who loves two women, we find that their love for him is not whole inasmuch as they are envious of one another. In order for a wife's love for her husband to be perfect, it is important that she see that he loves no other woman in the world besides her. She will then bind herself to him in a covenant of unrestricted love. In the same way, the *Shekhinah* will not bind Her love to a man who is devoted to worldly matters. Hence, the essential element in love consists in his not loving anything whatsoever in this world more than he does God, may He be blessed. His love of God ought to be greater than that which he bears for his wife and children and all other worldly things. For a man becomes separated from the love of the Holy One, blessed be He, while praying or studying the Torah, due to the evil, distracting thoughts which intrude upon his awareness.[18] This happens because he is not totally immersed in the love of the Holy One, blessed be He. Instead, his love is greater for matters of this world, for this or that thing. If only he would not love worldly things more than he loves the Holy One, blessed be He! When God sees that a person's love for Him is deficient, and that he abandons Him, He likewise departs and separates Himself from that individual. . . .

As in the case of cleaving to God, there are two aspects to one's "longing" for Him. First, a person should cleave to the *Shekhinah* with his soul by means of each and every commandment that he performs; he must carry them out with longing, heartfelt enthusiasm, and very great love. This is what is intended by the quality of "desire of the heart" of which the Zohar frequently speaks. It is not possible to attain such desire of the heart—which is what this longing is—unless a person initially sets his mind on God, may He be blessed, and upon the love which he feels for Him. This longing derives from the realm of love. The nature of this longing is discussed by R. Shimon bar Yohai in Zohar II, 198b. He also comments [II, 128a–b] that the means by which an individual draws upon himself the *Shekhinah* is primarily desire of the heart. We find there that the evil powers rest upon a man "for free," provoking him to act foolishly so that they might abide with him. Following this the Zohar comments:

> But the Holy Spirit is not like the evil powers. It demands a full price and great effort, purification of one's self and one's dwelling, desire of the heart and soul; and even so one will be fortunate to succeed in having it take up its abode with him.

Therefore, a person needs to gain control over his evil inclination and not be deflected from his goal by worldly considerations. Instead, his soul should continuously yearn for the *Shekhinah* whose name is "heart." That is what is meant by "desire of the heart."[19] . . .

With respect to "desire" for God, an individual must turn away from all wordly concerns and thoughts. This is in order for his soul's desire to gain in strength and to enable his soul to cleave to God. Thus, he will become so impassioned while carrying out the commandments that even if he were to be given all of the money in the world, he would still not stop performing them.

In reality, a man would not delay making love to his wife when he feels passion for her, even if he were given all the money in the world. In a similar manner, it is proper that he feel passionate about carrying out the commandments since, through their performance, he makes love to the King's Daughter, that is, the *Shekhinah*, the Daughter of Jacob; for every wife is her husband's daughter. It is not proper to postpone such lovemaking; rather, he must perform the commandments unhesitatingly and with intense zeal. In this way, he will cleave to the "upper life" and his soul will be illuminated by the upper light which shines upon a person when he performs a precept.

Just as "desire" may be found in connection with the performance of the commandments, so too when it comes to the study of Torah. Study will strengthen his soul's desire for God, causing all physical sensations to fade away. His soul will cleave to God in the course of the intensive study of Torah until he feels absolutely no worldly sensation. For just as an individual who longs for the one whom he lóves eliminates all other thoughts from his mind because of his preoccupation with his lover, and a fire of love burns in his heart even while he eats, drinks and sleeps, so should a person's love for God be likewise. We learn this from a story told by R. Isaac of Acco. Among the stories having to do with ascetics which this sage reported, he wrote that a person who has never experienced longing for a woman is like a donkey—even worse. The reason for this is that as a result of the feeling of longing for a woman, one learns to cultivate longing for God. We can learn from this that the man who loves the Torah with such great passion that he thinks of no worldly matters whatsoever, either by day or by night, will assuredly attain to a most wonderful grade of soul. He will have no need for mortification of the body or for fasts, for cleaving to God depends on nothing but the longing for and loving of the Torah. He should love the Torah with as great a passion as he loves his wife. One also expresses this love for God by rising regularly at midnight out of his great desire.

Chapters Five and Six

There are numerous reasons why a person is obligated to love God, may He be blessed. Firstly, he must love God on account of the soul which He created and implanted within him, and which is a divine portion from on high. He must also love God, may He be blessed, inasmuch as He desires that a person cleave to Him. An individual should say to himself:

Am I so worthy—a human being fashioned out of dust and ashes—that the Holy One, blessed be He, whom the heavens cannot contain, desires to dwell with me? And of what significance am I that the supernal King should come and reside in my dwelling place? It is only fitting that I prepare a lovely place for Him so that He will come to dwell with me. Concerning this King David said ". . . Oh, when wilt Thou come unto me?" [Ps. 101:2], in order to study Torah.

A student of Torah who is separated from his wife during the six days of the week while he is studying Torah is bound to the supernal union and the *Shekhinah* remains attached to him.[20] Upon learning this from the words of R. Simeon bar Yohai, it is proper for an individual to kindle his heart to love the *Shekhinah* as he loves his wife. And he should prepare a lovely dwelling place in his heart for the *Shekhinah* in order that She may be able to find somewhere to rest; for She does not abide in a place which is not pure.

Also, when you realize that the Holy One, blessed be He, provides you each day with the means with which to live, your love will grow stronger for Him. You will see that He demonstrates His compassion by providing an individual with the intelligence and the capacity with which to earn a living by means of craftsmanship and artisanship. In connection with the [spiritual] sustenance which God provides, see what R. Simeon bar Yohai taught (II, 61b), as we have recorded in Chapter 15 of the "Gate of Holiness."[21] From there one learns "that man doth not live by bread only, but by everything that proceedeth out of the mouth of the Lord doth man live" [Deut. 8:3]. In light of this, consider what it means when we observe penitents who fast for three days and nights—there are some who do so for six days—but do not succumb to death. A physician will argue that according to the rules of nature such a penitent place his life in danger through these physical mortifications. Nevertheless, such people remain in good health. It is all due to the help which God gives to them; for the *Shekhinah* descends below for the purpose of showering divine blessing upon Her children. "And to every individual God provides the sustenance which he requires in order that he may draw nourishment from the Torah, which, in turn, serves as nourishment for the soul. This is so that each person may be provided for according to his needs" [*Tiqqunim*].

Moreover, it is proper for an individual to ponder the number of miracles which the Holy One, blessed be He, has wrought on his behalf, and from how many life-threatening situations God has rescued him. How many sick people arrive at the brink of death and yet are miraculously restored to health? Similarly, how often do we find that highwaymen assault people and yet they are not harmed? Occasionally, the Holy One, blessed be He, will perform some miracle on a person's behalf without his even being aware of it.

Among those things which a person ought to recognize as deriving from God's providence are his dreams. That this is actually the case is evidenced by the fact that the accuracy of an individual's dream corresponds to the quality of his character. Hence, a person must examine his deeds.

Sometimes, a person will experience supernal visions while dreaming and will converse with the departed whom he will recongize, and who will disclose to him knowledge of Paradise and Hell, as has occurred frequently in our own time. Therefore, our Sages taught: "Whoever goes seven days without a dream is called evil" [Ber. 14a]. The reason for this is that the soul of an evil person fails to ascend on high; consequently he experiences no dreams. The soul of such an individual is like that of an animal which remains below.

A person must also reflect upon God's providential concern for Israel as demonstrated by the sharing of His knowledge with those who are worthy of it. Thus, our Sages taught: "On seeing the Sages of Israel one should say—Blessed be He who hath imparted of His wisdom to them that fear Him" [Ber. 58a]. In Safed, located in the Upper Galilee, there have already appeared Sages for whom it was appropriate to recite this blessing. They used to be capable of practicing the science of physiognomy and were able to inform a man concerning all that he had done—whether it was good or evil.[22] To be sure, these individuals did not merit this wonderful wisdom [which is akin to possessing the Holy Spirit] except on account of their virtuous deeds and saintly behavior.

Another kind of knowledge of this same sort is practical Kabbalah, that is, the formation of God's holy names which can be permutated in a number of different forms, such as the "fifty-two," "forty-two," and "seventy-two" letter names of God. And even though the truth is that it is not appropriate for every individual to practice the permutation of holy names—for who is worthy to use the King's sceptre other than one who is close to the King—nevertheless, we know with absolute certainty that a person who knows how to practice this science and is qualified to do so can bring about wondrous things, as I have personally witnessed and have heard from one who has done so.[23]

Still another thing which will stimulate a person to acknowledge his Creator and to fulfill God's Torah and commandments involves his recognition of death. For the death of human beings is unlike that of all other living creatures. When other living things experience a natural death, it is on account of some illness, such as having torn a limb, or due to a loss of strength by virtue of old age. It is not so, however, with Israel. We know that death overtakes young children as well as youths whose strength is undiminished and who are still vigorous. Yet they may suffer death all of a sudden without having been previously ill whatsoever. This is especially true in the case of those who fall ill from plague in which young people, the elderly, children, and women die without apparent cause. Such plagues, which occur from time to time, are brought by God on account of our many sins. It is important to realize that with respect to Israel in particular, death is a result of divine compassion insofar as it enables individuals to "mend" their souls. It is therefore said of God: "The Lord is righteous in all His ways . . ." [Ps.145:17]. . . .

Further, in this connection, R. Simeon bar Yohai commented at length in portion *Terumah* of the Zohar [II, 150a]. Briefly, his point is that when Adam sinned he became clothed in a thick material body which prevents the soul from envisioning the supernal holiness on high. By means of his death a person divests himself of this "clothing" and dons spiritual garments which are fashioned out of the deeds and precepts which he performed during the course of his lifetime. In this way, he is privileged to behold and to delight in the light of supernal life. Inasmuch as death effects the mending of a righteous individual's soul, by virtue of which he is privileged to be clothed in these spiritual garments, a wicked individual who fears death ought to turn in repentance. Another thing which should engender love for God is when a person considers what the Holy One, blessed be He, promised to Israel—through the Prophets, as well as through the words of the Holy Spirit—with respect to the good things of the world to come which the righteous are to inherit. . . .

Another dimension of God's compassion, may He be blessed, is that He welcomes a penitent individual after he has sinned, as it says in the rabbinic passage: ". . . the right hand of the Holy One, blessed be He, is stretched forth to receive the penitent every day . . ." [*Pirkei de-Rabbi Eliezer*, chap. 43]. That is, He stretches forth mercy even as far as the realm of evil for the purpose of extricating a soul from there. Other examples of God's compassion are provided by the author of the *Duties of the Heart:*[24] The creation of man out of nothing; the flawless formation of the different parts of his body; the perfect character of man's intellect; and the like. All this is a result of divine compassion, even though a person may be deserving of stern judgment on account of his transgressions. And even if an individual is lacking one of his limbs, he accepts his misfortune because of his love for God, as will be explained. For a person must accept his misfortunes by virtue of his love of God.

Chapter Seven

This chapter will treat the subject of God's love for Israel. Consult the *Beginning of Wisdom* itself for the details as I have decided not to deal with this at length. We find a lovely explanation there of the blessing: "Blessed art Thou, Lord our God, King of the Universe, by whose word all things come into being." On the basis of this you will be able to discern and understand how great God's compassion is for us, whether it manifests itself in the form of the miracles which were wrought on behalf of our forefathers, through the agency of our Prophets, or through the miracles which He has performed for us, those which He does each day as well as those which He will yet do. All these miracles are brought about through the medium of the *Shekhinah* to whom we are bound, the Mother who acts compassionately towards us.

Therefore, it is proper that we express our gratitude by reason of all the benevolent and loving things which we have received from God, may He be blessed. We should seek to carry out His will and to love Him, just as He loves us. We can awaken this love through our prayers and through our deeds, uniting the *Shekhinah* with the Holy One, blessed be He. Every act of unification constitutes an act of love; this is especially true given our current state of exile in which the divine union is severed and our Mother is in exile in this world, as it is written: "And for your transgressions was your mother put away" [Is. 50:1]. For we must take it upon ourselves to restore the unity of God through our prayers and religious deeds. This may be compared to a son who loves his mother and who requests from his father food, raiment, and conjugal rights on behalf of his impoverished mother. He becomes exceedingly angry with his father and weeps on account of his mother's exile, reminding his father about the love which they once shared in their youth. In this same way one is able to arouse the love of *Tif'eret* for the *Shekhinah*. The children are responsible for awakening this love through their prayers.

The *Tiqqunim* comments in this connection that the *Shekhinah* is the one who watches over us wherever we are; Israel is therefore obliged to unify Her through their fulfillment of the commandments and through their prayers. In addition, just as God answers us whenever we are in distress, so too when we repent and are filled with remorse on account of our transgressions, and when we engage in fasts and perform acts of penitence, the Holy One, blessed be He, immediately takes pity upon us. This phenomenon is attested in the course of Israel's experience innumerable times, especially in connection with droughts. For Israel is a holy and beloved nation to God; when they order three public fasts, they are answered. In this way, God's name is sanctified, and it demonstrates that God is surely in Israel's midst.

Chapter Eight

This chapter will deal with various ways for loving the *Shekhinah*, regardless of whether we are called "children" by virtue of possessing souls deriving from the divine world of "Emanation," or "servants" when we possess souls which derive from the *Shekhinah*.[25] An individual who seeks to cleave to the *Shekhinah* must continually perform some deed on Her behalf, be it the study of Torah or some other commandment, in order to arouse the "female waters" within Her; for the *Shekhinah* is not unified [with *Tif'eret*] except by means of the souls [that is, the deeds] of righteous individuals. Now, inasmuch as this love between *Shekhinah* and *Tif'eret* depends upon the righteous, it is important that they hasten to bind themselves to Her love.

Even during the period when the Temple still stood, following the completion of the sacrifice, there were Israelites within their divisions[26] and Levites in their choirs singing, such that there was continual arousal from below. How much more so now, on account of our many transgressions, during this great and bitter exile in which the *Shekhinah* is deprived of arousal from below through sacrificial activity—and is supported only slightly by means of the deeds of the righteous—must they raise Her up from Her fallen state. For She is "the tabernacle of David that is fallen" [Amos 9:11], who each day sinks even lower than the previous one. All this is because of our transgressions, as it says: "And for your transgressions was your mother put away" [Is. 50:1]. For on account of our sins She falls lower, and by means of our righteous deeds She becomes strengthened. Serve as a support for Her, as it says in the Zohar [III, 40a]. It is surely our responsibility to do so, inasmuch as the *Shekhinah* requests of Israel, Her children, that they provide Her with assistance. That is, we must help her by means of the *yihudim*[27] which accompany our prayers, and our study of Torah, for these serve to support and sustain Her. Even though there is no [perfect] intra-divine "marriage" in our state of exile, we must still fortify Her through acts of unification which provide Her with some degree of inspiration. Concerning this the *Tiqqunim* [146b] teaches: "But certainly, while the *Shekhinah* remains in exile, every individual who fulfills a commandment in order to extricate Her from there is regarded as one who pays homage to the Holy One, blessed be He." Such is the desire of the *Shekhinah*, namely, that we continually unify Her by means of prayer, performance of the commandments, including deeds of lovingkindness, and other precepts of the Torah. . . .

Chapter Nine

. . . A person ought to place his complete trust in the Holy One, blessed be He, because even though He desires His Shekhinah's love, He nevertheless grants us permission to draw Her close to us below by means of our prayer and righteous actions. He does so due to His love for Israel. He also does so in order to facilitate unification in the world above insofar as it is we who stimulate the love of the *Shekhinah* for Him, just as He chooses His people Israel in love. . . .

An individual's religious devotion, his prayer and his study, should vary in accordance with the changes in nature which take place at various times of day and night and at different seasons. To begin with, it is proper for a person to direct all of his attention, each day, to unifying the *Shekhinah* during the three prayer services: morning, evening, and afternoon. The reason for doing so during these three times is because the supernal governance of the world alternates between Mercy [*Ḥesed*], Judgment [*Din*], and Beauty [*Raḥamim*] in accordance with the earthly time rhythm. Thus, during the morning service we are capable of arousing the quality of Mercy, at the afternoon service, Judgment, and during the evening prayers, Beauty. And if a person rises early from his sleep for the purpose of studying Torah, so as to express his love for the *Shekhinah*, how good is his portion! . . .

There is a general rule which applies to all those who unify the *Shekhinah*, as we have already explained, and as we will explain further, with the help of God. Before a person begins to perform some act of unification he ought to recite the following out loud: "I am fulfilling this commandment in order to unify the *Shekhinah* and the Holy One, blessed be He."[28] And he should concentrate upon the unification of the letters *YAHDVNH"Y* with the intention that through this action the *Shekhinah* will elevate Herself from exile.[29] When he walks to the synagogue to pray the morning service a person should say: "I am about to unite the *Shekhinah* with the Holy One, blessed be He, by means of the right hand."[30] He should also have this intention in mind while reciting other prayers and performing other precepts.

It may be that there is some selfish motive in the performance of a commandment, for He who examines all hearts is aware of everything. But when—at the start of the performance of some deed—an individual says out loud that such action is for the purpose of serving God, and that his intention is to unify the *Shekhinah*, then all the evil shells will depart and be incapable of attaching themselves to this deed. For the evil shell possesses a desire to cling to the spiritual aspect of this deed even more than it does to something material in which there is no reality. Even when it comes to mundane activities, one should intend that these are also being carried out for the sake of God. This will ensure that evil does not attach itself to any of one's temporal activities. Similarly, you find that it was a custom of the early Sages, may they rest in peace, prior to performing some religious deed, to utter the proper meditative intention, as in the case of R. Abba who did so at the three festive Sabbath meals, as reported in the Zohar [II, 88a–b]. Rav Hamnuna did so as well with respect to the *Sukkah*.[31] From these examples we may learn to do the same with all the other precepts. . . .

Chapter Ten

We wish to explain in this chapter that all the stringent practices which an individual is obligated to perform so as to restore the *Shekhinah* have to be carried out with joy, as it is said: "Because you would not serve the Lord your God in joy and gladness over the abundance of everything, therefore shalt thou serve thine enemy . . ." [Deut. 28:47]. In connection with this verse, see the Zohar [I, 116a–b]. The meaning of this is that a person ought to derive greater pleasure from the joy of serving God and fulfilling His commandments than from all the money in the world, as it says concerning the Torah: "And all things desirable are not to be compared with her" [Prov. 8:11]. Likewise, no joy in the world may be compared with that of the commandments.

The means by which a person acquires joy consists in his contemplating the goodness which God, may He be blessed, bestows upon him, as in the case of the giving of the Torah. An individual should recite the following silently:

Cause of causes and Reason of reasons who created and brought into existence all creation—everything is for the sake of man and because of God's providential concern for me. Even though there is no beginning nor end to God's greatness, He protects a small mosquito such as myself—for I am as naught in comparison to His greatness, may He be blessed—so as to bestow upon me the benefits of this world as well as those of the world to come.

In connection with the source of joyful love, we find the following in the *Book of the Pious* [number 14]:

> In order to serve God joyfully a person ought to learn from analogy to mortal man. If a person becomes aware of the king's desire, he would not be silent nor rest until he fulfilled the will of the king [who is, after all, a mere worm like himself]. He would be full of great joy if the king noticed what he had done in order to fulfill his wish. How much more must a person go out of his way to inquire about the Creator who is eternal, asking, "How can I carry out His will?"

Moreover, an individual should reflect and say to himself: "Behold, all the heavenly hosts serve Him in great gladness and are joyful to perform the will of their Maker." Their heavenly devotion is twice as great as ours, for the heavenly spheres never cease their activity. Likewise, the sun eternally rotates and each morning when it rises, it does so in joy, as it says; "In them hath He set a tent for the sun, which is as a bridegroom coming out of his chamber, and rejoiceth as a strong man to run his course . . ." [Ps. 19:5–6]. The sun also sings before God, as it says in the Zohar [II, 196a]. Elsewhere in the Zohar [II, 232a] we learn that all the worlds praise, exalt, and extol the Cause of causes. Even with regard to Crown [*Keter*], which is elevated above all else, King David, may he rest in peace, said: "Praise Him, ye heaven of heavens," followed by, "Let them praise the name of the Lord, for He commanded and they were created" [Ps. 148:4–5]. The name Lord [*YHVH*] in this context refers to the first *Sefirah* [*Keter*] which cleaves to the Cause of causes [*'Ein-sof*], the mighty Ruler of the universe.

And inasmuch as all the heavenly spheres bring forth song out of their longing to cleave to God, so must a person also sing and praise God in order to gladden his Maker and to cleave to Him. For song facilitates cleaving to God in that a person recalls the many benevolent and compassionate things which He does for him, just as we recite:

> Were our mouths filled with song as the sea is with water, we should still be unable to thank Thee for one-thousandth of the countless favors which Thou hast conferred on us and on our fathers. The breath and spirit which Thou hast placed into our nostrils, and the tongue which Thou hast placed into our mouth, shall ever think, and bless and extol Thy name, our King.[32]

King David intended the same thing when he said: "I will be glad and rejoice in Thy lovingkindness for Thou hast seen mine affliction" [Ps. 31:8]. Joy derives from the realm of Mercy with which God invests a person with blessing. By virtue of Mercy, King David used to sing to God and enjoined us to sing and to be joyful, as it says in Scripture: "Rejoice in the Lord, O ye righteous," and "Sing unto the Lord a new song" [Ps. 33:1; Ps. 96:1]. Likewise, you find that whenever a miracle occurred to Israel they would immediately begin to sing: "Then sang Moses and the children of Israel this song unto the Lord . . ." [Ex. 15:1], as well as "Then sang Deborah . . ." [Judges 5:1]. It is not possible for a miracle to take place in which divine Mercy does not play a part.

In connection with joy, there is a general rule that God enables the joyful to effect His unification—a privilege not accorded all people. The joy which a person brings to the fore during his prayer [particularly when he is in the synagogue or house of study] becomes a crown for the King of the universe. It is fitting for one to ask himself: "Whence would I be privileged to provide the King of the universe with a crown were it not for the fact that He brings me close to Him by virtue of his enormous compassion? Consequently, it is only proper for me to serve Him joyfully." In the Zohar [II, 131b] you will learn that the assembling of groups of the supernal angels and of the *Shekhinah* on high depends upon the prayer of the righteous.

Whenever a person is present in the synagogue he should feel joyful that he is in the house of God. An individual should likewise be joyous in the course of fulfilling the Torah, as R. Nehuniah ben he-Kanah said in his prayer: "The divine Presence [that is, the *Shekhinah*] rests upon man neither in indolence nor in gloom nor in frivolity nor in levity, nor in vain pursuits, but only in rejoicing connected with a religious act" [Pes. 117a]. The commandments constitute the King's ornaments with which He regales Himself; it is thus good for an individual to be filled with happiness while performing them, especially when he is aware of the restitution which he accomplishes through the enactment of a particular commandment, as well as the personal benefit he derives on his soul's behalf. Then he will experience even greater happiness. Particularly when it comes to the act of giving charity should an individual be joyful. For by doing so he cleaves to the *Shekhinah*, as Scripture says: "As for me, I shall behold Thy face in righteousness" [Ps. 17:15].[33] . . .

It is already well known that our Sages, of blessed memory, taught that on a festival a man is obligated to enjoy himself by eating meat and drinking wine—he and all his household [Pes. 109a]. The reason for this is that the festival is regarded as a guest who visits from time to time. And just as we ought to welcome a guest with kindness, so must we welcome the festival. For on a festival a new light manifests itself, as taught in the Zohar [III, 93a]. In this connection, see the *Tiqqunim* [58b] as well. It is especially important to express joy on the Festival of Booths. Inasmuch as this holiday is called the "Festival of our Rejoicing," one should be particularly careful to avoid sadness.

One of the conditions associated with the celebration of the festivals is that a person should not indulge in frivolous behavior or travels away from home as is the custom of the gentiles when they rejoice during their holidays, as it is said: "Rejoice not, O Israel, unto exaltation like the peoples . . ." [Hosea 9:1]. Rather, rejoice in the holiday itself, inasmuch as it is a holy convocation, as explained earlier. One who experiences such joy may be compared to a person who stands in darkness and becomes filled with happiness when light appears to him. In the same way, a person should rejoice in the Torah during festivals more than at other times, for our Sages, of blessed memory, have explained that "the festivals were not given to Israel except in order to engage in the study of Torah" [Talmud Yerushalmi, Shabbat 15a].

A person who desires to gladden his soul ought to seclude himself for a portion of the day for the purpose of meditating upon the splendor of the letters *YHVH*, as is explained in Chapter 5 of the "Gate of Holiness." For our soul issues forth from the name *YHVH*, as it is said: "Ye are the children of the Lord [*YHVH*] your God" [Deut. 14:1]. Therefore, when an individual meditates upon this name his soul lights up and shines wondrously. The soul becomes filled with happiness, and by virtue of the power of this illumination, it is invested with the strength with which to emit sparks. This joy extends even to the body, as it says: "My flesh also dwelleth in safety" [Ps. 16:9], so that deceit is unable to govern it. Such is the status accorded the righteous who cleave to the name of God. For even in death the righteous are called "living." By virtue of their cleaving to the name *YHVH*—the wellspring of all life—they are invested with a degree of vitality.

Another practice which facilitates cleaving to God consists in a person's secluding himself for part of the day while he meditates upon the greatness of the Creator of all things, as is explained in the "Gate of Fear." One should recite the final replies given to Job by God, doing so out loud, with understanding and in a pleasant manner.[34] Similarly, one should recite several verses from King David's Psalms, which tell of God's wonders and greatness. It is beneficial, once each week, to recite the reply: "Then the Lord answered Job out of the whirlwind," and "Gird up now thy loins like a man . . ." [Job 38:1, 3]. Rabbenu Jonah[35] wrote that an individual should recite the following verse with proper intention on a daily basis: ". . . what doth the Lord thy God require of thee, but to fear the Lord your God" [Deut. 10:12]. Likewise, a person cleaves to God when he recites the "Verses of Praise" out loud with appropriate concentration.[36] In the same way, he should accustom himself to recite verses from the Psalms each day in a loud voice and with proper concentration while in the synagogue. How much better it is if he concentrates upon them according to their mystical meanings, by means of some of the divine epithets commonly found in the Zohar. For as a consequence of one's love for the King, a person should praise Him and sing before Him in the synagogue, just as it is the custom to sing before a king of flesh and blood. By [our] singing His praise, the King is glorified. In this connection, see the Zohar [I, 73a]. In any event, when one recites Psalms and the like, he ought not to raise his voice loudly unless it is pleasant, as is explained in the Zohar [I, 249b].

In the same way that songs of the Torah help facilitate cleaving to God, may He be blessed, the songs which women sing [inasmuch as they are concerned with lustfulness and obscentities] cause the soul to separate from the "bundle of life." At the very least, they constitute idle speech insofar as they possess no value. Some men, being meager of spirit, are attracted to these worthless songs, thereby ruining their souls. Concerning this the prophet said: "Take away from Me the noise of thy songs; and let Me not hear the melody of the psalteries" [Amos 5:23]. Our Sages, of blessed memory, taught that singing is forbidden. This applies, however, to songs having to do with love between friends and those which praise physical beauty. But a Jew should not desist from singing songs of praise for God, or those which speak of God's compassion. Indeed, it is a custom among all Israel to sing at weddings or at festive banquets in a melodic and joyous way. We have never seen anyone who opposed this.

Our Sages, of blessed memory, taught: "He who recites a verse of the Song of Songs and treats it as a secular air, and one who recites a verse at the banqueting table unseasonably, brings evil upon the world" [San. 101a].[37] Rabbi Akiba said: "He who sings from the Song of Songs at a banquet and treats it as a secular song has no place in the world to come" [San., Tosefta, chap. 12]. Regarding this matter King Solomon, may he rest in peace, said: "The heart of the wise is in the house of mourning; but the heart of fools is in the house of mirth" [Ecc. 7:4]. The prophet Jeremiah said: "I sat not in the assembly of them that make merry, nor rejoiced . . ."

[Jer. 15:17]. It is therefore improper to indulge in the joys of this world insofar as they are all transitory.

There is another kind of pleasure which is still more evil, such as that which one feels when one's fellow fails in his efforts to serve God, may He be blessed, or taking satisfaction at another's more limited learning. On the contrary, any individual whose desire accords with that of God will be distressed over the fact that God's will is not carried out. Even with respect to his enemies, an individual should pray for them to serve God. When reciting the blessings, "Thou favorest man with knowledge"; "Restore us, our Father, for we have sinned"; and all the others, a person should have in mind *all* Israel—his friends and enemies alike. For how is it possible for a person to pray "Blessed art Thou, O Lord, who healest the sick among Thy people Israel" without genuinely desiring that his fellowman be healed?

Since this tendency[38] is characteristic of all people, and because an individual is insensitive to such matters, it was necessary for Scripture to caution people about the fear of God, may His name be blessed, to wholeheartedly and sincerely train themselves to serve God, to pour out their souls before Him on behalf of all Israel, friends and enemies alike, thereby fulfilling the precept: "But thou shalt love thy neighbor as thyself," as well as, "And he that hath clean hands waxeth stronger and stronger" [Lev. 19:18; Job 17:9].

Appendix

Description of the Ten Sefirot

While *'Ein-Sof* cannot be named, the *Sefirot* can be imagined using a tremendous variety of symbols. *Keter* (Crown) is the first and highest of the *Sefirot*. So closely united with *'Ein-Sof* is *Keter* that many regarded it to be as much a part of the concealed God as it is an actual emanation from *'Ein-Sof*. In this view, *Keter* has two aspects to it, one that is bound to *'Ein-Sof* and one that turns outward toward that which is below it. The general opinion is that *Keter*, while intimately connected to *'Ein-Sof*, does indeed constitute a distinct emanation. One of the common names for *Keter* is primal Will, a term that expresses the conception that even the most subtle stirrings of volition can legitimately be applied only to that which is outside of *'Ein-Sof*. Another image associated with *Keter* is divine Nothingness; from the subjective point of view of an individual contemplating the *Sefirot*, *Keter* constitutes the point beyond which the imagination cannot penetrate. It is the barrier between the utter concealment of *'Ein-Sof*, on the one hand, and God's self-disclosure, on the other.

It is only with the second *Sefirah*, *Hokhmah* (Wisdom), that we can speak of actual "thingness" or existence within the sefirotic structure. *Keter* looks downward, so to speak, and brings forth *Hokhmah*, a greater degree of divine willfulness. *Hokhmah* is called the Beginning or the primordial Point, insofar as it constitutes the first truly discernible aspect of the Godhead. It is also imagined as an active masculine principle within God, and is thus known as the Upper Father.

As a masculine dimension of God, *Hokhmah* is said to "impregnate" the third *Sefirah*, *Binah* (Intelligence or Understanding), thereby sowing the seeds of further unfolding of the Divine. *Binah* is, then, the female counterpart to *Hokhmah*, the Upper Mother, the Womb from which all the rest of life—divine and earthly—will emerge. It is, in other words, the union of the "parents" *Hokhmah* and *Binah* that results in the birth of their "children," the seven lower *Sefirot*. In Her capacity as divine Mother, She

159

is called Building or Palace, images suggesting the many "rooms" within *Binah* that contain the lower *Sefirot*. The relationship between *Hokhmah* and *Binah* is also described as the flow of a stream of water from Eden (*Hokhmah*) into a river (*Binah*).

The fourth emanation, on the right side of the sefirotic structure, is called *Hesed* (Mercy). It symbolizes that aspect of the divine that is wholly filled with God's "abundance" (*shefa*) and loving light. It is the vessel through which God's unrestrained love flows down into the lower regions, a source of blessing and goodness. It is counterbalanced on the left side by the fifth *Sefirah*, *Din* (Judgment), also called *Gevurah* (Power). Were it not for the countervailing tendency of this *Sefirah*, the unbridled light of *Hesed* would be too overwhelming for human beings to receive. Thus *Din* serves as a restraint on the forces of *Hesed*.

While *Din* is absolutely necessary for all existence, it is at the same time regarded as the root of evil, or the potential for evil within the sefirotic structure. Here we confront what is one of the truly remarkable features of kabbalistic mythology. The Kabbalists do not hesitate to assert that the principle of evil resides with God. *Din* is capable of becoming full-fledged evil when it fails to remain in harmonious balance with *Hesed*. This occurs primarily as a result of human sinfulness. The quality of divine limitation or strictness becomes inflamed or aggravated and assumes the character of actual evil. *Hesed* and *Din* reveal more than something about God's moral nature. They express the intuition that love and strictness, flow and restraint, are dialectical principles that are part of the very nature of all existence.

Tif'eret (Beauty), sometimes called *Rahamim* (Compassion), stands in the middle of the divine structure. It is understood as a *harmonizing* principle that serves to blend the forces of *Hesed* and *Din*. Through it, equilibrium is maintained among the *Sefirot*. While all of the lower seven *Sefirot* are the offspring of *Hokhmah* and *Binah*, *Tif'eret* in particular is their "son." Its most common name is "The Holy One, blessed be He."

Nesah (Lasting Endurance) and *Hod* (Majesty), on the right and left sides respectively, are the seventh and eighth manifestations of divine existence. They symbolically express two aspects of divine kingship. As *Nesah*, God is the compassionate ruler, while as *Hod* God is a more regal and aloof king. *Yesod* (Foundation) is the ninth *Sefirah*, and is symbolized as phallus; it is the vehicle through which the procreative vitality of the divine life flows downward.

Malkhut is imagined as the receptive female, called also by the name *Shekhinah*. She is receptive in the sense that She possesses no light of Her

THE TEN SEFIROT

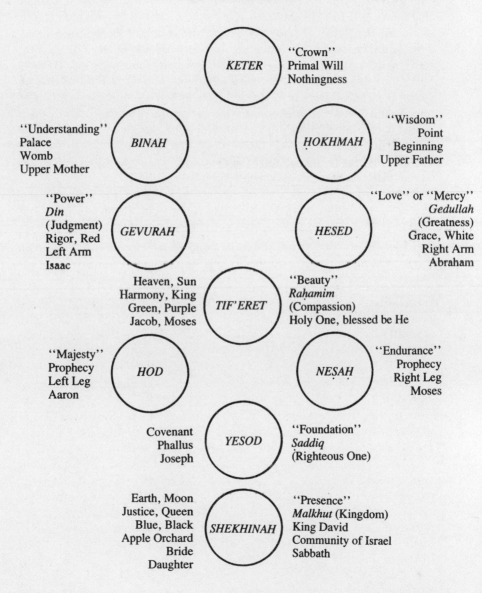

KETER
"Crown"
Primal Will
Nothingness

BINAH
"Understanding"
Palace
Womb
Upper Mother

HOKHMAH
"Wisdom"
Point
Beginning
Upper Father

GEVURAH
"Power"
Din
(Judgment)
Rigor, Red
Left Arm
Isaac

HESED
"Love" or "Mercy"
Gedullah
(Greatness)
Grace, White
Right Arm
Abraham

TIF'ERET
Heaven, Sun
Harmony, King
Green, Purple
Jacob, Moses
"Beauty"
Rahamim
(Compassion)
Holy One, blessed be He

HOD
"Majesty"
Prophecy
Left Leg
Aaron

NESAH
"Endurance"
Prophecy
Right Leg
Moses

YESOD
Covenant
Phallus
Joseph
"Foundation"
Saddiq
(Righteous One)

SHEKHINAH
Earth, Moon
Justice, Queen
Blue, Black
Apple Orchard
Bride
Daughter
"Presence"
Malkhut (Kingdom)
King David
Community of Israel
Sabbath

own, but is an empty vessel until She receives nourishment from the other *Sefirot*. She is filled with divine abundance from the upper *Sefirot*. In rabbinic literature *Shekhinah* is not an independent entity, no less female in character. It is merely the term applied to God in His nearness to the world. In the Kabbalah, however, *Shekhinah* is one of the ten manifestations of the Godhead, the "daughter" of *Ḥokhmah* and *Binah*. She goes by many names, including Lower Mother, Princess, Queen, Bride, Rachel, Earth, and Moon. She is, moreover, the lover of *Tif'eret*. Unlike that of *Ḥokhmah* and *Binah*, whose love is described as harmonious and perfect, the relationship between *Tif'eret* and *Malkhut* is one of tension. Under the proper conditions they are in perfect union, while at other times this union is rent asunder. They express the intuition that all life, patterned after the model of divine life, is constituted of male and female. And they reveal the eternal dialectic between male and female.

Glossary

'Amidah: essential part of Jewish liturgy, "Eighteen Benedictions."

'Arikh'Anpin: term for the *Sefirah Keter*, Crown.

Binah: third *Sefirah*, Intelligence or Understanding.

Devequt: attachment, cleaving or communion with God.

Din: fifth *Sefirah*, Judgment; also called by the name *Gevurah*.

'Ein-Sof: the "Infinite"; that aspect of the Godhead which is completely concealed and beyond human apprehension; source of all the *Sefirot*.

Gehinnom: hell.

Gerushin: "exiles," or wanderings carried out by the Safed Kabbalists in imitation of the exiled *Shekhinah*.

Halakah: Jewish law.

Hanhagot: lists of practical ritual and ethical customs of a prescriptive as well as a descriptive nature.

Ḥaqal Tappuḥin Qaddishin: "Field of Holy Apples"; appellation for the *Shekhinah*.

Ḥasidei Ashkenaz: medieval pietistic movement that flourished among the Jews of Germany.

Ḥavurot: organized mystical brotherhoods.

Ḥesed: fourth *Sefirah*, Mercy.

GLOSSARY

Ḥokhmah: second *Sefirah*, Wisdom.

Kabbalah: Jewish mystical movement beginning in twelfth-century Provence and thirteenth-century Spain; continued to flourish in various manifestations down through the centuries.

Kabbalat Shabbat: liturgical service introduced in sixteenth-century Safed, which ushers in the Sabbath on Friday evening.

Keter: first *Sefirah*, Crown.

Lekhah Dodi: kabbalistic poem composed by Solomon Alkabez; central feature of the Kabbalat Shabbat service.

Maggid: angelic voice that speaks through the voice of an individual, revealing kabbalistic teachings.

Malkhut: tenth and final *Sefirah*, also known as *Shekhinah;* feminine in character, containing the divine light of all the upper *Sefirot*.

Meṭaṭron: chief angel in the divine world of *yeṣirah*.

Mezuzah: a piece of parchment on which the first two paragraphs of the *Shema* are written. The parchment is rolled, put into a small case, and affixed to the right-hand doorpost.

Mishnah: code of Jewish law edited by Judah ha-Nasi in ca. 200 C.E.; the body of literature upon which the *Gemara* is based.

Miṣvah (pl. Miṣvot): commandments or precepts that constitute the practical injunctions of Jewish law.

Nefesh, Ruah, Neshamah: three divisions of the soul according to Kabbalah.

Qelippah (literally shell) (pl. *qelippot*): evil or demonic force that conceals the holy.

Qushia: difficult problem at the heart of a legal question.

Ra'aya Mehemna: portion of the Zohar.

Sama'el: the devil or evil power.

GLOSSARY

Sefirah (pl. *Sefirot*): ten aspects of the Godhead that emanate from *'Ein-Sof* and comprise the "Upper World" of kabbalistic theology and mythology.

Shekhinah: tenth and final *Sefirah*, *Malkhut*.

Tetragrammaton: *YHVH*, holy name of God; each of its letters represents different *Sefirot*; taken as a whole, symbolizes the entire sefirotic structure.

Tif'eret: sixth of the *Sefirot*; at the center of the sefirotic universe; male in character, "husband" or "lover" in relationship to *Shekhinah*.

Tiqqun: mending or restoration of the cosmos, especially by means of kabbalistic prayer and meditation.

Tiqqunim, Tiqqunei Zohar: anonymously authored addition to the Zohar, written in Spain near the beginning of the fourteenth century.

Yom Kippur Qaṭan: ritual enacted on the day before the New Moon; introduced by the Kabbalists of Safed.

Yiḥudim: letter combinations that form esoteric names of God, used for contemplative purposes.

Ze'ir 'Anpin: name for *Tif'eret*, representing the six *Sefirot* from *Ḥesed* through *Yesod*.

Zohar: classical work of the Kabbalah, composed in the latter part of the thirteenth century in Spain.

Selected Reading

This selected bibliography will enable the reader to pursue further the study of the religious life of sixteenth-century Safed. While the largest portion of scholarly work on Safed is in Hebrew, a fair amount of important reading is now available in English. While I have emphasized materials in English, Section C lists major works in Hebrew.

A. Political, Economic, and Historical Background

The historical setting of sixteenth-century Kabbalah is described well in Yizhak ben Zvi, "Eretz Yisrael Under Ottoman Rule, 1517–1917," in Louis Finkelstein, ed., *The Jews—Their History, Culture and Religion* (New York, 1966). Norman Stillman's *The Jews of Arab Lands—A History and Source Book* (New York, 1979) contains a number of primary documents related to the economic and political situation of the Jews of Safed. More detailed accounts of political and economic conditions of Safed Jewry are found in the following: *Population and Revenue in the Towns of Palestine in the Sixteenth Century* (Princeton, 1978) by Amnon Cohen and Bernard Lewis; *Ottoman Documents on Palestine,1522–1615* (Oxford, 1960) by Uriel Heyd; and *Notes and Documents from the Turkish Archives: A Contribution to the History of the Jews of the Ottoman Empire* (Jerusalem, 1952) by Bernard Lewis.

B. Secondary Works in English

A classic essay by Solomon Schechter, "Safed in the Sixteenth Century," is still worth reading, although it is somewhat dated. It is found in Schechter's *Studies in Judaism*, second series (Philadelphia, 1908). The sixteen-volume *Encyclopedia Judaica* (Jerusalem, 1972) is a treasure of information on all aspects of mysticism and Kabbalah. Volume 10 contains a book-length entry, "Kabbalah," by the great scholar of Jewish mysticism, Gershom Scholem (1897–1982). Scholem's *Encyclopedia* entries are conveniently collected in *Kabbalah* (Jerusalem, 1974). Scholem's classic work *Major Trends in Jewish Mysticism* (New York, 1941) contains the chapter "Isaac Luria and His School," which discusses Lurianic mysticism within the context of sixteenth-century Safed in general. Another detailed account of Lurianic Kabbalah and its repercussions in the seventeenth century is found in Scholem's monumental *Sabbatai Sevi: The Mystical Messiah, 1626–1676* (Princeton, 1973).

Other books by Scholem containing important essays on specific themes related to the Safed experience are *On the Kabbalah and Its Symbolism* (New York, 1965) and *The Messianic Idea in Judaism* (New York, 1971).

A valuable essay on Moses Cordovero is Kalman Bland, "Neoplatonic and Gnostic Themes in R. Moses Cordovero's Doctrine of Evil," *Bulletin of the Institute of Jewish Studies* 3 (1975). In this connection, see also Joseph Dan, " 'No Evil Descends From Heaven'—Sixteenth Century Concepts of Evil," in *Jewish Thought in the Sixteenth Century*, ed. B. Cooperman (Harvard, 1983). The Gnostic elements of Safed Kabbalism are discussed briefly in Isaiah Tishby's "Gnostic Doctrines in Sixteenth-Century Jewish Mysticism," *Journal of Jewish Studies* 6 (1955). A full-length study of Joseph Karo's unusual mystical experiences by R. J. Z. Werblowsky is *Joseph Karo—Lawyer and Mystic* (Oxford, 1962). It serves at the same time as a penetrating treatment of the spiritual life of the Safed community in general. This important book offers the unique insights of a comparative religionist who is also a scholar of the kabbalistic tradition.

The development of techniques of mystical experience played a primary role in the religious life of this community. One such technique having to do with the attainment of maggidic revelations is described in the present author's essay "Maggidic Revelation in the Teachings of Isaac Luria," in J. Reinharz and D. Swetschinski, eds., *Mystics, Philosophers, and Politicians—Essays in Jewish Intellectual History in Honor of Alexander Altmann* (Duke, 1982). Hayyim Vital's mystical experiences are analyzed in my "Recitation of Mishnah as a Vehicle for Mystical Inspiration: A Contemplative Technique Taught by Hayyim Vital," *Revue des Études Juives* 141 (1982).

Louis Jacobs discusses the idea of man in Safed sources in his article "The Doctrine of the 'Divine Spark' in Man in Jewish Sources," in R. Loewe, *Studies in Rationalism, Judaism and Universalism* (London, 1966). This same subject is treated by Alexander Altmann in "God and the Self in Jewish Mysticism," *JUDAISM* (1954). A study of the phenomenon of demonic possession is found in Raphael Patai, "Exorcism and Xenoglossia among the Safed Kabbalists," *Journal of American Folklore* 91 (1978).

C. Major Works in Hebrew

Sefer Sefat, two volumes on the history of the Jewish community in Safed, edited by Yishak ben Zvi and Meir Benayahu, includes a range of valuable essays by leading scholars (Jerusalem, 1962–1963). The first volume contains a lengthy bibliography of publications on Safed by Naphtali Ben Menahem. A study of Moses Cordovero's kabbalistic theology is found in Joseph Ben-Shlomo, *Torat ha-'Elohut shel R. Moshe Cordovero* (Jerusalem, 1965). *Sefer Toldot ha-'Ari* by Meir Benayahu is a study of the hagiographical literature that developed around the figure of Isaac Luria (Jerusalem, 1967). An important study of Lurianic Kabbalah is Isaiah Tishby's *Torat ha-Ra ve-ha-Qelippah be-Kabbalat ha-'Ari* (Jerusalem, 1960). Valuable discussions of Safed literature may be found in two books by Joseph Dan, *Sifrut ha-Musar ve-ha-Deush* (Jerusalem, 1975) and *Ha-Sippur ha-'Ivri be-Yemei ha-Benayim* (Jerusalem, 1974).

D. Primary Texts in Translation

Translation of primary Safed sources into English are few and far between. The only book to be translated in its entirety is Moses Cordovero's little treatise on kabbalistic ethics, *The Palm Tree of Deborah* (London, 1960), by Louis Jacobs. Another book by Jacobs, *Jewish Mystical Testimonies*, includes translations of writings by Joseph Karo and Hayyim Vital. Other translated material may be found in Ben Zion Bokser, *The Jewish Mystical Tradition* (New York, 1981) and Aryeh Kaplan, *Meditation and Kabbalah* (York Beach, Maine, 1982).

Notes

Rules of Mystical Piety

Introduction

1. A collection of such ethical wills can be found in I. Abrahams, ed., *Hebrew Ethical Wills* (Philadelphia, 1926). Reprint edition by The Jewish Publication Society (Philadelphia, 1976).

2. The practice of rising at midnight to study, as well as the custom of studying the night of the Feast of Weeks, is mentioned as early as the Zohar; it was not until the sixteenth century, however, that these rites assumed more concrete form and became more widely practiced. Concerning the development of these rituals, see G. Scholem, "Tradition and New Creation in the Ritual of the Kabbalists," in his *On the Kabbalah and Its Symbolism* (New York, 1965); Y. Wilhelm, "Sidrei Tiqqunim," *Sefer Yovel le-Shlomo Zalman Schocken* (Jerusalem, 1972); M. Benayahu, "Seder ha-Tiqqun le-Shevi'i shel Pesah," *Qiryat Sefer* 52 (1977)ı 818–33.

3. See, for example, *Tiqqun Leil Shavu'ot* and *Tiqqun Leil Hoshannah Rabbah* (Venice, 1648); *Tiqqun Leil Shevi'i shel Pesah* (Amsterdam, 1725); *Tiqqun Leil Lag Be-'Omer* (Izmir, 1775).

4. Moses ibn Makhir, *Seder ha-Yom* (Venice, 1599); Jacob Semah, *Shulhan 'Arukh ha-'Ari* (Jerusalem, 1961); *Naggid u-Mesaveh* (Amsterdam, 1712); Nathan Hannover, *Sha'arei Sion* (Prague, 1662).

5. *Shnei Luhot ha-Brit* (known also by the acronymn *SheLaH*) was published for the first time in Amsterdam in 1648 and thereafter in numerous editions as well as condensations. *Hemdat Yamim* was written by an anonymous author in the early part of the eighteenth century and was published originally in Smyrna in 1731. This fascinating book was the subject of much controversy; filled with the spirit of ascetic Sabbatianism, it was withdrawn from public circulation in Eastern Europe soon after its publication in 1742 in Podolia (although it continued to be studied). In Turkey, however, and other Jewish communities in the Near East, there was no reticence about according it great respect. Concerning this book, see I. Tishby, *Netivei 'Emunah u-Minut* (Jerusalem, 1964), pp. 108–68.

6. Some prominent examples include *Sha'arei Rahamim* (Salonika, 1741); *Hesed le-Avraham* (Smyrna, 1764); *Siddur ha-'Ari* of the Brody klaus (Zolkiew, 1781); and Isaiah Horowitz's *Siddur ha-Shelah* (Amsterdam, 1717). Concerning the use of kabbalistic and Lurianic prayer books among the Hasidim, see L. Jacobs, *Hasidic Prayer* (New York, 1973), pp. 36–45.

7. For an interesting set of remarks concerning the possibility of adapting certain aspects of kabbalistic *theology* for contemporary purposes, see A. Green, "The

NOTES

Role of Mysticism in a Contemporary Theology," *Conservative Judaism* 30:4 (1976): 10–24.

Moses Cordovero

1. Concerning Cordovero's activities, see G. Scholem, *Major Trends in Jewish Mysticism* (New York, 1943), pp. 251–55; J. Ben-Shlomo, *Torat ha-'Elohut shel R. Moshe Cordovero* (Jerusalem, 1963), pp. 7–22; L. Jacobs, *The Palm Tree of Deborah* (London, 1960), pp. 9–14.

2. J. Karo, *She'elot u-Teshuvot, 'Avqat Rokhel* (Leipzig, 1857), no. 91.

3. Moses Cordovero, *Pardes Rimmonim* (Salonika, 1584); idem, *'Elimah Rabbati* (Brody, 1881). The publishing of his *'Or Yaqar* began in Jerusalem in 1961 and is still in progress.

4. L. Jacobs, *The Palm Tree of Deborah*, p. 46.

5. Ibid., pp. 39–42.

6. An example of Cordovero's use of Abulafian writings is found in *Sha'ar Peratei ha-Shemot* of *Pardes Rimmonim;* this chapter is largely a direct quotation from Abulafia's contemplative manual *'Or ha-Sekhel*, although Cordovero refers to it as *Sefer ha-Niqud*.

7. Samuel Gallico, *'Asis Rimmonim* (Venice, 1601).

8. Concerning Mordecai Dato's relationship to Cordovero, see I. Tishby, "Rabbi Moses Cordovero as He Appears in the Treatise of R. Mordecai Dato," *Sefunot*, vol. 7 (Jerusalem, 1963), pp. 119–66. Hebrew.

9. Da Fano's major kabbalistic work is *'Asarah Ma'amarot*, of which portions have been printed (Venice, 1597).

10. S. Schechter, "Safed in the Sixteenth Century," in his *Studies in Judaism*, second series (Philadelphia, 1908), pp. 202–306.

11. I have drawn this translation from P. Birnbaum, *Ha-Siddur ha-Shalem* (New York, 1969), pp. 276–78.

12. Concerning Solomon Alkabez, see *Encyclopedia Judaica*, vol. 2 (Jerusalem, 1971), pp. 635–7.

13. As indicated earlier, there are actually forty-one rules altogether when the five found in the Jewish Theological Seminary manuscript are added.

14. The idea that the mystic's heart is God's true dwelling place is a typically Sufi notion. R. J. Z. Werblowsky suggests that "it is quite obvious that those among the Safed authors who used this kind of language drew heavily upon such writings of earlier kabbalists as have, in fact, absorbed Sufi influence." See his *Joseph Karo, Lawyer and Mystic*, (Oxford, 1962), p. 58.

15. The allusion to Moses refers to his alleged offense of having become angry in connection with procuring water for the Israelites in the wilderness (Num. 20:7–12). The nostrils were regarded as being the seat of wrathful anger.

16. *Sama'el* is a name for Satan.

17. The *'Amidah* (literally standing prayer) refers to the "Eighteen Benedictions," the central part of Jewish prayer.

18. Traditionally, the Reader who leads the congregation in prayer repeats the *'Amidah* after it has been recited silently by those praying. Phylacteries (*tefillin*) refer to two black leather boxes containing scriptural passages that are bound by black leather straps on the left hand and on the head for the morning services, excepting Sabbaths and festivals. In normative practice the prayershawl and phylacteries are worn *only* during the morning prayers.

19. The reason for doing so is that Sunday is considered the day on which the Sanctuary was destroyed. See the "Additional Customs From Safed," no. 4, this volume.

20. This is based on the following talmudic injunction: "Every feast which is not in connection with a religious deed, a scholar must derive no enjoyment thereof"; "Whoever partakes of a secular feast eventually goes into exile . . ." (Pesaḥim 49a).

21. The Talmud records ten saintly customs practiced not by Rav, but by another important sage, R. Jochanan ben Zakkai. One of these is that he completely avoided indulging in idle conversation (Sukkah 28a).

22. This is based on Soṭah 42a.

23. This is a typical rabbinic sentiment. Thus, for example, "All the almsgiving and loving deeds which the Israelites perform in this world are great advocates between them and their Father in heaven" (Baba Batra 10a).

24. Literally *"ben ha-meṣarim"* ("within the straits"), an expression derived from Lamentations 1:3. This expression is interpreted by the talmudic sages as referring to the three weeks between the seventeenth day of the Hebrew month *Tammuz* and the ninth day of the month *'Av*. These are considered days of mourning because they witnessed, according to tradition, the collapse of besieged Jerusalem, beginning with the breaching of the walls and ending with the destruction of the Temple on the ninth of *'Av*. It is a time during which weddings and other joyous celebrations should not take place.

25. This custom appears to foreshadow an important characteristic of spirituality associated with the Hasidic movement. This is the idea known as *"avodah be-gashmiut,"* according to which a person is called upon to transform material or physical activities, such as eating and drinking, into contemplative moments. Drink-offering refers to one of the many kinds of scripturally enjoined Temple offerings.

26. The Talmud (Qiddushin 30a) teaches that one should divide his study into three parts, Scripture, Mishnah, and Talmud, that is, Gemara.

27. As can be seen from the last four of Cordovero's rules and from several other *Hanhagot* the study of Mishnah became extremely popular among the Safed mystics. This is explained, in part, by the fact that the Kabbalists associated Mishnah with the last of the *Sefirot, Shekhinah*. Thus, for example, Joseph Karo identified the mentor-angel that revealed itself to him in the form of automatic speech as the Mishnah personified as the *Shekhinah*. Indeed, Karo induced the voice that spoke through him by study and repetition of the text of the Mishnah. Similarly,

Hayyim Vital developed a technique for communicating with the souls of departed rabbinic sages by the repetition of particular Mishnah passages.

28. The injuction concerning the Sabbath found in Exodus 20:8 begins, *"Remember* the Sabbath day to keep it holy" while in Deuteronomy 5:12 it reads, *"Observe* the Sabbath day. . . ."* According to rabbinic tradition (Shevu'ot 20b) both forms were miraculously communicated by God simultaneously.

29. "Beloved" refers, according to some commentators, to the *Sefirah Tif'eret*.

30. According to Jewish tradition, the Messiah will be a descendant of King David, the son of Jesse, of Bethlehem.

31. The imagery and wording in this and the following stanzas draw on the second part of Isaiah.

32. King David was descended from Perez through the biblical character Boaz (Ruth 4:18–22).

Abraham Galante

1. The commentary on Genesis was published under the title *Zoharei Hammah* (Venice, 1649–1650) while the commentary on Exodus was published in Przsemysl, 1883.

2. The commentary on Lamentations was published in *Qol Bokhim* (Venice, 1589). The commentary on *Pirqei 'Avot* (entitled *Zekhut 'Avot*) is found in *Beit 'Avot* (Bilgoraj, 1911).

3. See M. Benayahu, *Sefer Toldot ha-'Ari* (Jerusalem, 1967), pp. 357–358; G. Scholem, *Kitvei Yad be-Kabbalah* (Jerusalem, 1930), pp. 102–103.

4. S. Schechter, *Studies*, pp. 294–297.

5. According to rabbinic law, there are four different means of administering capital punishment, dependent on the nature of the transgression involved. These are stoning, burning, decapitation, and strangulation, the details of which may be found in the Mishnah, Sanhedrin 7:1. Compare Berukhim's customs, number 3.

6. "Men of action" *('anshei ma'aseh)* refers to individuals who went out of their way to observe these customs and rituals.

7. RaMBaM is an acronym for the famous medieval rabbi, philosopher, and physician Moses Maimonides (1135–1204). This acronymn is also used to refer to his important code of law, the *Mishneh Torah*. The "great" afternoon service refers to the entire period during which this service may be prayed, between 12:30 P.M. and sunset. Unleavened bread refers to the special bread eaten on Passover, while "guarded unleavened bread" is that which has been made from flour which has been overseen at every stage to ensure that it came into no contact with any leavening agent. Gleanings, the Forgotten Sheaf, *Pe'ah*, Heave-Offering, Tithes and *Halah* all refer to laws having to do with either charity to the needy or required Temple offerings. These laws are all agriculturally based and obtain only in the Land of Israel.

8. A medieval midrashic compilation consisting of an exposition of Exodus 14:30–15:18.

9. While Schechter transcribes the word *todah* (thanksgiving) after "songs of," the manuscript has Torah, a preferable reading of this phrase.

10. The *'Omer* refers to the period of forty-nine days beginning with the second night of Passover and concluding with the eve of the Feast of Weeks, *Shavu'ot*. A brief ceremony called "Counting of the *'Omer*" is held each night. In ancient times the *'Omer* was accompanied by the bringing of a measure (*'omer*) of the first barley harvest to the Temple. Psalm 67 does indeed consist of forty-nine words if the first four introductory words composing verse one are not counted.

11. While Schechter's text has the sixteenth day of *Tammuz*, it should read seventeenth. As noted elsewhere, the seventeenth of *Tammuz* marks the beginning of the destruction of Jerusalem, this being the day on which the Romans breached the walls of the city according to tradition (Mishnah, Ta'anit 4:6).

12. The ninth day of *'Av* is the supreme day of mourning in Jewish tradition, the day on which the Temple was destroyed and Jerusalem burned. Concerning the custom mentioned here, the Talmud contains the following tradition: "The following was the practice of R. Judah bar Ilai. On the eve of the Ninth of *'Av* there was brought to him dry bread with salt and he would take his seat between the [baking] oven and the [cooking] stove and eat, and he would drink with it a pitcher full of water and he would appear as if a near relation were lying dead before him" [Ta'anit 30 a–b]. The position described is intended to be a humble one, an expression of an individual's lowly state, one suitable for mourning.

13. *Sefer Ben Gurion* refers to *Sefer Jossipon* [The Book of Josephus], a historical narrative composed in Hebrew by an anonymous author in Southern Italy in the tenth century. The author ascribes the work to Josephus, the famous Jewish historian of the Second Temple period, whom he calls by the name Joseph ben Gurion. The study of it by the Safed Kabbalists on the Ninth of *'Av* is explained by the fact that it was the primary source of information for the Jews of the Middle Ages concerning the events of the final years of the Second Temple period. *Shevet Yehudah* [The Rod of Judah] is another historical chronicle compiled by Solomon ibn Verga, a sixteenth-century Spanish historiographer. It provides accounts of the persecutions undergone by the Jews from the destruction of the Second Temple until his own day.

14. According to the Talmud, "Some of the worthiest of Jerusalem did not go to sleep all the night [of the Day of Atonement] in order that the high priest might hear the reverberating noise, so that sleep should not overcome him suddenly" [Yoma 19b].

15. *Hoshannah Rabbah* is the name for the seventh and last day of the Feast of Booths. According to rabbinic tradition, this day is considered to be the end of the period of atonement ushered in by the holiday of *Rosh Hashanah*, the New Year.

16. The three pilgrimage festivals are the Festival of Booths, Passover, and

the Feast of Weeks, occasions on which Jews would go up to the Temple in Jerusalem with their festival offerings.

17. According to Jewish practice, it is a duty to make an effort to pray with a *minyan*, that is, a quorum of ten adults. To be counted among the first ten to arrive at synagogue is considered especially praiseworthy.

18. Similarly, the Talmud teaches: "Make thy study of the Torah a fixed habit" [*Chapters of the Fathers* 1:15].

19. The *mezuzah* is a piece of parchment on which the first two paragraphs of the *Shema'* (Deut. 6:4–9, 11:13–21) are written. The parchment is rolled, put into a small case, and affixed to the righthand doorpost.

20. The expression "fence around the Torah" refers to the rabbinic concept of ensuring the observance of religious commandments by requiring behavior that goes beyond the minimal obligation. Each letter of the twenty-two letters of the Hebrew alphabet possesses a numerical equivalent, a system known as Gematria. The numerical equivalent of the Tetragrammaton, *YHVH*, is twenty-six, the number of rules thus far delineated.

21. "Our holy teacher" refers to R. Judah ha-Nasi who edited the Mishnah about 200 C.E. Again, Galante employs Gematria by associating the word "power" (*CoaH*), which equals twenty-eight, with the total number of rules which he describes.

Abraham ben Eliezer ha-Levi Berukhim

1. Abraham ben Eliezer ha-Levi Berukhim should not be confused with another important figure from the same period, Abraham ben Eliezer ha-Levi, who lived in Jerusalem beginning in 1515 and wrote a number of apocalyptically oriented kabbalistic treatises.

2. *Tiqqunei Shabbat* was published for the first time at the end of Jacob Poyetto's *Reshit Hokhmah ha-Qasar* (Venice, 1600).

3. Abraham Berukhim, *Zohar Hadash* (Salonica, 1597).

4. *Sha'ar Ruah ha-Qodesh* (Tel Aviv, 1962), pp. 36b, 52b.

5. These are found in *Sha'ar Ruah ha-Qodesh* and *Sha'ar ha-Yihudim* (Jerusalem, 1970).

6. A. Yaari, *'Iggrot 'Eres Yisrael* (Ramat Gan, 1971), p. 205.

7. Ibid. This is reported in Berukhim's *Tiqqunei Shabbat* as well. See his rules, number 10.

8. Hayyim Vital, *Sefer ha-Hezyonot* (Jerusalem, 1954), pp. 130, 252.

9. Yaari, *'Iggrot 'Eres Yisrael*, pp. 205–206.

10. Concerning the *Hasidei Ashkenaz*, see Scholem, *Major Trends*, Third Lecture, pp. 80–118; I. Marcus, *Piety and Society* (Leiden, 1981).

11. Benayahu, *Sefer Toldot ha-'Ari*, pp. 226–27.

12. Schechter, *Studies*, pp. 297–99.

13. The Mishnah is comprised of six orders, each one a book of considerable length. According to one anonymous Safed pietist, there were a number of scholars

who knew all six orders of the Mishnah by heart, though "most have memorized only one." See Y. M. Toledano, *'Osar Genazim* (Jerusalem, 1960), p. 51. Hayyim Vital reports that Isaac Luria instructed him to learn by heart the order of Mishnah *Nashim* (Women). See *Sefer ha-Ḥezyonot*, p. 158. Finally, Joseph Karo's mentor-angel informs him that there are others who know the entire Mishnah by heart as he does. See Werblowsky, *Joseph Karo*, p. 274.

14. Whereas ritual immersion *(ṭevilah)* is traditionally obligatory for women only, it is an optional practice for men. Many Safed sources attest to the importance of ritual immersion for men on a variety of occasions. See, for example, Isaac Luria's customs, nos. 20 and 32, this volume.

15. As indicated earlier, Berukhim was reported to have behaved this way himself.

16. "Secular" food refers to unconsecrated food consumed by non-priests. In Temple times the priests were required to eat their consecrated food while in a state of ritual purity. One of the characteristics of the Pharisaic sect, however, was its concern for eating meals in a state of ritual purity as if they were Temple priests, believing that one is obligated to maintain the purity laws outside of the Temple. The custom described here suggests the same kind of behavior as that of the Pharisees, although on a much more limited basis. The Ten Days of Penitence refers to the first ten days of the Hebrew month *Tishri*, from *Rosh Hashanah* until the Day of Atonement.

17. Bridegroom and Bride may refer to the *Sefirot Tif'eret* and *Malkhut* respectively.

18. *Nisan* is the Hebrew month during which the festival of Passover is celebrated.

Joseph Karo

1. Concerning Karo's activities in Turkey and his relationship to Solomon Molkho, Joseph Taitazak, and Solomon Alkabez, see Werblowsky, *Joseph Karo*, pp. 84–121. With respect to Karo's longing for martyrdom, see also pp. 151–154.

2. This injunction clearly qualifies the previous one according to which Karo is instructed to concentrate on *nothing* but the Mishnah, Torah, and commandments.

3. Karo appears to have been married three times. Concerning the comments of Karo's *maggid* about his wives, see Werblowsky, *Joseph Karo*, pp. 94–95; 112–116.

Additional Customs from Safed

1. J. M. Toledano, *'Osar Genazim* (Jerusalem, 1960), pp. 48–51.
2. The currency indicated here is *peruṭah*.
3. So that his back is not turned to the Torah.
4. *Simḥat Torah* (Rejoicing in the Torah) is the final day of the holiday season that begins with the Festival of Booths, *Sukkot*. Since the concluding portion of the

NOTES

Five Books of Moses is read on this day, it is an occasion for celebrating the Torah through song and dance.

Isaac Luria

1. For an introduction to Lurianic Kabbalah, see Scholem, *Major Trends*, Seventh Lecture, pp. 244–286. Concerning the influence of Lurianism on the Sabbatian movement, see Scholem, *Sabbatai Sevi* (Princeton, 1973), chap. 1 and *passim*.

2. For an enumeration of Luria's legal writings, see G. Scholem, *Kabbalah* (Jerusalem, 1974), p. 420.

3. Concerning Luria's relationship to Cordovero, see G. Scholem, "Luria's Authentic Kabbalistic Writings," *Qiryat Sefer* 19 (1953): 187, 192–193. Hebrew.

4. See *Sefer ha-Hezyonot*, p. 8.

5. Published in Hayyim Vital's *Sha'ar Ma'amarei Rashbi*.

6. *Liqqutei Shas* (Livorno, 1790), 3c.

7. The major original versions of Luria's teachings are those by Moses Jonah, Joseph ibn Tabul, Israel Sarug, and Hayyim Vital. The version by Moses Jonah, *Kanfei Yonah*, was printed in an edition compiled by Menahem Azariah Da Fano (Kores, 1786). A complete authentic text is extant in many manuscripts, among which there is MS Sasoon 993 copied by the author himself in Constantinople in 1582. Joseph ibn Tabul edited a systematic account of Lurianic doctrines that was for a long time erroneously attributed to Vital under the title *Derush Hefsi-Bah*, and was published in his name at the beginning of Masud ha-Kohen al-Haddad's *Simhat Kohen* (Jerusalem, 1921). Israel Sarug taught Lurianic Kabbalah in Italy and several European countries following 1590. Though he claimed to have been a disciple of Luria's in Safed, evidence indicates that his version of Luria's teachings was based on his reconstruction of those versions of Luria's true disciples that came into his hands. Nevertheless, his version was considered by many as authoritative and formed the basis for most of the earlier works on Lurianism, such as *Ta'alumot Hokhmah* and *Novelot Hokhmah* by Joseph Solomon Delmedigo (Basle, 1629–31) and *'Emeq ha-Melekh* by Naftali Bacharach (Amsterdam, 1649). Sarug's own version, *Limmudei 'Asilut*, was published under Vital's name in Munkacs, 1897.

It was Vital, however, whose writings were ultimately most influential. In contrast to the more limited nature of the other versions, Vital's work is extremely detailed. His version is known as the *Shemonah She'arim* [Eight Gates], the version in which Lurianic teachings were circulated widely from about the year 1660. It was published in Jerusalem between the years 1850–1898. For a full discussion of the numerous and complex corpus of Lurianic "writings" see the entries by G. Scholem in the *Encyclopedia Judaica*, vol. 11, pp. 575–78, and vol. 16, pp. 173–76. The account given here is indebted to Scholem's bibliographical investigations.

8. For the gnostic character of these doctrines, see I. Tishby, "Gnostic Doctrines in Sixteenth Century Jewish Mysticism," *Journal of Jewish Studies* 6 (1955): 146–52.

9. Reference has already been made to the letters of Solomon Shlomiel of Dresnitz. These letters were published under the title *Shivḥei ha-'Ari* [In Praise of the 'Ari], and contain both legendary material and some more historically reliable information. Vital's accounts of Luria's practices and activities are, in general, highly reliable.

10. See *Sha'ar Ruaḥ ha-Qodesh*, 14a–18b; 39aff.

11. See *Sha'ar ha-Gilgulim* of the *Shemonah She'arim* and Vital's *Sefer ha-Ḥezyonot*, part 4.

12. Thus, for example, Nahman of Braslav (1772–1811) regarded himself as the last great religious leader in a series of five illustrious individuals that included Moses, R. Simeon bar Yohai, Isaac Luria, and Israel Baal Shem Tov, the founder of the Hasidic movement. See A. Green, *Tormented Master, A Life of Rabbi Nahman of Braslav* (University, Alabama, 1979), pp. 10, 186, 209.

13. Benayahu, *Sefer Toldot ha-'Ari*, pp. 315–344. I have translated selected paragraphs from Benayahu's collection and used my own numbering system. Benayahu's edition indicates the primary sources from which each of the texts derives. Unbracketed dotted lines in the translation are the same as indicated in the Benayahu edition. Bracketed dotted lines indicate material which I have omitted.

14. The translation of Luria's Sabbath eve hymn is based, in part, on that found in Scholem, *On the Kabbalah and its Symbolism*, pp. 142–144.

15. This idea goes back to the Talmud (Makkot 23b) according to which there is a relationship between the commandments and the limbs of the body. The 365 negative commandments correspond to the number of days in the year while the 248 positive precepts correspond to the supposed number of man's limbs. In a similar way, Targum Jonathan ben Uziel on Genesis 1:27 draws a parallel between the 613 commandments and the supposed 613 parts of the body. This theme is also taken up by the author of the Zohar I, 170b.

16. Just as an animal that has been torn by beasts of prey is considered unfit for consumption according to Jewish law, an individual who "tears" his soul through anger renders himself unfit morally. Elijah de Vidas reports the same tradition in Luria's name (*Reshit Ḥokhmah*, "The Gate of Humility," chap. 2).

17. Moses Vital.

18. Vital alludes here to the scriptural injunction: "Thou shalt not curse the deaf, nor put a stumbling block before the blind . . ." [Lev. 19:14].

19. Hillel was an important sage who lived at the end of the first century B.C.E. and the beginning of the first century C.E. The incident alluded to is reported in the talmudic tractate Ketubot 67b.

20. This moral obligation is based on an injuction in Deuteronomy 24:15 that requires one to pay a hired servant what he is owed before sundown.

21. This appears to reflect the talmudic teaching "A man should always eat and drink less than his means allow, clothe himself in accordance with his means, and honor his wife and children more than his means allow . . ." [Hullin 84b].

22. *Havdalah* (literally separation) refers to the ceremony that ushers out the

Sabbath on Saturday evening. Blessings are recited over a candle made of two intertwining pieces of wax, producing a double flame, a box of spices, and a glass of wine. *'Etrog* is a lemonlike citrus fruit that is one of the "Four Species" used on the Festival of Booths.

23. This custom suggests the talmudic teaching [Berakhot 34b]: "A man should not pray save in a room which has windows, since it says, 'Now his windows were open in his upper chamber towards Jerusalem' " [Dan. 6:11]. *Midrash ha-Ne'elam* refers to a particular section of the Zohar; the reference is to Zohar I, 113a.

24. According to Lurianic mythology, the initial step in the process of creation was actually the "withdrawal" *(ṣimṣum)* of the divinity away from a point, a shrinkage in God, so to speak, producing a primeval space in which the universe could come into existence. That is, God had to "contract" Himself in order to create room in which to return in the act of self-revelation. The figure of supernal Adam, or primordial man *(Adam Qadmon)*, refers to that initial configuration of divine light which flowed from within the deepest recesses of the Godhead into this space. *Tiqqun* can be conceived of as the restoration of this first and highest form to its original state of being.

25. The term *qelippah* is a technical one in Lurianic Kabbalah, referring to the realm of the material in which the fallen sparks of divine life have become entrapped. This text, along with the next two, suggests a highly interesting theory concerning the role played by the logical puzzle *(qushia)* characteristic of rabbinic legal discourse. It serves as a mask or barrier separating an individual from the holy light which lies at the heart of all things. In this case, the hidden inner core is defined as the esoteric or kabbalistic interpretation of the Torah. Far from rejecting the study of Jewish law, the mystic Luria virtually transforms the study of *halakha* into an esoteric activity.

26. According to Elijah de Vidas, *Reshit Hokhmah*, "The Gate of Repentance," chap. 6, it is especially desirable to be the *first* to arrive at synagogue.

27. The widespread concern for this matter is suggested by the frequency with which it is mentioned in our sources. See Cordovero, nos. 6 and 9, and Galante, no. 20, this volume.

28. *Beḥukotai* is the section of the Torah from Leviticus 26:3–27:34. The curses mentioned refer to the delineation of various calamities that will befall the Israelites should they fail to heed God's commandments (Lev. 26:14–43).

29. According to Luria, true knowledge of Torah was taught in a public fashion until the death of R. Simeon bar Yohai, the second-century sage regarded by tradition as the author of the Zohar. From that time on this knowledge went underground and only a few were priveleged to acquire esoteric wisdom. In this way esoteric knowledge was transmitted from one generation to the next until the time of Moses Nahmanides (1194–1270), the last in a succession of genuine Kabbalists. All others based their work on human perception and intellect and were thus unworthy of attention. Eleazar Kallir was among the greatest of the medieval liturg-

ical poets; Luria believed that he was identical with R. Simeon bar Yohai's son Eleazar.

30. The custom of reading the Torah portion in Hebrew and Aramaic in anticipation of the coming Sabbath is mentioned in the Talmud (Berakhot 8a).

31. The "extra holiness" refers to the notion that every individual is invested with an additional soul on the Sabbath.

32. The Aramaic expression "field of holy apple trees" (*haqal tappuhin qaddishin*), as indicated earlier, alludes to the *Shekhinah*. "In this metaphor the 'field' is the feminine principle of the cosmos, while the apple trees define the *Shekhinah* as the expression of all the other *sefirot* or holy orchards, which flow into her and exert their influence through her. During the night before the Sabbath, the King is joined with the Sabbath-Bride, the holy field is fertilized, and from their sacred union the souls of the righteous are produced" (Scholem, *On the Kabbalah and its Symbolism*, p. 140).

33. The use of myrtles on the Sabbath drew its inspiration from the following talmudic account: "On the eve of the Sabbath before sunset, they saw an old man holding two bundles of myrtle and running at twilight. 'What are these for'? they asked him. 'They are in honor of the Sabbath,' he replied. 'But one should suffice you?' One is for 'Remember' and one for 'Observe.' " [Shabbat 33b]

34. Rabbinic custom requires making a blessing over *two* Sabbath loaves known as *Hallah* at the festive meal. Luria deviated from this tradition out of a desire to have his table resemble "the table of show-bread" in the Temple on which twelve loaves were arranged in two rows of six.

35. The use of Hebrew over the vernacular appears to have been an ideal among the Safed pietists in general. See Cordovero, no. 37 and "Additional Customs From Safed," no. 9, this volume.

36. So too, the Talmud: "Thy Sabbath garments should not be like thy weekday garments" [Shabbat 113a].

37. See the rules of Abraham Galante, no. 13, this volume.

38. Meron is a short distance from Safed and is held to be the gravesite of R. Simeon bar Yohai and his son Eleazar. *Lag Be-'Omer* is the thirty-third day of the counting of the *'Omer*. According to tradition, the Hadrianic persecutions that began after the failure of the Bar Kochba revolt in 135 C.E. were interrupted on this day, as a result of which it was declared a semi-holiday. It is also believed that *Lag Be-'Omer* is the date of R. Simeon bar Yohai's death, helping to account for the custom of visiting Meron on this day. It is customary not to have the hair cut during the *'Omer* except on *Lag Be-'Omer* because of its festive character. Even today, in Israel, a great celebration is held at Meron on this holiday.

39. This invocation points to the sacred action that is represented by the meal, and calls for the *Shekhinah* to share the meal with Her Bridegroom *Tif'eret* as well as the "Holy Ancient One."

40. The Sabbath morning meal, celebrated following the morning prayers, focuses on the "Holy Ancient One."

NOTES

41. The final meal, celebrated in the late afternoon as the Sabbath begins to wane, focuses on the "Impatient."

42. The Sabbath table is prepared for the *Shekhinah*.

43. Her Husband *Tif'eret* (or "Impatient") embraces her.

44. The unification of Bride and Bridegroom causes the forces of impurity to depart and the power of holiness to emerge; the Sabbath revitalizes the soul.

45. The union of Bride and Bridegroom results in the creation of new souls. The thirty-two paths refer to the thirty-two paths of Wisdom mentioned in the *Sefer Yeṣirah* [Book of Creation]. The three branches are *Ḥesed*, *Din* and *Tif'eret*, the three main pillars of the sefirotic realm.

46. That is, six on each side.

47. The sacred action carried out on the Sabbath incapacitates all evil.

Elijah de Vidas's Beginning of Wisdom
as condensed by Jacob Poyetto

Introduction

1. These references to Isaac Luria are collected by M. Benayahu in his *Sefer Toldot ha-'Ari*, pp. 356–57.

2. For these *yiḥudim*, see *Sha'ar Ruaḥ ha-Qodesh*, pp. 156–60; 186–88.

3. De Vidas provides this information at the conclusion of the introduction to the book.

4. A list of the editions of *Reshit Ḥokhmah* is provided following "A Note about the Translation." De Vidas authored another book called *Toṣa'ot Ḥayyim* (Amsterdam, 1650). According to a tradition established by either one of the early copyists or the first printer of this volume, *Toṣa'ot Ḥayyim* was long regarded as a condensation of *Reshit Ḥokhmah* written by de Vidas himself. Actually, it is an entirely independent work having to do with practical aspects of repentance and prayer. This brief book is of relatively little significance in the history of kabbalistic-ethical literature. See M. Wilensky, "Mi-Tokh Kitvei Yad," *Hebrew College Annual* 14 (1939), pp. 459–60.

5. The most extensive analysis to date of the literary sources, style and structure of *Reshit Ḥokhmah* is found in the doctoral dissertation (Hebrew) of Mordecai Pachter, "Homiletic and Ethical Literature of Safed in the Sixteenth Century," (Hebrew University, 1976, second section, ch. 4, pp. 363–78. I have used a microfilm copy found in the Joseph Regenstein Library, University of Chicago. As the notes below indicate, I am indebted to Professor Pachter's study for several insights and observations.

6. For a full discussion of de Vidas' literary sources, see Pachter, "Homiletic and Ethical Literature," pp. 367–72.

7. Concerning de Vidas' use of the Zohar, see Pachter, "Homiletica and Ethical Literature." pp. 371–74; J. Dan, *Sifrut ha-Musar veha-Drush* (Jersualem, 1975), pp. 223–24.

NOTES

8. Concerning this question, see Pachter, "Homiletic and Ethical Literature," pp. 365–67.

9. On the history and nature of these adaptations and condensations, see M. Pachter, "Elijah de Vidas' *Beginning of Wisdom* and its Abbreviated Versions," *Qiryat Sefer* 47 (1972), pp. 686–710 (Hebrew).

10. A list of the editions of this work is provided following "A Note about the Translation." It is interesting to note that while no editions of the original were, to our knowledge, printed between 1593–1703, seven editions of the *Abbreviation* were published during this period. This fact suggests the importance of the role which Poyetto's book held in the developing popularity of de Vidas' work.

11. See Pachter, "Abbreviated Versions," pp. 697–8.

12. As in the original, the early chapters of each Gate preserve discussion of a theoretical nature.

13. Ample documentation of the role played by *Reshit Hokhmah* in the works of these and other scholars is provided by J. Elbaum in his doctoral dissertation (Hebrew), "Trends and Courses in Jewish Speculative and Moralistic Literature in Germanic Lands and Poland during the Sixteenth Century," (Hebrew University, 1977). See chapter 7, pp. 197–208; chapters 13–15, *passim*. I am grateful to Professor A. Altmann for kindly permitting me to borrow a copy of this dissertation in his possession.

14. For a partial listing of such references, see Pachter, "Abbreviated Versions," p. 686, n. 4.

15. Pachter, "Abbreviated Versions," p. 687.

16. Pachter, "Abbreviated Versions," p. 687.

17. M. Piekarz, *Be-Yemei Ṣemiḥat ha-Ḥasidut* (Jerusalem, 1978), p. 102.

18. Pachter, "Abbreviated Versions," p. 687, n. 12.

19. *Sefer Torat ha-Maggid*, ed. I. Klapholtz (Tel Aviv, 1969), *Hanhagot* of the Maggid, #7, p. 1; Elimelech of Lizensk, *No'am Elimelech* (Jerusalem, 1960), *Hanhagot*, #4. Regarding Nahman of Braslav's study of *Reshit Hokhmah* as part of his education as a youth, see A. Green, *Tormented Master—A Life of Rabbi Nahman of Bratslav* (University, Alabama), p. 30.

The Gate of Repentance

1. Vital-soul *(nefesh)*, spirit *(ruaḥ)*, and super-soul *(neshamah)* are three aspects of the soul according to Kabbalah. The lowest grade of soul is the *nefesh;* every individual is inherently endowed with this quality of soul. The other two aspects however, *ruaḥ* and *neshamah*, are latent within a person and need to be activated. The *neshamah* is aroused and enlivened when a person prays with appropiate kabbalistic intention, studies Torah, and observes the commandments properly. These activities assist in the development of the higher intuitive powers of cognition and represent the fullest maturation of the soul. Concerning these three dimensions of the soul, see, for example, Zohar I, 83b; II, 141b.

2. *Gehinnom* refers to the netherworld or hell.

NOTES

3. According to rabbinic legend, repentance was one of seven things brought into existence before the creation of the world. "Seven things were created before the universe came into being. They are: Torah, repentance, Paradise, *Gehinnom*, the Throne of Glory, the Sanctuary and the name of the Messiah" (Pes. 54a).

4. Portion *Mishpatim* refers to Exodus, chapters 21–24. In the original text of *Reshit Hokhmah*, De Vidas cites Zohar II, 96b–97a, which clarifies the meaning of our text here: "When the Holy One, blessed be He, came to create the world, it pleased Him to form all the souls which were destined to be allotted to the children of men, and each was shaped before him in the very outline of the body she was afterwards to inhabit. He examined each one, and saw that some of them would corrupt their ways in the world. When the time of each had arrived, the Holy One summoned it, saying: 'Go descend into such and such a place, into such and such a body.' But ofttimes it chanced that the soul would reply, 'Lord of the world, I am satisfied to be here in this world, and desire not to leave it for some other place where I shall be enslaved and become soiled.' Then the Holy One would respond: 'From the very day of your creation you have had no other destiny than to go into that world.' At this the soul, seeing that it must obey, would descend against its will and enter this world. The Torah, which counsels the whole world in the ways of truth, observed this, and proclaimed to humankind: 'Behold, how the Holy One has pity upon you! He has sold to you for nothing His costly pearl, for you to use in this world, namely the holy soul.' 'If a man sell his daughter to be a maidservant'—that is, when the Holy One delivers His daughter, the holy soul, to be a maidservant, enslaved in bondage unto you, I adjure you, when her time comes, let her 'not go out as the menservants do,' polluted by sins, but free, illumined, and pure, in order that her Master may be able to find joy in her. . . . But should she 'not please her Master,' being polluted with sin, then woe to the body which has lost its soul for ever! For when the souls ascend from this world in a bright and pure condition, they are entered into the King's archives, each one by name; and He says: 'This is the soul of such a one' she belongs to the body which she left'; as it is written: 'Who hath betrothed her to himself.' But 'if she pleased not her Master,' that is, if she became polluted by sin and guilt, He does not again appoint that same body for her, and so she loses it for ever, *unless* the person should be roused to repentance, for then 'shall she be redeemed'—as it is written: 'He will deliver his soul from going into the pit' [Job 33:28]. This signifies that man is advised to redeem his own soul by repentance and atonement. In fact, the words 'he shall redeem her' have a double significance. They point to a man's own redemption of his soul by repentance, followed by the redemption from *Gehinnom* effected by the Holy One."

5. *Tiqqunim*, or *Tiqqunei Zohar*, refers to an imitation of the Zohar proper. It was written in Spain at the beginning of the fourteenth century by an anonymous author.

6. These prayers are all petitionary in nature.

7. Jabez (d. 1507) was a homiletic author who wrote after the expulsion from

Spain. His works deal with theological questions concerning exile and redemption. His commentary to 'Avot (*Chapters of the Fathers*) appeared in Constantinople in 1533.

8. He is no longer able to practice the Torah as before. Hence, an individual must prepare his way and accumulate merit through study and righteous deeds in this world.

9. Rashi, an acronym for Solomon ben Isaac (1040–1105), was an important French scholar whose rabbinic commentary accompanies the text of the Talmud.

10. Duma refers to an angel of silence and the stillness of death. The Zohar depicts him as having tens of thousands of angels of destruction under him, and as being the chief of demons in *Gehinnom*. The word *She'ol* is another term for the netherworld.

11. In the biblical context, Isaiah denounces those who indulge in sacrificial devotion while neglecting social and ethical obligations. De Vidas echoes this sentiment by warning against prayer that is not preceded by proper heartfelt repentance.

12. De Vidas is referring here to Zohar II, 131b, in which we read the following: "When the *Shekhinah* comes and finds in the synagogue one person who has arrived there before anyone else, it is to Her even as though all (that is, all ten persons required for a prayer quorum) were present, for the holy *Shekhinah* joins company with him and together they wait for the others to come, that the prayers may be started. She becomes closely acquainted with him, and promotes him to the grade of "Righteousness." But if no one had come in time, She would have said, "Why, when I came, was there no man?" [Isaiah 50:2]; and note that it does not say "there were no *ten* men," but "no man," meaning, "There was no one man waiting to unite himself with Me and and become My companion and friend, to be a "man of God" in the grade of Righteousness." Moreover, if one day the favoured man is missing, She is greatly concerned, and makes inquiries about him. . . ."

13. It is an individual's soul which induces feelings of repentance. A bad dream is, presumably, one which frightens a person so that he will want to repent.

14. Psalm 92 is one of the Psalms sung at the service on Friday afternoon which ushers in the Sabbath, *Kabbalat Shabbat*.

15. Bahya ibn Paquda, *Duties of the Heart*, "The Gate of Love," chaps. 2–3.

16. The fifth letter of the Hebrew alphabet. The *heh* actually has two openings, one at the top left side and one at the bottom.

17. The Greek *exedra* refers to a covered porch in front of a house, open in the front. Here the letter *heh* is compared to an *exedra;* the opening at the top of the letter permits repentance.

18. *Yado* ("His hand") rather than *Yede* ("the hands of"). *Hayyot* refers to the angels that bore the Divine Chariot as described in Ezekial, chap. 1.

The Gate of Holiness

1. This verse is in reference to Mt. Sinai, where the Israelites were cautioned

not to draw near to the mountain, nor to have relations with women during the period preceding God's revelation.

2. According to Jewish tradition, 365 commandments are formulated in the negative, over against 248 commandments that are expressed in positive language.

3. According to kabbalistic tradition, Adam and Eve wore "garments of light" *(qotnot 'or)* prior to their commission of sin. It is this garment, "woven" by one's righteous deeds, that the soul wears once again following death.

4. Evil shells, *qelippot,* refer to the realm of materiality and evil.

5. Evil One, literally *Sitra Aḥra,* or the "Other Side."

6. That is, the evil forces, the powers of strict judgment are placated or overpowered by virtue of the study of Torah. At the same time such devotion constitutes a means of repentance.

7. Thus, tractate Berakhot 57b: "Sleep is one-sixtieth of death."

8. According to rabbinic tradition, David used to rise at midnight for purposes of prayer and study. See, for example, Berakhot 3b–4a.

9. According to the Zohar, when a man rises to study at midnight the *Shekhinah* awakens and joins the Holy One, blessed be He *(Tif'eret).* A person who does not arise fails to contribute to this heavenly union.

10. The forty-two-letter name of God *(Shem mem bet)* is referred to as early as the Talmud (Qiddushin 71a), and by Hai Gaon in the ninth century. According to the Kabbalists, this name is formed by rearranging the first forty-two letters in the book of Genesis. These letters are used acrostically in the liturgical poem *'Ana be-Coaḥ,* ascribed by tradition to the second century sage R. Nehunia ben ha-Kanah.

11. The "female waters" *(mayyim nuqvin)* refers to divine flux which forms within *Shekhinah* and arouses the desire of *Tif'eret.* Human actions are responsible for stirring up the female waters in the first place. At night, when an individual goes to sleep, he surrenders his soul to the *Shekhinah* as a pledge that he trusts will be restored to him when he awakens.

12. Berakhot 60b.

13. The Aramaic version of Scripture is known as the *Targum.* It was traditionally studied alongside the Hebrew text.

14. *Duties of the Heart,* "The Gate of Abstinence," chap. 5.

15. This echoes the sentiments found in Berakhot 24a concerning the various aspects of a woman that are sexually exciting to a man.

16. The figurative meaning of this appears to be that as a result of hearing unworthy things one may be led to speaking in such a way oneself. The ear is the first organ of the body to fall prey to sin.

17. This refers to an incident recorded in the Talmud (Baba Meṣia 84b). Eleazar's wife would not permit her husband to go to the study house lest the other sages criticize him on account of a controversy in which he was engaged.

18. In reference to the legions of angels on high who receive a person's prayers, the Zohar [II, 202a] teaches: "All these legions are winged, part of them are full of eyes, and by their side are others full of ears. These are called "ears" be-

NOTES

cause they listen to all those who pray in a whisper, from the heart, so that the prayer should not be overheard by anyone else. Only such a prayer is accepted by these "all-eared" legions, whereas a prayer that is heard by the ears of a man is not listened to on high, and so remains unheard by anyone save by him who overheard it at first. Hence it behooves a man to be careful not to let others hear his prayer."

19. The Hebrew expression *"ḥarah 'af"* which literally means "snorting with the nose," is a term for anger.

20. Foods that are prohibited in accordance with the traditional dietary laws of *kashrut*.

21. Prayer and the "scent" it provides are understood here as a substitute for the sacrifices that once took place in the ancient Temple. Just as the scent of animal sacrifices used to be pleasing to God, so too the "scent" of prayer.

22. According to the Zohar, performance of the commandments pacifies and appeases the forces of judgment and evil.

23. In certain parts of the Zohar, the *'Idra Rabba* and the *'Idra Zuta*, the ten *Sefirot* are reorganized into different configurations and called by different names. *Keter*, the first *Sefirah*, is called *'Attiqa Qaddisha* ("The Ancient Holy One") or *'Arikh 'Anpin* ("The Long Face" or "The Patient One"). The *Sefirah Tif'eret* (including the *Sefirot* from *Ḥesed* through *Yesod* is known as *Ze'ir 'Anpin* ("The Short-Face One" or the "Impatient One"). *Ze'ir 'Anpin* is described as having various anatomical features, including hair, a forehead, eyes, nose, ears, and a beard.

24. Incense *(qeṭoret)* was used as part of the sacrificial offerings in ancient times. The cultic use of incense is described in many places in the Torah, including Ex. 30:34–38; Lev. 16; Num. 16:16–18 and Num. 17:11–12. According to the Zohar [II, 218b–219b], just as the use of incense in the Temple had powerful atoning effect, so too *study* of the section of the Torah describing the incense. "There is nothing so beloved by the Holy One, blessed be He, as the Incense. It is able to banish sorcery and all evil influences from the house. Seeing that perfumes prepared by men possess the virtue to counteract, by their odour and fumes, the ill-effects of evil things, how much more so the Incense! It is a firmly established ordinance of the Holy One, blessed be He, that whoever reflects on and recites daily the section of the Incense will be saved from all evil things. . . . But it must be read with devotion."

25. Lev. 9–11.

26. According to the Zohar [II, 62b], *both* study and prayer prior to eating constitute means by which one satisfies the soul. See also Zohar II, 62a.

27. According to Jewish law, it is forbidden to eat either a *nevelah*, an animal that dies a natural death or that has been killed by a method other than ritual slaughtering (Deut. 14:21), or a *trefah*, an animal that has been torn by a wild beast or is suffering from an injury that may lead within a specific time to its death. The Talmud, tractate Ḥullin (37a forward), nevertheless, contains a lengthy discussion over whether the flesh of a dying animal that was ritually slaughtered may indeed be consumed or not. In this context, the words of Ezekial 4:14 are understood to

mean that Ezekial was especially strict on this question, abstaining from eating the flesh of a dying animal which was slaughtered that a Sage had pronounced to be permitted.

28. It is also forbidden to eat certain *portions* of "clean" or permitted animals. For example, the fat portions *(ḥelev)* attached to the stomach and intestines of an animal are forbidden. De Vidas's point appears to be that if Ezekial restrained himself from eating food concerning which there was any question whatsoever as to its permissibility, others must certainly avoid eating that which is *clearly* forbidden.

29. Hebrew, *'Aḥaronim*.

30. See tractate Bekhorot 35a–b.

31. Rabbinic judges, *Poskim*. The traditional prohibition against eating cooked food prepared by a non-Jew was intended, in part, to guard against intimacy between Jew and Gentile. See Avodah Zarah 29b, 34b, 38a.

32. "The more flesh the more worms . . ." ['Avot 2:7].

33. The "hard shell of evil" is that which resides within the "final" shell, the material world. It is this inner shell that gains dominion over those who attach themselves to worldly evil.

34. There are two medieval works by the name *Candelabrum of Light (Menorat ha-Ma'or)*, one by Isaac Aboab (end of the fourteenth century), and one by Israel al-Nakawa (d. 1391). De Vidas utilized both of these books, although in this instance he is alluding to the work of Israel al-Nakawa.

35. Moses ben Nahman, also known as Nahmanides (1194–1270), was one of the greatest rabbinic scholars of Spain. He wrote, among other things, an important commentary on the Torah that included kabbalistic interpretations.

36. That is, human beings are capable of subduing their evil impulse in contrast to other animals.

37. The word "beaten" in Numbers 28:5 is interpreted here as referring to the ascetic avoidance of pleasurable things.

38. The rich man benefits the poor one with his charity, while the poor man benefits the rich one by affording him the opportunity of performing a righteous deed.

The Gate of Humility

1. That is, contrition is tantamount to sacrifice as a means of atonement.

2. *Midrash Tanḥuma*.

3. The bush that "burned with fire" but was not consumed, according to Exodus 3:2. These are taken to be examples of God's humility.

4. The first three *Sefirot* refer to *Keter* (Crown), *Ḥokhmah* (Wisdom), and *Binah* (Intelligence).

5. One of the most important symbols of the *Shekhinah* is that of moon. Like *Shekhinah*, the moon has no light of its own. Concerning the motif of the moon's "exile" as a basis for the sixteenth-century ritual known as *Yom Kippur Qatan* (Minor Day of Atonement) on the eve of the New Moon, see G. Scholem, *On the Kabbalah*,

pp. 151–53. See also Abraham Galante's customs, no. 1, this volume.

6. That is, righteous individuals will be called "the Small" after the moon, which was reduced in size.

7. Exodus 34:6–7, according to the rabbinic view, refers to thirteen attributes of divine compassion that are to be recalled during prayer (Rosh Hashanah 17b). In addition, the Kabbalists speak of thirteen higher attributes that belong to the *Sefirah Keter*, in which there is no element of divine judgment whatsoever. The thirteen attributes of Mercy are also recorded in Michah 7:18–20.

8. The title *Ga'on* (pl. *Ge'onim*) refers to the heads of the Babylonian rabbinical academies from about the seventh century through the eleventh.

9. It is the *imitation* of God's moral personality that induces God's compassion toward human beings.

10. Just as *Ze'ir 'Anpin* is described as possessing various anatomical features (see note 23 to the "Gate of Holiness"), so too *'Arikh 'Anpin*. It has a head, hair, forehead, eyes, nose, and beard. As indicated above, *'Arikh 'Anpin* is another name for the *Sefirah Keter*. The symbol of the beard is used to denote the various "strands" of divine mercy that flow from within the inner recesses of *'Arikh 'Anpin*. The entire section is based, in part, on Moses Cordovero's discussion in *Tomer Devorah* (The Palm Tree of Deborah), chap. 2.

11. Cause of causes refers to *'Ein-Sof*, the concealed realm of the Godhead from which all the *Sefirot* emanate. *Keter* is called *'ayin*, "Nothing" or "Nothingness," the contemplative void standing between *'Ein-Sof* on the one hand, and the lower nine *Sefirot* on the other.

12. Divine Thought refers to the *Sefirah Hokhmah*, which derives its nourishment from *Keter*.

13. See note 19 to the "Gate of Holiness."

14. Jerusalem Talmud, Mo'ed Qatan 3:1, 81d. Rabbinic literature depicts this third-century sage as especially concerned with humility and the avoidance of every kind of impure speech. See, for example, Sotah 5b, Avodah Zarah 20b, Pesahim 3a, Zevahim 88b.

15. This is a play on words. While the word *ruhacham* denotes "your mind" in this verse, it also means "nothing." Thus, *ruah* is mere vanity, that which has no substance.

16. Jeroboam (tenth century B.C.E.) was the first king of post-Solomonic Israel. The conceit referred to here is reported in Sanhedrin 101b.

17. By virtue of his arrogance.

18. That is, the Messiah who will be a descendant of King David.

19. The Eighteen Benedictions *(Shemonah 'Esreh)*.

The Gate of Fear

1. According to the Kabbalah, the four letters of the Tetragrammaton, *YHVH*, represent the totality of the *Sefirot*. *Yud* symbolizes the *Sefirah Hokhmah*,

Heh represents *Binah*, *Vav* stands for *Tif'eret* (and the middle six *Sefirot* as a whole), and the final *Heh* represents *Malkhut*.

2. Generally, *neshamah*, the highest part of the soul, is considered to derive from *Binah*, although some Kabbalists taught that its source is *Hokhmah*.

3. This is because the *misvot* are understood to be organically related to one another, different "limbs" of a single organism.

4. The Tree of Life corresponds to the right side of the sefirotic structure, the side of divine mercy. According to the *Ra 'aya Mehemna* and *Tiqqunei Zohar*, whereas during the period of exile the world is dominated by the Tree of Good and Evil, in the time of the redemption dominion will pass over to the Tree of Life.

5. Gematria is the technique of assigning Hebrew words numerical value by adding up the numerical equivalent of each letter and associating it with another word of the same value. In this instance, the word *tov* equals seventeen, as does *YHVH* when the *Yud* in the Tetragrammaton is assigned the value of one rather than its customary ten. This maneuver is known as taking the "small" number by discounting the tens or hundreds.

6. The Tree of Good and Evil corresponds to the left side of the sefirotic structure, the side of strict judgement.

7. The general concern of this chapter is the various ways in which to cultivate the fear of God by honoring Him. One of the ways to honor God is to treat sacred books with care and reverence.

8. I am unable to find such a report in this book. On the contrary, the *Book of the Pious* (paragraph 28) suggests the very opposite, namely, that although one is not normally supposed to meditate on Torah in the bathhouse, it is permitted in order to prevent a man from committing a transgression by thinking about something sinful. See also *Sefer Hasidim*, paragraph 157, which does echo the sentiment in Berakhot 24b, as well as paragraph 18.

9. That is, it is divine in nature.

10. The negative attitude toward the body evidenced here contrasts rather significantly with the generally positive rabbinic view of the physical body. This is consistent with the kabbalistic claim asserted here that the real object of human attention should be the spiritual realm, the realm that is the source of the soul's life.

11. Hebrew, *miqdash m 'at*.

12. The *Book of the Pious* (paragraph 128) speaks of Jacob son of Rabbi Yaqar as having practiced this custom. This individual was actually Rashi's teacher, not his grandfather as our text suggests.

13. Elderly people represent the "Holy Beard on high."

14. The "Glory" that takes up its abode in the synagogue.

15. See Tosefta, Sanhedrin, chap. four.

16. This verse serves as the basis for the rabbinic injunction to don phylacteries.

17. This talmudic passage is omitted by Poyetto; I have included it on the basis of the original text.

18. That is, a fear that is not heartfelt.
19. The *Book of the Pious*, paragraph 46.

The Gate of Love

1. The *Sefirah Gevurah*.

2. Hananiah, Mishael and Azariah are the three companions described in the book of Daniel who were willing to sacrifice their lives rather than pay homage to the golden idol erected by Nebuchadnezzar (Dan. 3). They were miraculously delivered from harm after having been cast into a fiery furnace as punishment for their disobedience.

3. The divine appellation *'Elohim* refers to *Gevurah*.

4. According to rabbinic tradition, Abraham underwent a series of ten trials or temptations ('Avot 5:3) of which different lists are given in various accounts (*'Avot de-Rabbi Natan* 33:2; *Midrash Psalms* to 18:25; *Pirqei de-Rabbi Eliezer*, 26). Through these trials Abraham proved his selflessness.

5. *Hasadim*, forces of mercy.

6. *'Ein-Sof*. The suggestion that an individual can cleave to the *'Ein-Sof* is highly unusual.

7. Hebrew, *Gan 'eden shel ma 'alah*.

8. Hebrew, *Ruah ha-Qodesh*. The Holy Spirit is a form of divine inspiration.

9. According to rabbinic theology, after the advent of the messianic age the dead will be resurrected and reunited with their souls.

10. We find the following discussion of these three aspects of love in Zohar II, 162b–163a: "R. Isaac happened to be in the company of R. Eleazar, and said to him: 'Verily, the love of man to the Holy One arises out of the emotions of the heart, for the heart is the source of the awakening of love. This being so, why does it say also "with all thy soul," as though there were two sources from whence love could emanate, the heart and the soul? If the heart is the source, why mention the soul?' R. Eleazar replied: 'There are indeed two sources, yet they are united as one, for heart, soul, and possessions are united as one, though the heart remains intrinsically the center and basis of all. "With all thy heart" means with the good and the evil inclinations, each of which is called "heart." "With all they soul"—the "all" includes all aspects of the soul, *nefesh*, *ruah*, and *neshamah*. As to "with all thy possessions," these also have various aspects, each one different from the other. True love to the Holy One, blessed be He, consists in just this, that we give over to Him all our emotional, intellectual, and material faculties and possessions, and love Him.' "

11. The Kabbalists conceived of four "worlds": (1) *'Asilut*, the world of emanation, of the *Sefirot*; (2) *Beriah*, the world of creation, the Throne of God and the Chariot; (3) *Yesirah*, the world of formation, the domain of the angels; and (4) *'Asiyyah*, the world of making, the terrestrial realm. The world of *'Asiyyah* is sometimes considered to occupy a place above the terrestrial sphere and to be filled with

the lower ranks of angels, of which Sandalfon is dominant. *Nefesh*, the vital-soul, is that dimension of the soul which is closest to the world of matter.

12. Meṭaṭron is considered to be the chief angel in the world of *Yeṣirah*.

13. The body and its needs are associated with the mundane and the material, the profane time of the weekdays, whereas the Sabbath is the time in which the soul delights.

14. In kabbalistic thought, the bond of eternal life is sometimes synonymous with celestial paradise and, at others, understood as referring to one of the *Sefirot* to which the soul returns after death.

15. Hebrew, *deviqah, hashuqah, hafiṣah*.

16. The situations in which the *Shekhinah* and the individual find themselves are parallel to one another; each must be divested of evil and impurity.

17. These two phrases from Nedarim 20b are intended to teach that a person must not have in mind a woman other than the one with whom he is making love. Similarly, a person must have only the *Shekhinah* in mind so as to cleave to Her.

18. It is interesting to note the ease with which de Vidas switches from speaking of the love for the *Shekhinah* to speaking of the Holy One, blessed be He. Insofar as a person's arousal of the *Shekhinah* brings about love between Her and the Holy One, blessed be He (*Tif'eret*), he simultaneously binds himself to *Tif'eret*.

19. That is, desire for the *Shekhinah*.

20. According to the Zohar, when a man is with his wife, her presence ensures his attachment to the *Shekhinah*. During time of separation from his wife, the study of Torah suffices to sustain his relationship to the *Shekhinah*. See, for example, Zohar I, 49b.

21. Concerning this spiritual sustenance, the Zohar teaches as follows: "Every day dew from the "Holy Ancient One" (*'Attiqa Qaddisha*) drops into the "Lesser Countenance" (*Ze'ir 'Anpin*) and all the holy apple fields are blessed. It also descends to those below, and it provides spiritual food for the holy angels, to each rank according to its capacity of perception. It was this food of which the Israelites partook in the wilderness: "each of them ate the food of celestial princes" (Ps. 58:26). Said R. Simeon: 'Even at this time there are those who partake of similar food, and that in a double measure. And who are they? Fellows of the mystic lore, who study the Torah day and night.' "

22. De Vidas is almost certainly referring to Isaac Luria, who was well known for having such abilities.

23. "Practical" Kabbalah refers to purely motivated "white" magic, usually having to do with the manipulation of various esoteric names of God. The Kabbalists were wary of engaging in such activity, except in the case of the most pure and highly qualified persons.

24. *Duties of the Heart*, "On Self-Examination," chap. 3.

25. According to Zohar III, 82b, "children" are those who serve God selflessly, out of pure love. "Servants" are those who serve God for the sake of a re-

ward. The devotion of a child is, therefore, greater than that of a servant. See also Zohar II, 94b.

26. Hebrew, *ma 'amadot*. These were made up of nonpriestly Israelites who visited the Temple in Jerusalem to serve for a period of time as representatives of the people. Their task was to accompany the daily Temple services with prayers.

27. The *yihudim* refer to meditative combinations of esoteric names of God.

28. This is one of the very earliest references to this important liturgical formula. It eventually became a standard formula used to introduce the performance of various kabbalistic rites. Concerning this, see the discussion in L. Jacobs, *Hasidic Prayer* (New York, 1973), pp. 140–53.

29. *YAHDVNH"Y* is a word that combines two divine names by interspersing their letters, the Tetragrammaton *(YHVH)* and *'ADoNaY*, representing *Tif'eret* and *Malkhut* respectively. By contemplatively depicting this combination of names, the Kabbalist united these two *Sefirot*.

30. That is, by donning phylacteries. Even though the phylacteries of the arm are placed on the left hand (except in the case of a left-handed person), the essential commandment, according to rabbinic tradition (*Menahot*, 36b–37a), is the act of *binding*, which is done with the *right* hand. In general, the use of the right hand is considered preferable in the performance of the *misvot*.

31. Rav Hamnuna (the elder) was a third-century Babylonian sage. The Talmud preserves a number of prayers that he recited and apparently composed (Berakhot 11b, 17a, 58a). He figures in the Zohar, where he is frequently referred to as a great authority of esoteric teaching, and several original ritual acts are attributed to him. See, for example, I, 6a, 7b, 250a. In Zohar III, 103b, we read that Hamnuna Sava used to begin his celebration in the Sukkah by "welcoming" the patriarchs—who represent various *Sefirot*—into the booth to share the festival. Concerning this, see D. Matl, *Zohar, The Book of Enlightenment*, pp. 148–52, 268–71.

32. This is a passage from the Sabbath and Festival liturgy.

33. The Hebrew word for righteousness in this verse is *sedeq*, a term associated kabbalistically with *Shekhinah*.

34. Job 40:6–41:26.

35. Jonah Gerondi (1200–1263), author of the moralistic treatise *Sha 'arei Teshuvah* (Gates of Repentance).

36. The "Verses of Praise" *(Pesuqei de-Zimra)* are biblical verses that are recited prior to the beginning of the formal prayer service.

37. According to Rashi's commentary, "as a secular air" means singing it with a melody other than its traditional cantillation. "Unseasonably" means making it the subject of jest or secular amusement.

38. To experience joy at the misfortune of others.

Index to Preface, Foreword, and Introduction

INDEX

INDEX

Index to Texts

INDEX

INDEX

INDEX

203

and the elderly, 132; and the evil impulse, 94; and longing for God, 143; and love, 136; and the midnight vigil, 43, 169*n*2, 184*n*9; and repentance, 98; and the *Sefirot*, 83; and *Shekhinah*, 33; mentioned, 30, 41, 62, 64, 83, 90, 149, 154–55

Zohar Ḥadash, 47

Other Volumes in this Series

Francis and Clare ● THE COMPLETE WORKS
Gregory Palamas ● THE TRIADS
Pietists ● SELECTED WRITINGS
The Shakers ● TWO CENTURIES OF SPIRITUAL REFLECTION
Zohar ● THE BOOK OF ENLIGHTENMENT
Luis de León ● THE NAMES OF CHRIST
Quaker Spirituality ● SELECTED WRITINGS
Emanuel Swedenborg ● THE UNIVERSAL HUMAN AND SOUL-BODY INTERACTION
Augustine of Hippo ● SELECTED WRITINGS